European Identity

Why are hopes fading for a single European identity? Economic integration has advanced faster and further than predicted, yet the European sense of "who we are" is fragmenting. Exploiting decades of permissive consensus, Europe's elites designed and completed the single market, the euro, the Schengen passport-free zone, and, most recently, crafted an extraordinarily successful policy of enlargement. At the same time, these attempts to de-politicize politics, to create Europe by stealth, have produced a political backlash. This ambitious survey of identity in Europe captures the experiences of the winners and losers, optimists and pessimists, movers and stayers in a Europe where spatial and cultural borders are becoming ever more permeable. A full understanding of Europe's ambivalence, refracted through its multiple identities, lies at the intersection of competing European political projects and social processes.

JEFFREY T. CHECKEL is Simons Chair in International Law and Human Security in the School for International Studies, Simon Fraser University, and Adjunct Research Professor in the Centre for the Study of Civil War, International Peace Research Institute, Oslo.

PETER J. KATZENSTEIN is Walter S. Carpenter, Jr. Professor of International Studies in the Department of Government, Cornell University.

CONTEMPORARY EUROPEAN POLITICS

Consulting Editor:
Andreas Føllesdal, University of Oslo

Contemporary European Politics presents the latest scholarship on the most
important subjects in European politics. The world's leading scholars provide
accessible, state-of-the-art surveys of the major issues which face Europe now
and in the future. Examining Europe as a whole, and taking a broad view of its
politics, these volumes will appeal to scholars and to undergraduate and
graduate students of politics and European studies.

European Identity

Edited by

JEFFREY T. CHECKEL

AND

PETER J. KATZENSTEIN

CAMBRIDGE
UNIVERSITY PRESS

CAMBRIDGE UNIVERSITY PRESS
Cambridge, New York, Melbourne, Madrid, Cape Town, Singapore, São Paulo, Delhi

Cambridge University Press
The Edinburgh Building, Cambridge CB2 8RU, UK

Published in the United States of America by Cambridge University Press, New York

www.cambridge.org
Information on this title: www.cambridge.org/9780521709538

First published 2009

Printed in the United Kingdom at the University Press, Cambridge

A catalogue record for this publication is available from the British Library

ISBN 978-0-521-88301-6 hardback
ISBN 978-0-521-70953-8 paperback

Contents

Figures

Tables

Contributors

Holly Case, Department of History, Cornell University

Dario Castiglione, Department of Politics, University of Exeter

Jeffrey T. Checkel, School for International Studies, Simon Fraser University

Adrian Favell, Department of Sociology, University of California, Los Angeles

Neil Fligstein, Department of Sociology, University of California, Berkeley

Douglas R. Holmes, Department of Anthropology, State University of New York at Binghamton

Hartmut Kaelble, Department of History, Humboldt University

Peter J. Katzenstein, Department of Government, Cornell University

Juan Díez Medrano, Department of Sociology, University of Barcelona and Institut Barcelona de Estudis Internacionals (IBEI)

Preface

When John Haslam, social sciences editor at Cambridge University Press, and Andreas Føllesdal, consulting editor for this series, first approached us to write a book on European identity, our response was along the lines of "been there, done that, why bother to do it again?" Yet, as we thought about the possibility, we began to warm to the idea. We relished the prospect of collaboration. Furthermore, existing scholarship seemed compartmentalized and missed one central feature of identity in the new Europe. European Union (EU) specialists, typically political scientists and often funded by the EU Commission, focussed overwhelmingly on the Union and the effects its institutions had in crafting senses of allegiance from the "top down," as it were. At the same time and from a variety of disciplinary perspectives, students of immigration, nationalism, and religion explored how feelings of community in Europe arose from the "bottom up," outside of or around EU institutions. Moreover, almost everyone was taken by surprise at how the return of Eastern Europe was profoundly and irrevocably changing European identity politics.

This book makes a start at addressing these omissions and oversights. We do not favor either top-down or bottom-up storylines. Instead, we explore the intersections and interactions between the two, and do so through the lens of multiple disciplinary perspectives. This approach allows us to capture the reality of identity in today's quasi-constitutionalized, enlarged, and deeply politicized Europe, where senses of "who we are" are fracturing and multiplying at one and the same time. This book is thus a statement on how we should be studying European identity rather than an overview of research on it. Our intent has been to open up rather than close down opportunities for inquiry.

All chapters have been through numerous rounds of revision. Chapter 1 started as a brief conceptual memo for a first project workshop, held at Cornell University in October 2006. At this meeting, contributors, Cornell faculty and graduate students, and some colleagues from universities within easy reach of Ithaca responded critically to our memo and presented short papers of their own. Our rewritten and expanded memo was discussed at a workshop for PhD students convened in May 2007 by the Wissenschaftszentrum Berlin. That expanded memo and the short papers of our authors became full draft chapters, discussed at a second workshop held at the University of Oslo in October 2007.

We owe thanks to many people and institutions. Our most important intellectual debt goes to our authors. As a self-consciously designed multidisciplinary project, our enterprise was not free of risk. Throughout, our contributors actively and enthusiastically engaged in our conversations about European identity, while graciously responding to endless editorial requests for changes and improvements of their chapters.

Michael Barnett and Thomas Risse gave indispensable help at a crucial later stage. At our Oslo meeting, they acted as discussants not only of individual chapters, but also of the framing chapters. Their trenchant criticisms and constructive suggestions, made in detailed written form and during our spirited discussions, have made this a much better book than it would have become otherwise. We often agreed with their criticisms; when we did not, their help made us more aware about our central aim.

During the Cornell workshop, we were helped greatly by the memos and active workshop participation of Chris Anderson, Mabel Berezin, Dominic Boyer, Martin de Bruyn, Valerie Bunce, Timothy Byrnes, Alan Cafruny, Mai'a Cross, Matthew Evangelista, Davydd Greenwood, Liesbet Hooghe, Gary Marks, Mitchell Orenstein, Hans Peter Schmitz, Nina Tannenwald, and Hubert Zimmermann. At the Oslo meeting, we received critical, unfailingly constructive, extensive written criticism from Svein Andersen, Andreas Føllesdal, Iver Neumann, and Ulf Sverdrup, both on the framing chapters and on the various contributions of our authors.

Last and certainly not least, we owe a huge debt of gratitude to Sarah Tarrow, who copyedited and formatted the entire manuscript with cheerful grace and in record time prior to submission.

In Ithaca, we thank Donna Decker, Tammy Gardner, Pam Kaminsky, and Elaine Scott for their administrative help, and we acknowledge the financial support of Cornell's Carpenter Chair for International Studies. In Berlin, we thank Jürgen Kocka, Johannes Moses, and

Dagmar Simon for offering us the opportunity of presenting our work and for providing welcome administrative assistance, and to Klaus Eder and Georg Sørensen for co-directing the dissertation workshop. In Oslo, the Department of Political Science at the University of Oslo provided financing through its small grants program, and Bjørn Magne Forsberg helped with innumerable administrative tasks. At Cambridge University Press, we thank John Haslam for organizing an efficient review process and Carrie Cheek for overseeing the production of the book.

Differences in how the two of us confront intellectual problems – brashly marshalling the attack versus meticulously plotting the advance – are reflected in some of our other passions as well – competition on squash courts versus conquest of Swiss mountains. Such differences can make intellectual collaboration an ordeal to be suffered through or a dream come true. At the end of our journey, we are happy to report that this book has cemented a friendship many years in the making.

PJK & JTC
Ithaca and Oslo
February 2008

1 | The politicization of European identities

JEFFREY T. CHECKEL AND
PETER J. KATZENSTEIN

The ship of European identity has entered uncharted waters. Its sails are flapping in a stiff breeze. Beyond the harbor, whitecaps are signaling stormy weather ahead. The crew is fully assembled, but some members are grumbling – loudly. While food and drink are plentiful, maps and binoculars are missing. Officers are vying for rank and position as no captain is in sight. Sensing a lack of direction and brooding bad weather, some passengers are resting in the fading sun on easy chairs thinking of past accomplishments; others are huddling in an openly defiant mood close to the lifeboats, anticipating bad times ahead. With the journey's destination unknown, the trip ahead seems excruciatingly difficult to some, positively dangerous to others. Anxiety and uncertainty, not hope and self-confidence, define the moment.

Many European elites, deeply committed to the European Union (EU) as a political project, might reject the vignette we sketch above. They see the EU as institutional machinery for the solution of problems that in the past had shattered peace, destroyed prosperity, and otherwise proven to be intractable for national governments. For them, it is a project rooted in the European Enlightenment, and an emphatic way of saying "never again" to the disastrous wars of the twentieth century. While the Union has not yet succeeded in crafting a common European sense of "who we are," time is on its side.

A smaller counter-elite might be more comfortable with our identity tale. Exploiting growing mass concerns and fears, it has in recent years begun to define an alternative agenda for European identity politics – one inspired by multiple currents, including nineteenth-century romanticism. The image of Europe as a shining city perched on the hill of

We thank all of the project participants, and, especially, Michael Barnett, Holly Case, Adrian Favell, Thomas Risse and Ulf Sverdrup for their insightful comments on earlier versions of this essay. The remaining shortcomings are due to our thick-headedness rather than their acts of intellectual generosity.

1

perpetual peace, social welfare, and inalienable human rights is replaced with the cry of "Europe for Europeans."

Various forces and claims are thus fragmenting the possibility of one European identity even as European economic integration has proceeded faster and farther than anyone expected. Why? Politics, we argue, is the answer.

European economic and political integration has proceeded in a technocratic fashion. At least initially, this was an understandable strategy, given the need to solve the German problem and to cope with the geopolitics of the Cold War. Exploiting a decades-long permissive consensus, elites designed and completed the single market, the euro, the Schengen passport-free zone, and, most recently, crafted an extraordinarily successful policy of enlargement. National political and economic elites as well as other winners from this project have closed ranks behind it. At the same time, these attempts to de-politicize politics, to create Europe by stealth, have produced a political backlash that has increased over time. In this contentious and expanding political narrative, Europeans need to take back their nation-states and resist the unnatural imposition of rule from Brussels.

We explore the politics of European identity by adopting a multidisciplinary perspective. While the work of political scientists and the survey techniques upon which they rely are important, in this book we largely turn elsewhere – to anthropology, sociology, and history. This approach allows us to capture the experiences of the winners and losers, optimists and pessimists, movers and stayers in a Europe where spatial and cultural borders are becoming ever more permeable. A full understanding of Europe's ambivalence, refracted through its multiple, nested identities, lies at the intersection of competing European political projects and social processes.

Politics – specifically, various forms of politicization – are redefining, remaking, and expanding these intersections. Politicization makes issues part of politics, and it involves a number of different actors and processes. Bureaucrats crafting a Europe centered on Brussels, and intellectuals theorizing and normatively justifying a new kind of (cosmopolitan) European allegiance, play key roles. Yet, their projects intersect with xenophobic nationalists, anti-globalization Euroskeptics, and a (Western) European public that for decades has been indifferent to the evolution of a European polity. Beyond elites and their projects, identities are also being crafted and politicized by ongoing social processes related to the lived experiences of Europeans. These may include watching Europe's top-ranked soccer clubs (many with precious few national players); following the annual Eurovision Song Contest; meeting in Europe-wide social and business networks; mobilizing at the grass-roots level across national borders to celebrate or protest Europe; and shopping in supermarket chains increasingly organized on a continental scale.

We are self-conscious in the use of project and process here. Sometimes European identity is a political construction project undertaken by various national or supranational elites. Talking about the construction of identity suggests an engineering view of politics – one that emphasizes purposeful actors and their political choices. At other times, though, we are dealing with processes along different scales of social mediation and exchange, including deliberation and communication, social networks, commodity circulation, and political bargaining. These may occur along European, national, subnational–regional, as well as transnational–global lines. From this vantage point, the evolution of European identities is the result of open-ended processes that give space to actors pursuing their specific political projects, without assuming either that they will come to full fruition, or that they will end in total failure.

Despite our focus on Europe, we recognize that its identity dynamics are not unique – an appreciation driven home when we locate the continent in a number of different contexts. These include the historical context of contemporary Europe; the spatial context of other world regions in which borders are fluctuating and contested; the cultural context of other civilizational polities seeking to define their coherence against relevant others; the rapid currents of globalization and inter-nationalization that make all state borders porous; and the context of a world order defined by an American imperium that combines the military traits of traditional European empires with commercial char-acteristics of the novel American emporium.

To deny Europe's uniqueness, however, does not mean to deny its distinctiveness. And that distinctiveness has two very different parts. Europe's past leads through luminous and dark periods; it encompasses the good and the bad; it inspires hope and despair. European ambiva-lence today reflects this legacy. And with Europe once again united, the store of collective memories has broadened enormously and will make the emergence of a collective European identity even more problematic than it had been before enlargement.

In sum, ours is not a state-of-the-art volume on European identities, but a statement on how we should go about studying them. We are interested in political and social rather than psychological notions of self-understanding. Identities refer to shared representations of a collective self as reflected in public debate, political symbols, collective memories, and elite competition for power. They consist also of collective beliefs about the definition of the group and its membership that are shared by most group members. We understand identities to be revealed by social practices as well as by political attitudes, shaped by social and geographical structures and national contexts.

Different analysts and different academic disciplines disagree on where to locate and how to measure identity. Is it to be found in European institutions, with their ability to foster and construct a sense of what it means to be European? Or should we search for it in a variety of everyday social practices such as co-ownership, joint political action, and shared consumption practices? Wherever we look for European identity, its form varies significantly across different social, geographic, and national domains. To capture this diversity, we have encouraged pluralism and a crossing of disciplinary boundaries in this book, with the intent to open new lines of inquiry and raise novel questions. Research on European identity – and especially that centered on the EU – could benefit from a fresh look. Our hope is to make a modest start in that direction.

In the remainder of this opening chapter, we develop our arguments in three parts. A first section surveys major theoretical approaches to European integration, assessing what we have learned about identity in Europe. In the second section, we explore the importance of politicization for understanding the contemporary construction of European identities and advocate a multidisciplinary approach to the topic. The last section previews the main lines of argument in the various chapters that follow.

Theorizing European identity

Over the last five decades, Europe has changed dramatically. A continent divided by national hatred, ravaged by war, and bereft of a firm psychological basis has evolved into an increasingly peaceful, prosperous, and confident polity in which various nation-states are experimenting with a novel kind of international relations. This dramatic change is reflected in the world of scholarship, which has moved from the discussion of European integration theory in the 1950s and 1960s to analyses of multilevel governance and Europeanization since the early 1990s. Below, we briefly survey these literatures, highlighting what they do – or do not – say about the politics of European identity construction.

European integration theory in the 1960s

A generation ago, one of the most important debates in international relations focussed on the future of Europe, including the evolution of European identity. It built on the foundations laid in the interwar years by David Mitrany and his technocratic vision of functional integration, and on a vibrant nationalism literature developed by Hans Kohn, Carleton Hayes, and others. The central protagonists were Ernst W. Haas and Karl W. Deutsch, who articulated two very different theories of European integration.

Haas's (1958, 1961) neo-functional theory focussed on the elite- and group-centered politics of a newly emerging European polity, specifically the various functional imperatives that were propelling the European integration process forward. In contrast to Mitrany, Haas deliberately inquired into the political pressures acting on politicians. Political elites in various nation-states, he hypothesized, would learn new interests and adopt new policies as they were pushed by the functional dynamics of integration. The political costs of staying outside or behind in the process of European integration were extraordinarily high. Like bicycle-riders, elites were condemned to pedal lest they fall off the bike altogether. Identity played a minor role in Haas's theory. What drove the process of integration were functional pressures and the redefinition of actor interests. Moreover, while Haas allowed for changes in interests, his rationalist ontology ruled out, or at least made very unlikely, any deeper changes of identity.

Haas's theory inspired a cohort of energetic and brilliant younger scholars to refine and operationalize his seminal work. Two synthetic statements summarized the progress of a decade of research. Lindberg and Scheingold (1970a, pp. 24–63) argued that Europe's would-be polity was compatible with the reconsolidation of the nation-state after the horrors of World War II; in terms of public support, it was operating within a permissive public consensus – one built upon instrumental rather than emotional ties. Joseph Nye (1987 [1971], pp. 94–5) placed the European experience with regional integration into a broader comparative perspective, developing a sophisticated version of a dynamic regional integration process model. The gap between the increasing complexity of the theoretical models (Lindberg and Scheingold 1970b; Puchala 1972) and General de Gaulle's stubborn refusal to let himself be integrated into integration theory led to a sharp decline in scholarly interest in European integration even before Haas's (1975) premature post-mortem on the obsolescence of regional integration theory.

In contrast, Deutsch and his collaborators developed an approach to regional integration that focussed on the flow of information and goods and services as proxies for the level and growth of a European community (Deutsch *et al.* 1957; Deutsch, 1953, 1967; Cobb and Elder 1970; Fisher 1969; Caporaso 1971). Informed by a cybernetic theory of politics and a belief in the absolute limits of all channels processing communications and transactions, Deutsch insisted on statistical measures that normalized absolute increases in European communications and transactions against the growth of comparable national figures. In the voluminous statistical studies that he and his students published, the growth of European interdependencies of various kinds was found to be lagging behind that of national interdependencies.

On the question of European identity, Deutsch was arguably both more explicit and more pessimistic than Haas. Indeed, he remained deeply skeptical about a possible shift of mass loyalties from the national to the supranational level. Deutsch and his collaborators recorded some gains in attitudinal integration of selected mass publics and elites in Europe in the mid-1960s (Deutsch *et al.* 1967). But even at the level of elites which, then as now, tend to be more internationalist than publics, a major empirical study at the end of the 1960s found the emergence of no more than a pragmatic transnationally oriented consensus that tolerated the persistence of national diversity (Lerner and Gordon 1969, pp. 241–61).

While the argumentative lines between the neo-functionalist and communication theories of European integration were clearly drawn, neither view offered a well-developed perspective on politics or politicization. Neo-functionalism relied on pluralist theory, an ahistorical and anti-institutional view of politics that made it difficult to incorporate issues of identity. Although Deutsch's theory of identity was powerful in terms of both conceptualization and operationalization, his theory of politics relied for the most part on political metaphor, couched in the language of cybernetics and Skinnerian behavioral psychology. Moreover, neither Haas nor Deutsch developed a more fine-grained understanding of the politicization of identities.

In sum, the distinction between elite and mass politics was central to two different visions of European integration in the 1960s. Since then, Europe has made strides that to some extent support the expectations of neo-functionalism, even though European politics is evolving into something quite different from a federal or confederate union. At the same time, although these advances in European integration have proven wrong the skepticism of Deutsch's cybernetic theory of integration, his insistence on the staying power of nationalism is supported by its continued vitality and the occasional vigor of national opposition to the European project. European identities are evolving at a complex intersection of elite and mass politics.

Europe as an emerging multilevel polity

Since the early 1990s and in response to a relaunched European project, a vibrant theoretical literature on questions of European integration and identity has emerged. Here, we highlight several theoretical contributions that might shed light on identity dynamics in Europe, including research on multilevel governance, historical institutionalism, ideational-constructivist frameworks, and arguments about deliberation.

Work on multilevel governance explores the complex institutional structure of the evolving European polity (Marks, Hooghe, and Blank 1996; Kohler-Koch 2003). It has helped us to conceptualize and document empirically how policymaking has spread across supranational, intergovernmental, transnational, and regional levels in post-Maastricht Europe (Leibfried and Pierson 1995). However, because of its rationalist foundations – stressing transaction costs, informational asymmetries, and principal–agent relations – this scholarship can tell us little about how European dynamics may be changing identities on the continent.

Research by historical institutionalists has brought a time dimension to studies of Europe and the EU. While historical institutionalism has always sat somewhat uneasily between rationalist and sociological understandings of institutions (Hall and Taylor 1996), the theorizing of prominent Europeanists moves it decisively closer to the former. Consider the work of Paul Pierson. Within the context of the EU, his discussion of unanticipated consequences, adaptive learning, institutional barriers to reform, and sunk and exit costs is entirely consistent with – and, in fact, premised on – a rationalist perspective. EU institutions are all about constraints and incentives (Pierson 1994, 1996). While Pierson is to be commended for providing solid microfoundations to a largely descriptive historical-institutionalist EU literature, the costs are quite significant. His rationalist take essentially destroys the bridge that links the analysis of institutions to sociological insights – a bridge that might make it possible to gauge how European institutions, over time, affect identity.

One might think that ideational and social constructivist work would be ideally placed to help us understand identity dynamics in Europe (Adler 2002). Yet, this is not necessarily so. For some, ideas are simply an important variable in helping to explain causal dynamics in the EU's development (McNamara 1998; Parsons 2003), but not identity per se. Other scholars do examine identity, but focus too much on the EU and its institutions (Risse 2004; Checkel 2007b), thus missing other, perhaps more important arenas of identity construction. Even more problematic, this scholarship too often underspecifies or brackets out altogether political dynamics, an implausible analytic move in today's Europe (Checkel 2007a).

Consistent with a central theme in this volume, multidisciplinary work by a smaller group of constructivists has come closest to capturing the true face of identity in contemporary Europe. Ted Hopf (2002), for example, integrates linguistic theory with political science in a way that drives home what many others miss: that identity in Europe starts at home. Bridging anthropology and political science, Iver Neumann (1996, 1999) helps us see that identities do not simply nest in the positive-sum way seen by all too many EU scholars (Laffan 2004). Identity construction often begets a process of "othering" rather than "nesting." Identities can be sharply conflictual rather than snugly complementary.

Finally and most recently, some scholars have developed deliberative arguments that address Europe's identity politics. More normative than empirical in orientation (Eriksen 2006; Pensky 2008), these arguments draw heavily upon the social theory of Jürgen Habermas, specifically his argument about constitutional patriotism, to sketch a European identity that is both post-national and non-malignant. Yet, they miss conceptual problems in Habermas's argumentation (Castiglione, this volume). Too often, these arguments fail to connect their social theory to politics, where contestation, conflict, and power play central roles (Hyde-Price 2006) and where a de facto constitution has long existed in the form of the frequently amended Treaty of Rome (Moravcsik 2006).

Closely related to this deliberative school of thought, another group of Europeanists seeks to find the EU's identity in its status as a civilian or normative power (Manners 2002). The close relation between these two lines of arguments blurs the distinction between normative ideal and empirical reality. If one actually tests for a correspondence between what the EU says and what it does, normative power as a basis for European identity comes up short (Erickson 2007).

While making important starts in theorizing European identity, these various literatures consistently underplay the importance of politics and processes of politicization. In some cases, the reason for this omission is an exclusive focus on institutions; in others, it is the theorist's penchant for neglecting the complexities of domestic politics; in still others, it is the adoption of a benign view of politics that, while normatively appealing, is simply out of touch with European and world politics.

Europeanization

Last but certainly not least, there is work on Europeanization, which in many senses provides the state of the art on how Europe might be reshaping deeply held senses of community – national, local, regional, and otherwise. The concept describes a set of interrelated processes that go well beyond the traditional focus of scholars interested in how state bargaining and elite identification affect the evolution of the EU (Olsen 2002, 2007; Graziano and Vink 2006). It shifts our attention to an examination of the effects Europe has on the contemporary state – its policies, institutions, links to society, and patterns of individual–collective identification (Caporaso, Cowles, and Risse 2001; Knill 2001; Börzel 2002; Schimmelfennig and Sedelmeier 2005).

Europeanization portrays a complex dynamic through which Europe and the nation-state interact. It is not a story that can be told relying on binary distinctions. The EU does not dominate over its members by steadily wearing down the barriers of the nation-state. And nation-states do not succeed in fending off attacks on their untrammeled sovereignty. Rather, both the EU and the nation-state play crucial roles.

Work on Europeanization has generated important new empirical findings on European identity.[1] Perhaps most intriguing is the argument about its positive-sum nature. That is, one can be French – say – and, at the same time, European; identities, European or national, do not wax

---

[1] We stress empirical because, until the mid-1990s, work on European identity tended to stress the normative – the kind of identity Europe ought to have (Delanty 1995, pp. 2–3).

or wane at each other's expense. Instead, they are often nested in complex and variegated patterns for different individuals and groups, and are triggered in specific situations leading to different kinds of politics (Herrmann *et al.* 2004, pp. 248–53; see also Risse and Maier 2003; Soysal 2002; Caporaso and Kim 2007).

Yet, several analytic biasses limit the ability of this scholarship to fully capture identity dynamics in contemporary Europe. Substantively, it focusses too much on EU institutions. Methodologically, it is hindered by excessive reliance on survey instruments such as the Eurobarometer polls. To be sure, cross-national surveys and refinements to them are useful for helping to understand basic distinctions in the political orientations of mass publics in Europe and toward the EU (Moravcsik 2006; Bruter 2005). But polls risk imposing a conceptual unity on extremely diverse sets of political processes that mean different things in different contexts. Indeed, survey questions may create the attitudes they report, since people wish to provide answers to questions that are posed (Zaller 1992; see also Meinhof 2004, pp. 218–19; Favell 2005, p. 1112; and Hopf 2006).[2]

In addition, Europeanization is nearly always portrayed as a top-down process, with the causal arrows pointing from EU institutions and policies to the nation-state. This focus on the EU level leads to an emphasis on elites and institutions. On the specific question of a possible Europeanization of identities, there thus exists a strong tendency to privilege EU institutions or political-bureaucratic elites (Hooghe 2005).

Finally, many important political elements are left unexamined. With its strong institutional focus (Fligstein, Sandholtz, and Sweet 2001), Europeanization research misses the politics and conflict that often accompany transformational dynamics. In a recent conversation, a specialist on the Middle East decried the way in which Europeanists study identity. "For you folks, identity is something nice; it's all about institutions, deliberation and elites. Where I study identity, people die for it!" Although it is true that European identity politics are today typically not a matter of life or death, they do incite strong political reactions. And as those living in London and Madrid have learned

---

[2] Survey research in particular insists on agreed-upon working definitions of the concept of identity as well as unambiguous and explicit operational indicators, in full awareness that the concept "takes on different meanings to different people in different contexts, under different historical, social, economic and political conditions" (Anderson 2006, p. 1).

firsthand, such politics can easily become a matter of life and death even in contemporary Europe.

Politicization of European identities

Our conception of the politicization of European identities broadens conventional understandings focussing on Western Europe and on the interplay of political institutions and practices in the European Union. The 2004 and 2007 enlargements, the EU's ongoing constitutional process, and the resurgence of religion have politicized European identities in significant ways. Building upon but moving beyond the contributions of political science, this book thus seeks out other social science disciplines and their fresh perspectives on the dynamic evolution of European identities.

Politicization is a process that makes issues part of politics (de Wilde 2007). Apart from working its effects through national and EU institutions, it may be found in dynamics of exclusion and boundary drawing; in structural effects of mobility and migration; or in reactions to various lived experiences and daily practices. This complexity makes the analysis of European identity contingent upon many factors that resist easy categorization by any one academic discipline.

Politicization of "who we are"

European identity has become intensely politicized in recent years. Consider the debates over the EU constitution in France and the Netherlands during the first half of 2005. These revealed two very different European identity projects. One was an outward-looking and cosmopolitan *European identity* project captured by the spirit and text of the EU's then constitutional treaty (Fossum and Menendez 2005). A second was an inward-looking, national-populist European *identity project* that focussed on the economic and cultural threats posed by the infamous Polish plumbers and Islamic headscarves (Thomas, forthcoming; Berezin and Schain 2003; Kastoryano 2002; Cederman 2001; Neumann 1999).

These cosmopolitan and populist conceptions of identity differ in both the form and the content of politicization. Cosmopolitan conceptions appeal to and are motivated by elite-level politics. Populist conceptions reflect and respond to mass politics. Cosmopolitan conceptions focus on political citizenship and rights. Populist conceptions center on issues of social citizenship and cultural authenticity.

Cosmopolitan European identities are shaped in part by the liberalization of national markets in the wake of the Single European Act (1987) and the process of market opening in an era of globalization. Identity change in response to market developments reflects shifting economic self-interests. As Neil Fligstein argues in chapter 6, European professionals, drawn largely from the upper social strata, tend to identify more with and be more supportive of Europe. In comparison, the new sources of oppositional politics that Douglas Holmes examines in chapter 3 are clear losers in the liberalization of national markets. Identities rooted largely in interests will wax and wane with market developments. Lacking other sources of identification, they can be likened to party hats that we put on and take off with relative impunity.

Beyond these economic sources of cosmopolitan and populist identities, however, Europe also shapes enduring senses of loyalty and obligation, linking individual to community. In contrast to the nation, dying for Europe is not a political litmus test; not killing Europeans is. One of the most surprising developments in Europe has been the rapid growth of a European security community (Deutsch 1957; Adler and Barnett 1998), based on a relatively thin conception of collective identity that is lacking in emotional strength. Europeans have made peace in what Dario Castiglione calls in chapter 2 a community of strangers.

Populist conceptions of European identities have cultural and ethnic rather than political content. In Douglas Holmes's analysis in chapter 3, Europeans are experimenting now with multiracial, multicultural, and other novel forms of identity. Many of Europe's young, in particular, are exploring alternative lifestyles that take an apolitical or anti-political form today, but that conceal a reservoir of oppositional politics ready to be tapped by political leaders. With holes in the welfare net growing at the same time that the size of socially marginalized and politically vulnerable populations increases, the appeal of "integralism" (Holmes 2000) is now firmly embedded in European politics. The political and social integration of ethnic and cultural minorities is a task that populist conceptions of European identities regard as a threat. "Europe for Europeans" rallies the supporters of an illiberal political project.

In its original eighteenth-century meaning, cosmopolitanism referred to tolerance toward strangers. Today, it is grounded in the principle of humanity.[3] These are not the meanings of the term in the political vocabulary of contemporary Europe. European cosmopolitanism often refers to a growing acceptance of cross-border exchanges, not only of goods and services but also of Europeans. But what is Europe and who are the Europeans? Recent EU enlargement has close to doubled the number of member states and increased greatly Europe's social heterogeneity. And Europe is not an island in a globalizing world. Old stereotypes are reappearing and new ones are being forged – as Holly Case illustrates in chapter 5.

Populist European politics draw boundaries between "Europe" and the "other," a fact illustrated by the highly charged debate over Turkish accession to the EU and, more generally, the difficult relations between Europe and Islam. "Europe for Europeans" is a slogan that captures more than nationalist backlash, as Doug Holmes argues in chapter 3. It incorporates broader European elements appealing to deeply felt political sensibilities. Hungary is a good example. Traditional chauvinistic nationalism in Hungary is now donning a European mantle, recognizing the political cover Europe offers for the pursuit of political influence in neighboring countries with significant Hungarian ethnic minorities.

Cosmopolitan and populist forms of European identity politics have varied in their salience. In the 1980s and 1990s, cosmopolitanism appeared to be winning out over populism. During the last decade, however, debates concerning a possible European constitution and controversies surrounding the process of enlargement have created a deeply politicized environment where the future of European identity looks anything but settled. Today, neither identity project can avoid the inescapable social fact of a growing number of migrants who are attracted by the vision of a social, prosperous, and peaceful Europe. These contrasting identities draw on different layers of memories and political practices, which are activated politically in the context of a relevant, or threatening, "other."

The liberal and illiberal tendencies in contemporary Europe thus are yielding a novel politics of immigration that differs sharply from the forced migrations that Stalin, Hitler, and World War II and its aftermath had created. The Iron Curtain and Cold War politics prevented comparable massive demographic shifts from occurring in the second half of the twentieth century. However, since 1990, as Adrian Favell argues in

---

[3] We thank Michael Barnett for discussions on these points.

chapter 7, legal and illegal immigration is leading to an unforeseen and largely unwelcome Americanization of Europe. Different kinds of migrants create less (as in the case of ethnic Germans migrating from Eastern Europe and Russia after 1990) or more (as in the case of illegal immigrants from Africa at the outset of the twenty-first century) political backlash. "Europe for Europeans" as a political project and the growth of multiracial and a multicultural Europe as a social process thus feed on each other.

Politicization of religion

In a Europe of changing borders, religion and religious identities are taking on new and deeply politicized roles. Toward the east, Christianity, or Catholicism, defines a civilizational boundary that is intuitively plausible to many Europeans. However, just as plausible is a non-confessional, secular European identity that, for many elites, offers a welcome contrast to a United States that is an unfathomable religious manifestation of the extreme west. Whether we focus on cosmopolitanism or populism, religion or secularism, Europe's multiple and often contradictory identities are readily apparent.[4]

Students of religion remind us that the politicization of European identities is affected profoundly by confessional dynamics. European Protestants have embraced a secular universalism, marking a transformation of their religion into one that can be substantially freed from individual faith or faith-based churches. Yet the historical foundations of the European Union are undeniably Christian-Democratic, a capacious political tradition that accommodates temperate offshoots of conservative political Catholicism as well as a social Catholicism that has proven in the past to be remarkably progressive in outlook and practice.

European enlargement has given renewed political importance to the connexion between religion and European identity (Byrnes and Katzenstein 2006). Pope John Paul III, for example, wanted Poland not simply to rejoin Europe, but to rejuvenate a Christian Europe. Poland and the other Central and Eastern European countries, in the Pope's vision, were not mere supplicants to Brussels, but had every right

---

[4] A similar point can be made by looking at Europe's multiple language regime as an indicator of the multiplicity of identities. See Laitin 1997.

to bring their own understandings of Europe and their own distinctive European identity to the entire apparatus of the European Union. Indeed, before the European constitution was shelved by French and Dutch voters, EU member states found themselves in a bitter political debate about how to balance their different views on the secular and Christian roots of European identity.

Religion is relevant not only for how Europe relates to its new members, but to the outside world as well. The continental European welfare state has broad, bipartisan support among Left and Right. Its ideological foundation is firmly rooted in Christian Democratic doctrine and political practice. American and British neoliberal policies and economic globalization have posed a great challenge to this welfare state. European anti-Americanism is thus tied not only to the divisive personality of President Bush and his policies, but also to a value conflict between two different types of societies (Katzenstein and Keohane 2007).

In addition, there are the complicated and delicate relations between the Catholic Church and Islam in contemporary Europe. Pope Benedict's repeated attempts to apologize for offending many Muslims at his address in the fall of 2006 might be seen as an attempt by "purportedly secular Europeans grasping for ways to resist what they see as Muslim encroachment on compacts that lay at the heart of what it means to be European" (Byrnes 2006, p. 2).

Politicization of national politics

In national elections, mainstream political parties have smartly avoided simplifying the multiplicity we describe above into zero-sum pro- or anti-European slogans or platforms. Such a politicization strategy most likely would divide support for any major party. The layering of European and national identities makes between 15 and 65 percent of the population Europeans, either by holding to an exclusively European identity or, more typically, by grafting a European identity onto a national one. Instead, political parties focus their energies on politicizing which kind of Europe they would like to bring about – social, green, democratic, liberal-capitalist, xenophobic, cosmopolitan, law-abiding, civilian, or military. The politics concerning Europe have thus become more contested. What once was a "permissive consensus" has become a "constraining dissensus" (Hooghe and Marks, forthcoming).

A persistent elite–mass gap, an increased scope of EU policies, and populist right-wing counter-mobilization have made Europe and European identities politically more salient than in earlier periods.

In making identity a subject of political contestation, parties have been responding to the politicization of Europe in elite and mass politics over the past fifteen years. Starting with the Maastricht Treaty of 1991 and ending with the signing of the Treaty of Lisbon in December 2007,[5] elites have focussed on the deepening and broadening of Europe, and on an increase in the EU's decision-making capacity. In the intervening years, elite concerns shifted from containing unified Germany as a putative hegemon to enhancing the political legitimacy and efficacy of an enlarged Europe. Mass publics, meanwhile, had very different concerns left largely unaddressed: Europe's economic downturn in the early and mid-1990s, the putative erosion of the welfare state under the impact of an aging society and international competition, and increases in immigration in the wake of enlargement.

Put differently, since the early 1990s, European politics has been marked by a growing political disjuncture. Elite politics has centered on a strategy of depoliticizing Europe, most clearly through the creation of the euro zone and a European Central Bank. At the same time, mass publics have experienced the effects of an EU that was beginning to regulate in policy domains – border controls, currency, citizenship, fundamental rights – that hit home in new and personal ways. This disjuncture has been heightened by the growing sense of a shift of power away from national parliaments to an unaccountable bureaucracy in Brussels.

Europe, the EU, and European identity have become focal points of contestation and politicization; they are no longer topics reserved for experts. Democratic politics has prevailed over technocratic politics, with the latter shown to be nothing more than a special kind of politics – trafficking, often disingenuously, in the appearance of neutrality. Politicization and contestation in contemporary Europe are an indication of normal rather than crisis politics. They indicate powerfully that, while falling short of a federation and confederation, Europe is nonetheless a polity-in-the-making. Novelty and volatility are its political hallmarks.

---

[5] This treaty resulted from the negative responses to French and Dutch referenda on the European constitution in 2005.

Multidisciplinary perspectives

It would appear, then, that the politicization of European identities invites more and different forms of analysis than political scientists focussing on the EU have provided. We adopt here a conceptualization of politicization that encompasses approaches from various disciplinary traditions. They enrich our understanding of the politics of European identity construction. For sure, the actions of strategically calculating elites, partisan competition, and bureaucratic infighting – all proper subjects for conventional political science analysis – play central roles. However, other important perspectives highlight deliberation (normative political theory), everyday practice (anthropology), lived experience (sociology), and contingency (history).

Deliberative and normative political theories have used the topic of the politicization of European identity as a provocation to inquire into questions of citizenship and the European public sphere. Scholars interrogate both the contents and the challenges to European solidarities as they are affected by principles of voluntarism, the effects of migration, constitution-making practices, the resurgence of religious politics, and the global impact of the rights revolution (Pensky 2008). More recently, these normative concerns have been analyzed empirically, through detailed investigations into the emergence of European-wide public spheres and their influence on pre-existing senses of community and belonging (Koopmans 2004b; Trenz 2004, 2006; "The Great Debate Begins" 2005; Beiler, Fischer, and Machill 2006).

Anthropologists explore the politicization of identity construction by asking ordinary people whether they think at all of their identities in European terms. Their ethnographic research reports the results of observing and listening to people directly. It has the virtue of being able to specify the substantive content of identity as well as the relevant individual or group that holds a particular identity. It thus captures variability in meanings, as well as avoiding or minimizing the often large inferential leaps of conventional survey research.[6]

The work of Douglas Holmes attests to the value of such an anthropological approach. His field research recovers the various romantic, fascist, and national manifestations of oppositional practices, activated

[6] Our argument here should not be read as favoring either research tradition over the other. Indeed, the best research on identity utilizes both ethnography and survey research. See Symposium 2006.

by a ruptured sense of belonging that opposes a cosmopolitan European identity. The political foundations for protesting European integration and enlargement are linked to a sense of political alienation rooted primarily in cultural rather than socioeconomic forms of estrangement. At stake in these modern rather than atavistic oppositional political movements is resistance against a multicultural and multiracial Europe, as well as against the flattening of existing social frameworks brought about by globalization's "fast capitalism" (Holmes 2000). Holmes traces these anti-materialist, authoritarian oppositional movements in various research sites, including the rural districts of Friuli in Italy, the bureaucratic and political precincts of the European Parliament, and the urban wards of London's East End.[7]

Sociologists offer slightly different, but equally revealing insights into the politicization of European identity. For example, Adrian Favell's inquiry into the lives of well-paid professionals in Amsterdam, London, and Brussels looks at the politicization of identity from the privileged vantage point of "Eurostars." He tracks the lives of more than sixty young and mobile Europeans, exploring what happens to this group as its members exploit their European citizenship rights to move under the most favorable economic and political conditions. The short-term benefits of mobility, Favell reports, soon run up against longer-term social barriers and identity issues that crop up as the Eurostars must choose whom to marry, where to settle, how to raise their children, and when and where to start laying the foundations for their eventual retirements. The politicization of identity in this case occurs at the intersection of a market with free labor movement and a deep-seated resistance in European society to free labor mobility (Favell 2008a).[8]

When exploring the politicization of identity, historians remind us of long-term trends in the development of European commonalities that have to date failed in shaping a distinctive social identity (Kaelble 2004, p. 278). They also point to the important effects of historical contingency and memory. The European enlargements of 2004 and 2007 could have happened in other ways. They have brought into play very different historical memories from those shared by West Europeans. The encounter

---

[7] For another important ethnographic study – in this case, of EU institutions – see Shore 2000.

[8] Medrano 2003 and Fligstein 2008a offer additional state-of-the-art sociological studies whose findings bear critically on issues of European identity.

with Islam, the experience of delayed modernization, occupation by Nazi Germany, and the Soviet Union have created a vast storehouse of potentially differentiating memories. Contingency – in the form of individual leaders (De Gaulle, Thatcher, Kohl, Blair, Merkel, or Sarkozy) or unexpected epochal events (the 1973 energy crisis, the 1983 French U-turn, the end of the Cold War, the Balkan wars, 9/11) must also be given their due in any analysis of the politicization of European identities.

Summary

At a moment when Europe is being transformed dramatically by the process of enlargement and the resurfacing of religious and civilizational issues, students of European identity need to capture more adequately such facts in their accounts. Yes, the European Union plays a central role and, yes, increasingly sophisticated surveys and similar techniques can provide important insight. However, if the purpose is to understand fully the dynamics of European identity construction and its politicization, we should cast our net more widely and probe more deeply. This volume thus relies on multiple disciplinary traditions to offer fresh perspectives, raise new questions, and develop unexpected insights on "who we are" in today's Europe.

Project, process, and European identities

The two sections above reviewed the terrain on which this book explores European identities; this one describes how we and our collaborators advance new perspectives on them. We organize the contributions in three parts: identity as project, identity as process, and European identity in context.

Identity as project

Dario Castiglione argues in chapter 2 that the construction of European political identity does not need to rest on a definite conception of what it means to be European. This is so for two reasons: one has to do with the transformation of the very nature of political identification with one's community in modern societies, the other with the mixed nature of the European Union as a multilevel polity comprising both intergovernmental and supranational levels of governance. Any normative discourse about political identity in Europe, he argues, will have to accommodate these facts.

Castiglione develops this argument in several stages. He begins by showing how the debate on European identity is intrinsically connected to that on the nature of the European Union as a political project, and that it therefore suffers from the same ambiguities and uncertainties. In this debate, a key role has been played by the German social theorist Jürgen Habermas and his notion of constitutional patriotism.

Castiglione's reading of Habermas is both sympathetic and highly critical. While it is true that constitutional patriotism offers a more sensitive understanding of how we identify with political community and of the basis for political allegiance in the contemporary world, Habermas's post-national position fails to come to terms with the mixed nature of the European Union and with the profound differences that exist within the European polity. In such conditions, European political identity cannot be constructed based on putative European values – as Habermas suggests – but needs to be supported by the more conflictual mechanisms of democratic politics. Building on this critique, Castiglione then suggests a different way of conceptualizing European political identity, one more attuned to living with persisting conflicts and politicization.

In chapter 3, Douglas Holmes explores the genesis, articulation, and political salience of an identity project that differs dramatically from that of Habermas and other public intellectuals. As an anthropologist, Holmes sees identity mediating the struggles by which emergent configurations of European society gain political articulation – thus becoming politicized – as moral frameworks, analytical constructs, and empirical facts.

At the outset of the twenty-first century, Holmes argues, the people of Europe are continually negotiating among liberal and illiberal registers of identity; these shifting configurations of consciousness typically do not succumb to a single, stable, and unambiguous expression. There are now countless experiments with identity unfolding across Europe. Almost all of them are in some way related to European integration, though not necessarily the outcome of any EU policy initiative per se or, for that matter, under EU institutional control or supervision.

Holmes then explores in some detail one – increasingly important – identity project in today's Europe. It covers wider-ranging experiments with identity aimed at defining a fully elaborated, supranational political agenda, and is circumscribed by what Holmes terms integralism. Particularly as constructed by Jean-Marie Le Pen, integralism draws authority from a diverse range of collective idioms encompassing family, town and country, ethnic and linguistic assemblages, religious communities, occupational statuses, and social classes. The insurgency inspired by Le Pen reveals paradigmatically how identity mediates the struggles by which emergent configurations of European society gain political articulation. For Holmes, identity in Europe has become increasingly disconnected from the stabilizing influence and control of the nation-state. In these circumstances, it has assumed a volatile dynamic able to impel a supranational politics that speaks powerfully to the predicaments of a new generation of Europeans.

Analyzing European identities from the perspective of the public sphere, Juan Díez Medrano examines in chapter 4 the broad contours of the Europe that elites and citizens imagine, the degree of consensus on such a Europe, and its advocates. Medrano's chapter holds the middle ground between the cosmopolitan and nationalist alternatives that Castiglione and Holmes discuss, respectively, in chapters 2 and 3. He begins with a synthetic overview of the parameters of the 2005 EU constitutional referendum outcomes and the political confusion that followed. This discussion challenges prevalent views and proposes an alternative interpretation that stresses the role played by elites.

The core of the chapter is a rigorous public-sphere analysis, one with implications for identity dynamics at both the elite and mass levels. For elites, Medrano documents divisions over further transfers of sovereignty to the EU. In the post-Enlargement era, there is also evidence that elite consensus on the civic/republican conception of European identity may be breaking apart and giving way to conflict with ethnic conceptions. At the mass level, Medrano argues that an open debate on Europe's political identity that would engage and enlighten the citizens is not taking place, with representatives of civil society conspicuously absent from public discussions. These features of the public sphere are consistent with the citizens' growing propensity to contest elite proposals for further integration.

These competing conceptions of Europe offer a complex set of alternatives that belie the notion of a simple choice between supranationalism and nationalism. Medrano's empirical study thus dovetails with and supports Castiglione's normative and Holmes's anthropological analysis. Binary distinctions get little traction in the muddy fields of European identity politics.

Identity as process

Moving beyond the focus on a European project by Castiglione, Holmes, and Medrano, three additional chapters explore different intersections of political identity in various spheres of European social and political life. Elites still matter, but they are now more fully embedded in ongoing historical, social, political, and even personal dynamics and processes.

In chapter 5, Holly Case adopts a historical perspective to demonstrate that East and West Europeans often understand European identity in different terms. These perspectives stem from the different ways in which groups of people have experienced revolution and supranational entities, as well as how they remember and position themselves in Europe, past and present. From the many axes along which these distinctive experiences can be drawn – North and South, big states and little states, rich states and poor states – Case chooses to explore that between East and West.

This axis may seem ephemeral to some, the product of a forty-year detour from centuries of common experience, and one that can easily be erased by mutual investment in the European project. From this perspective, the European Union allows for dissonant perspectives to coexist without creating major conflict. In essence, it serves as a great shock absorber for contentious politics, especially around old boundary disputes and minority issues. Nevertheless, and especially after the recent enlargements, competing political visions now emerge of what it means to be European, of what Europe is and what it does or should do – visions that are on a collision course with the technocratically devised structures of European unity.

These differences mean that, while certain shared concepts remain central to understandings of "Europeanness" in both East and West, they carry radically different meanings, informed by regional experience and politicized memory. Revolution, supranationalism, and revised or centrally manipulated historical memory form a nexus around which European identity projects have been built, rebuilt, and dismantled with awe-inspiring frequency in the modern era. From this historical perspective, Case argues that European identity is largely rooted in national experience and is likely to become more explicitly so in the future, even if the institutions of the European Union were to remain relatively unaffected by the exigencies of nationalist activism.

The identity-as-historical-process perspective so nicely sketched by Holly Case is then followed by two chapters – both written by sociologists – that give it analytic grounding. In chapter 6, Neil Fligstein asks why, after half a century of European integration, political support for a more united Europe remains so tepid. The reason, he argues, is that integration has acted very unevenly in bringing individuals together. The main beneficiaries of European integration have been the managers, professionals, and white-collar workers who have had the opportunity to travel, speak second languages, and interact with their counterparts across Europe. One consequence of this social change is Europe's rich associational life. Fligstein shows that professional, scientific, and trade associations have created a European civil society in which educated citizens from different countries meet to discuss issues of common interest.

The political consequences of this development have been complex and play themselves out in very different ways across the partisan spectrum and in European associations. While center-right and center-left parties are largely supportive of the European project, parties of the Left and of the Right oppose Europe, if on different grounds. The Left sees Europe as a capitalist plot that seeks to eliminate the welfare state, the Right sees Europe as a frontal attack on the nation-state.

Such complexities in party and interest group politics can cut both ways, creating common European positions – for example, in the opposition to Austria's Jörg Haider and his populist xenophobia – or undermining European solidarity, as in the reaction to BSE Creutzfeldt-Jacob mad cow disease. Grounded in a provocative and rich sociological framing, the chapter concludes by drawing out some alternative European futures, with the suggestion that we may be at the limit of European identity. The European project in the image of the national state may never be realized.

Adrian Favell examines in chapter 7 the crucial impact of migration on European identity. After sketching the role of population movements in the making and unmaking of Europe historically, he explores in depth the three kinds of migration/mobility that are most salient to the continent today and its structural transformation: the ongoing, traditional "ethnic" immigration of non-Europeans into European nation-states; the small but symbolically important emergence of new intra-European "elite" migrations; and the politically ambiguous flows of East–West migrants – which fall somewhere between the other two forms – that have been connected to the EU enlargement process.

Since the enlargements of 2004 and 2007, many East Europeans have become EU citizens. But their ambivalent status is shared by migrants from all candidate countries and associate members of the EU. Are they free movers, like the privileged West Europeans, or just immigrants, like the rest? Is their presence helping to construct an integrated Europe or rebuild a Europe of nation-states? Even though they are (mostly) white, Christian and hold EU passports, they often encounter the prejudices and exclusionary practices traditionally faced by immigrants coming from outside the EU.

Favell's analysis thus points to a complex set of effects that migration has on European identities – effects that are equally far removed from the simple economic and social models that motivated the Single European Act or from Habermasian–cosmopolitan notions of constitutional patriotism.

European identity in context

In chapter 8, Hartmut Kaelble analyzes from a historical perspective the cross currents between politicization and depoliticization that define European identity as both project and process, and that have shaped European politics since the early 1980s. Kaelble unravels five different strands of identification with Europe. Identification with a Europe superior to all other civilizations is perhaps the oldest of these. Second, identification with Europe's internal heterogeneity as a sign of vitality and strength may well be the harbinger of a new form of Euro-centrism. Third, identification with a distinctive European lifestyle and European values is at times so much taken for granted that Europeans are not even aware of it. A fourth characteristic is the caution and restraint of identification with Europe: Europe has no resemblance to a traditional nation-state (where the formation of a national consciousness precedes the process of state formation) and only a faint resemblance to a state-nation (where the temporal sequence processes of state and nation creation are reversed). Finally, identification with Europe is no longer grounded either in violence and death or in strong political hierarchies. Remarkably, Kaelble argues, in comparison with the nation-state, identification with Europe shows, a stronger sense of trust in European institutions and policies. Here lies the promise for a future evolution of European identity.

In chapter 9, Peter Katzenstein and Jeff Checkel briefly review the book's main findings before placing European identity in a broader, comparative framework. Domains of identity construction can be found in the projects of political entrepreneurs and in social processes such as discourses, institutions, and European daily practices. This book supports the conclusion that European identities are shaped by factors that are too inchoate to replicate processes of nation-state identity formation. Instead of one strong European identity, we encounter a multiplicity of European identities. Far from being unique or unusual, this multiplicity is in fact the hallmark of civilizational identities in other world regions such as Asia and the Americas. Those civilizational polities also develop self-conscious ideas in their encounters with other such polities. While in comparison to other civilizations, the EU as an expressly political arrangement makes Europe distinctive, it does not make it unique. Far from narrowing our focus only to Europe, the analysis of European identities thus opens a window on a broader set of political phenomena in world politics.

PART I

European identity as project

2 | Political identity in a community of strangers

DARIO CASTIGLIONE

In this chapter I argue that the construction of European *political* identity does not necessarily rest on a definite conception of what it is to be European. This is so for two reasons – one related to the transformation of the very conception of political identification with one's own community in modern societies, and the other to the mixed nature of the European Union as a multilevel polity comprising both intergovernmental and supranational levels of governance. Any normative discourse about political identity in Europe must accommodate these two realities.

Political identity is both a social and a historical construct. As a social construct, it reflects the institutional nature of the political community As a historical construct, its emergence and consolidation is bound up with historical contingencies and with the way in which competing narratives and ideologies shape the self-perceptions of the members of the community. As suggested in the introductory essay to this volume, Europe's identities exist in the plural; and so it is for the more specific sense of political identities.

But there is an important functional element to political identity, insofar as this plays an important role in sustaining citizens' allegiance and loyalty to their political community. In this respect, the different kinds of motivations and cultural and psychological constructions that make different people identify with a political community may be irrelevant, as long as political identity helps to bring the members of a community together. On the other hand, the content of political identity may

This piece would have never been written but for the encouragement, good advice, and infinite patience of the editors of this volume. I also wish to acknowledge the input provided by all participants in the Oslo meeting, when the first drafts of the chapters of this volume were discussed; and in particular by Andreas Føllesdal and Thomas Risse, who gave me extremely valuable written comments. The usual caveat about my exclusive responsibility for the shortcomings of this piece applies.

matter a great deal in determining the character and self-understanding of a political community.

The purpose of this chapter is to examine the state of the debate about European political identity, concentrating on its more normative aspects. In the first section, I show how this debate is intrinsically connected to that of the nature of the European political community, therefore suffering from the same ambiguities and uncertainties. The following two sections present two different conceptions of European political identity, reflecting nation-based and post-national understandings of politics in the European Union. As I argue throughout, the nation-based conception fails to appreciate the changing nature of political identity in a more globalized and internationalized world – the first "reality" mentioned at the beginning of this chapter. In this respect, the kind of "constitutional patriotism" propounded by Jürgen Habermas offers a more sensitive understanding of how we identify with our political community and what is the basis for political allegiance in the contemporary world. However, as I discuss in the essay's fourth section, Habermas's post-national position fails to come to terms with the second "reality": the mixed nature of the European Union and the profound differences that exist within the European polity. Under such conditions, European political identity cannot be constructed on the basis of putative European values but must be supported by the more conflictual mechanisms of democratic politics and inter-institutional balance.

The concluding part of the chapter builds upon the critical analysis of constitutional patriotism by suggesting a different way of conceptualizing European political identity, one more attuned to living with persisting conflicts. This is partly due to the diminished role that force (both internal and external) plays in the self-understanding of modern political communities, making it easier to reconcile the demands of different nested political identities despite their occasional tendency to conflict with one another.

Political identity and political community

The idea of political identity is a complex one. It contains two distinct forms which for good reasons are often conflated, but whose analytical distinction is nonetheless important. One refers to the way in which political action and institutions contribute to processes of individual and collective *identification* and differentiation; the other to how this process of identification provides the grounds for political *allegiance* in a political community.

Different forms of political identification do not need to clash. As an individual, one can simultaneously play different political roles, in the same way as one has different social and personal roles in life. There is no contradiction in feeling a sense of belonging to functionally different organizations. In some respects, certain political roles – for instance, being a political activist, a member of a trade union or of a pressure group, a partisan voter, and a citizen of a political community – can even support each other insofar as they all contribute to determining the way in which one makes sense of one's political identity. The case is not dissimilar when we consider identification with territorially, rather than functionally different entities: with the city, the region, and the nation; or even, though sometimes more problematically, with the different levels of either a federal or a composite political system (Katzenstein 2005, p. 81). In fact, in the latter cases, dissonance may be due to cultural rather than strictly political aspects of personal or group identification.

When we take political identity in the specific sense of allegiance, however, it is a different story. This is because political communities – communities that claim the legitimate use of force over their members – require some form of allegiance and loyalty, which has a somewhat exclusive nature both in its claims over our solidarity with our fellow citizens (that is, internally) and in its demands for defending our own community against external threats (Taylor 1998).

Differentiating between these two senses of political identity has some relevance when we come to the European case. European political identification is in itself unproblematic. It has rightly been argued that it does not need to be in direct opposition to either national or regional identities, since they can all easily cohabit in a nested structure causing neither psychological nor cognitive dissonance (Risse 2004, pp. 248–9). This represents what in the introduction to this volume is called the "positive-sum nature" of European identity; and although the development of a particular attachment to Europe, or more specifically to the EU as a political entity, may impact on the way in which we perceive other forms of institutional and territorial identification, the latter need not be either abandoned or subordinated to the European level. It is, after all, possible to be and feel both British and English (or Spanish and Catalan; or Italian and Sicilian) at the same time, although these are complex historical constructions that conjure up various kinds of

meanings and associations, resting on political and cultural experiences
that have on occasion taken divergent or even opposite directions (on
the relationship between Britishness and Englishness, cf. Colley 1992;
Pocock 1995; Aughey 2007, among many).

As one would expect, the issues are somewhat more complex with
regard to European identity in the sense of political allegiance to the EU.
In modern democratic societies, this sense of political identity is bound
up with the practices of citizenship and has a recognizably "projectual"
nature resulting from elites' attempts to ensure the popular support
for a political system or project. Moreover, the projects and narratives
of political identity have been adapted and made functional to the
requirements of sovereignty and territoriality, and therefore conceived
as exclusive to either a particular state or a particular nation. The
emergence of a distinctive European political identity thus necessarily
enters into some kind of collision with the more historically and politically sedimented allegiances toward the nation-state.

Such a conflict and its resolution can be conceptualized in two ways.
The first, and most obvious one, is a conflict of content, so to speak. From
this perspective, European citizens are asked to change the priority of their
political allegiances by identifying with a different territory and expressing
loyalty toward different sovereign institutions. Hence, the EU and its
institutions come to take the place of the nation and the nation-state.
The second is a more radical conceptualization in which the EU, as a
transnational entity, does not simply take the place of the nation-state, but
effectively undermines the very principles of territoriality and sovereignty.
This changes both the form and the function of political identity, as the
latter would seem to play a different role within the political system.

From a more theoretical and normative perspective, the current
debate about European political identity oscillates between these two
positions: a more traditional statist and nation-like conception of identity, which sees the European Union as a nation writ large; and a post-
national conception that sees the EU as a new form of state. Indeed, since
Maastricht (though not just because of Maastricht), the question of the
political form of the European Union has become part of a Europe-wide
debate. Even though it remains true that the "quasi-constitutional"
structure and institutional organization of the European Union have
been stable for some time, its political form – between an international
organization and a full-grown political community – remains both controversial and largely unresolved (Castiglione and Schönlau 2006).

As became even more evident in the course of the ratification debate about the now abandoned Constitutional Treaty, there are many reasons why such stabilization appears either unsatisfactory, or threatening, or illusory, depending on the point of view. For many, the Constitutional Treaty was meant to bring some kind of closure to the protracted phase of economic and political integration and to establish the limits of geopolitical enlargement, processes that had proceeded piecemeal and "functionally" since the 1950s but accelerated dramatically with German unification and the collapse of the Soviet sphere of influence at the end of the 1980s. It could be argued that the supremacy of the member states as the "masters of the Treaty" was re-established with the failure of the Constitutional Treaty and with the retreat into the more traditional territory of intergovernmentalism during the preparation of the Treaty of Lisbon. But this is more likely to be a temporary swing of the pendulum. Intergovernmentalism and supranationalism remain poised in an uneasy equilibrium within the institutional structure of the European Union, and, from this perspective, the Treaty of Lisbon (even if approved) does not change the status quo.

The debate about European identity is part and parcel of this conundrum of the political nature of the European Union. Indeed, it is one aspect both of the debate on how to interpret the nature of the EU, and of the political attempt to influence what the EU will become. For, if the European Union is or is becoming a political community of sorts, its stability and sustainability require that its members share some sense of being part of it. But if the nature of such a community is unclear, people's sense of belonging may be equally confused. Hence the present sense of anxiety and uncertainty of which the introduction to this book speaks. The image that is evoked in the introduction, of a ship losing direction, is not unfamiliar in the European debate, conjuring up similar images of journeys, crossroads, and destinations that have been part of the discourse of European *finalité*. Nonetheless, when these images, or the very discourse of *finalité*, are applied to political identity, they tend to become somewhat paradoxical, or at least circular (Walker 2002; Castiglione 2004).

In the European case, this circularity takes two forms. On the one hand, it is unclear what comes first, a European political identity or the consolidation of the European Union as a political community – the well-known discussion about the European demos (Weiler 1999). On the other hand, as remarked in the introduction to this volume, there appears to be a double movement of politicization and de-politicization involving political identity. European identity is increasingly becoming an issue of deep political controversy both across Europe and within individual member states. At the same time, the search for a European identity is intended to be a way of establishing a common ground for overcoming political differences. Thus, European identity becomes politicized at the very same time as it is invoked as the de-politicized ground on which Europeans should recognize each other. This paradox of politicization and de-politicization is not peculiar to European political integration. It was already present in the process of nation-state formation, but there it was often solved (or perhaps obscured) by appeals to the more cultural aspects of national identities as the substratum of political identities, something that, as we shall see, is more problematic in the European case.

Nation-like conceptions of European political identity

The difficulty of matching cultural and political identity in Europe is particularly evident when we examine those positions that look at European political integration as a process of scaling up the dimension of the political community. The implication here is that the European integration process poses the question of the scale of politics but does not change the fundamental categories of sovereignty and nationhood, which remain dominant in European politics, inscribed as they are within the more general context of the international system of states and of international law (Grimm 1995b).

These positions are important because they remain extremely influential at a political and popular level. Indeed, from a strictly political perspective, the debate about political identity has been dominated by the simple alternative between national and European identity – the former favored by the Euro-skeptics, the latter by the Euro-federalists. In spite of their political division, both Euro-skeptic and strongly federal conceptions of the EU tend to agree on the nature of the issue at stake: whether or not the center of political gravity, and therefore of primary allegiance, should be moved from the national to the European level. They disagree, of course, on the advisability of such a move. This way of looking at the EU as a direct challenge to national identity is a zero-sum game between European and more local political identities. It reproduces an older discussion about dual citizenship (see Aron 1974) that applies to federal as well as to multinational systems of state govern-ance, where the component parts are strong or distinctive enough, in terms of language or other historical and cultural features, that their existence poses a more acute problem of political allegiance.

In terms of the conception of political identity, Euro-skeptics and enthusiastic Euro-federalists share a similar belief in the dominance of traditional conceptions of (national) statehood and sovereignty, accor-ding to which politics (and democratic politics at that) needs a "thick" conception of political identity, necessary to guarantee both political allegiance and social solidarity. This belief can either take a more cultura-list (even ethnic, and narrowly nationalistic) turn, or be articulated in a more liberal or civic-democratic language (Thibaud 1992; Tamir 1993; Millar 1995, 2000).

Of course, for the Euro-skeptics and for those who set great store by a historical conception of nationality as the cement of the political com-munity, a European political identity is out of the question. If anything, this kind of deep-seated Euro-skepticism, based on an "integralist" agenda (see Holmes in this volume), has developed a kind of European anti-identity, arising from a vision of Europe as a centralizing bureau-cratic empire. But the possibility of a European political identity in its traditional sense is at the core of a federal vision of the European Union, what is sometimes referred to by its opponents as Europe as a superstate. This position predicates a fully sovereign EU with an inde-pendent foreign policy on the grounds that this arrangement, in contrast to a loose confederation, would be capable of delivering security and welfare to all European citizens in a way in which the member states no longer can (Morgan 2005). This position is sometimes identified with a vision of "Fortress Europe" that replicates at the EU level some of the nation- and state-based categories such as sovereignty and the congru-ence between territory and culture, in order to preserve Europe as an area of political influence and prosperity within the context of twenty-first-century international politics.

"Fortress Europe," or Europe as a "superstate," would seem to require a positive sense of political identity not dissimilar to the one that has traditionally operated at the nation-state level. The debate about the cultural and religious origins of Europe that was sparked by the drafting of the Preamble of the Constitutional Treatise (Castiglione *et al.* 2007, ch. 10), and by the question of Turkey's membership in the European Union, highlights a conception of political identity as fundamentally rooted in a shared and largely homogeneous cultural background, offering positive motives for identification as a strong basis for political allegiance. What is important in this context is that this conception makes no distinction between the process of identification and that of securing political allegiance, so that loyalty toward a community is possible only if there is some strong element of identification that holds people together, beyond the mere fact of belonging to the same political community. In this sense, political identification is always, to a certain degree, based on cultural aspects of mutual recognition, and therefore European political identity is hardly distinguishable from a more general idea of European identity.

Naturally, the idea of a common European identity can be presented as either the result of the historical uncovering of a common past (Christian Europe, Enlightened Europe, and so on), or as a more constructivist operation identifying the European roots in a narrative whose starting point is Europe's present. Indeed, the latter process is often presented in the guise of the former. Whether rooted in its historical and cultural past or "imagined" (Anderson 1991), the political identity of a European superstate seems nonetheless to require not only strong positive identification, but also a certain sense that such an identity is distinct from that of others. Recent events have provided interesting opportunities for the formation of an oppositional political identity, where anti-Americanism and anti-Islamism can easily form the content for a political identity mainly conceived in opposition to an "other." Yet, it is evident that deep divisions in Europe may undermine both projects. From this perspective, Enlargement provides a telling paradox for Europe as a superstate (see Case in this volume). On the one hand, it has offered a vision of Europe as a definite geopolitical entity, finally reunited within its "cultural" and "historical" confines; on the other, it has introduced in the EU very different self-understandings of Europe, of its history and of its mission. In this respect, the relationship with the US is a crucial one, and one that divides European countries (against each other) and European society (within each country) more than it may unite them. The same is true of religion, an issue that has become even more complex since Enlargement.

But, from the point of view of the construction of a European political identity, one should not dismiss the role that negative elements play alongside more positive ones. Despite being articulated in entirely negative and oppositional terms, the influence of Euro-skepticism as part of a discourse on European identity should not be underestimated. It is plausible to imagine Euroskepticism as a permanent feature of EU politics, one articulating in a populist language, or in the form of anti-politics, a strong resistance against some of the centralizing and bureaucratic tendencies of the European integration process. Issues such as migration and how to deal with a multicultural society provide the integralist position with ammunition for their defense of traditional conceptions of national sovereignty, territorial integrity, and cultural nativism, thus making discourses of a dominant European identity rather vulnerable for the foreseeable future.

In this perspective, it is interesting to note two particular phenomena linked to the recent process of Enlargement. From the point of view of many of the "old" member states (those comprising the area traditionally described as "Western Europe"), the issue of internal mobility – so central to the ideological construction of a "common market" – has recently become much more controversial as large numbers of skilled and unskilled workers from new East European member states have started making use of the freedom of movement allowed them by the integration process (see Favell in this volume). Thus, integration has paradoxically contributed to reactivating a number of "national" reflexes in the attempt to provide social protection for local populations.

Enlargement has also produced paradoxical results in Central and Eastern Europe. The rather protracted process of integration, and the emergence of deep divisions in international affairs between what have come to be know as "New" and "Old" Europe, have contributed to the emergence of Euro-skepticism in some of the new member states. This has partly undermined the prevalent conviction in those countries soon after 1989 that there were no tensions between the rediscovery of their national sovereignty and their joining the European "family," in the form of the EU. In fact, for many of these countries, joining the EU was meant as an assertion of national sovereignty, something that they may not be prepared to relinquish too readily by diluting it within the larger confines of the European Union.

This discussion of the contradictory ways in which Enlargement and integration seem to have affected the construction of a European political identity and a sense of belonging to the European Union shows how difficult it is for a European identity conceived in a nation-like fashion to displace more traditional national identities and allegiances.

This is probably a reflection of the fact that, whether conceived as an intergovernmental or as a supranational organization, Europe is not a nation writ large. From a normative perspective, a post-national conception of European political identity looks more promising.

Constitutional patriotism as European political identity

The main exponent of a post-national conception of European political identity is probably Jürgen Habermas, who has deployed the idea of constitutional patriotism – an idea originally developed in the context of German constitutional culture (Müller 2007, ch. 1) – as the centerpiece for a normative conception of political identity adapted to post-national conditions. This section will explore the analytical and normative elements of Habermas's position. However, his position does not stand in isolation; it is part of a longer history of positions that, contrary to what we have seen in the previous section, maintained that the European process of integration undermined a purely national and state-based view of politics (Haas 1958). The neo-functionalist literature, in particular, offered a reading of the integration process that tried to capture the piecemeal way in which postwar (Western) Europe was being created as a single economic and political space. As part of this process, it was suggested that the emergence of the European Communities, and later of the Union, weakened territoriality and sovereignty as the unifying principles of both internal and external political action.

As noted in this volume's introduction, the gradual construction of a European identity – not in opposition to national and local identities but as the natural reflection of the emergence of new supranational political structures and practices to which people grew increasingly accustomed, and which they supported more on the basis of rational calculations than emotive attachments – was part of this vision of functional integration (Haas 2000, pp. 322–52; Marks 1999, pp. 69–71). Such a vision of political identity does not deny that national borders matter in the reality of politics and in people's own self-understanding as political agents; but, in the words of Robert Schuman, it suggests that the importance of borders and of nation-states was "de-emphasized" in the new architecture of political space and political action (Haas 2000, p. 322). The conception of political identity that follows from this vision is the reverse of the one we saw in the previous section. Whereas a nation-based conception collapses identification and allegiance together, the post-national conception separates the two, conceiving allegiance and loyalty in a more rationalistic and abstract, rather than an emotive way – somewhat detached from the cultural and psychological processes of identification (Benhabib 2004).

This position gives very little importance to political identity as an "exclusionary" identity. The allegiance we may have to the system of laws and rights developed by the EU (even against our own government/ country) comes from the universality of the principles upheld by that system, or by the efficiency-driven imperatives of the market and of bureaucratic administration. According to such a perspective, all we need to do in order to sustain social and political obligations at the European level is to cultivate a kind of universal citizenship attuned to the rights of others; or to disregard altogether the discourses of democratic citizenship and political identity, while relying entirely on other mechanisms of formal and substantive legitimacy.

But there is a different and more "republican" conception of post-national politics, which does not devalue the importance of identification as part of the political integration process, and does not completely separate identification from allegiance. It insists instead on the importance of a politics of identity as part of a new normative framing for democratic politics at a supra- and post-national level. Habermas (1996, 1997, 1998) has developed such a version by proposing "constitutional patriotism" as the basis for political identity at a European level. This is a kind of patriotism (hence a particular attachment to the European polity), but one that in Habermas's view should be based on a "civic" (and cosmopolitan) understanding of the principles underlying the European polity. It should therefore be open to the inclusion of the "other" but remain rooted in a self-understanding of the European perspective, thus combining both universalist and particularist instances. This is what it makes it both attractive and distinctive as a normative reading of European identity.

In a recent treatment of the issue, Habermas (2006, ch. 6) distinguishes two elements of his argument. He first addresses the question of whether European identity is "necessary," and second, whether it is "possible." The first part of the argument is implicitly directed against the kind of liberal and functional conceptions of post-national citizenship that, as already argued, put little emphasis on the emotional attachments that ground citizens' loyalty toward the community and the political system. The second part is an answer to those who believe that national attachments are still the only viable basis for political identity.

Habermas's demonstration of the need for a European political identity starts from the observation that both the explanatory value and the political force of the once influential neo-functional theory of European integration as self-propelling process are now exhausted. He identifies the three main challenges facing the European Union as governing Enlargement; managing the political consequences of increasing economic unification; and redefining the role of Europe within the new geopolitical situation created by 9/11 and the Bush administration's foreign policy (particularly in the Middle East). While the spillover character of economic and social integration as envisaged by the neo-functionalist model did not require a "common European consciousness" (2006, p. 68), each of these challenges requires a definite awareness on the part of citizens, who are increasingly asked to recognize the discipline of majorities and minorities within a much enlarged community and to accept the redistributive effects of more "positive" forms of integration. Moreover, a common foreign and security policy needs more overt forms of opinion- and will-formation, and therefore the development of a European public sphere.

For Habermas, the decision taken at Laeken in 2001 to start a more overt discussion about writing a European constitution was therefore a timely way of addressing the shortcomings of the neo-functionalist narrative of, and approach to, European integration. A Constitution (or a Constitutional Treaty, as it emerged from the Convention on the Future of Europe) offered a moment of closure to the debate about *finalité*, providing the basis for a new form of statehood at a supranational level and for fixing the structure of internal power in the EU. But Habermas stresses another aspect to the overt process of constitution making that has relevance to our discussion of why Europe needs political identity. According to him, a normative conception of constitutional politics needs a constitutional moment, something that breaks the routine of normal politics and introduces an important aspect of symbolism in constitutional politics (Castiglione *et al.* 2007, ch. 2). "As a political collectivity" – Habermas writes – "Europe cannot take hold in the consciousness of its citizens simply in the shape of a common currency. The intergovernmental arrangement at Maastricht lacks that power of symbolic crystallization which only a political act of foundation can give" (Habermas 2001, p. 6). In this sense, the Constitution represented a catalytic point in the creation of Europe as a political community, coming at the end of an already advanced process of social, economic, and political integration and helping to put in motion the construction of a European-wide civil society, a common public sphere, and a shared political culture (Habermas 2001, pp. 16–21).

As we know, that opportunity was not seized; but this does not necessarily contradict the first part of Habermas's argument about political identity: that Europe *needs* to activate citizens' consciousness in the process of political integration, requiring an explicit form of political identity. However, it does pose a problem for the second part of his case: that such a political identity is *possible*.

Habermas's argument on the feasibility of European political identity moves in three stages. The first concerns the post-national nature of the political identity itself. The second stage engages with the substance of a European political identity, and the final one with the political forces most likely to generate it. I shall try to briefly summarize these three parts in the remainder of this section, and I shall address what I take to be its shortcomings and a possible alternative conception in the following two sections.

Regarding the post-national nature of European political identity, there is a sense in which this is not very different from national forms of political identity. Against those who stress the more culturalist and communitarian aspects of national political identity, Habermas remarks that, historically, national consciousness emerged as a form of "solidarity amongst strangers," of a fairly abstract nature with strong legal mediations (2006, pp. 76–7). From such a perspective, the real issue about the feasibility of a European political identity is not whether it exists already, but what are the conditions for it to exist.

There are, however, as Habermas admits, important ways in which the nature of a European political identity may depart from its national counterparts. Such an identity may need to be more overtly "constructed" and more "cosmopolitan" in nature. The former aspect is largely due to changed historical and political conditions. Whereas national political identity has often emerged in situations of revolutionary struggle and through processes of democratization that conferred on it an important element of pathos, this is not so in the case of the construction of European political identity, which needs to emerge more mundanely from the everyday dealings of the European citizens, in conditions that are already governed by democratic principles and practices.

The second departure of European political identity from its national counterpart follows, according to Habermas, from a series of developments that can already be observed in the nation-states, particularly since the second half of the twentieth century. This is its more universalistic character, due mainly to the "internal dynamic" of the democratic process, which contributes to shaping the references for public discourse in terms of issues of justice, rather than simply of national interests (Habermas 2006a, p. 77). Habermas also detects a "peculiar switch in emotional fixation from the state to the constitution" (p. 78), which corresponds to the way in which civic solidarity grows not so much out of identification with a national community, but out of membership in a democratic polity – in other words, a shift from processes of identification that see the state and the community in relation to the outside, to processes that emphasize the preservation of a particular liberal and democratic order within the community. In sum, Habermas believes that European political identity is feasible insofar as it is an extension of national forms of consciousness.

The second stage in Habermas's argument is concerned with the more substantive values that make Europe distinctive in the present historical and geopolitical conditions. This is an important point, since it engages directly with the question of how the more cosmopolitan kind of political identity that Habermas believes Europe is developing relates to its historical roots, and how these are identified. The nearest that Habermas has come to defining such roots is in his "manifesto" on "what binds Europeans together," which he co-signed with Jacques Derrida at the height of the European debate on the war in Iraq (Habermas 2006a, ch. 3).[1] Here (pp. 46–8) Habermas highlights a number of European achievements and values as part of Europe's distinctive historical legacy: a secular politics; politics and the state as correctives to market outcomes; a diffuse awareness of the paradoxes of progress, instilling ideological competition among political parties; social solidarity emerging from a history of class struggle; rejection of capital punishment; domestication of state power through international

---

[1] The context is important, since at the time Habermas maintained that the diffuse European popular opposition to the invasion of Iraq was perhaps the first real manifestation of a European public opinion, and of the possibility of the formation of a pan-European public sphere. Moreover, in spite of the divisions among the European governments, the expression of the European voice in the form of popular protest seemed to be a moment of both self-assertion and self-confidence.

organizations; and a capacity for self-reflexivity in the face of global decline.

The third and final stage in Habermas's argumentation for the feasibility of a European political identity is of a more immediate political nature and seems to be based on the conviction that the political core of European integration remains firmly in the Franco-German axis. As he responds to a question about the role that different countries (particularly the Eastern European ones) may play in the EU, "the changing tempo of European unification has always been determined by the agreement between France and Germany to keep the process moving forward ... as the Eurozone demonstrates, there is already a Europe of different speeds" (Habermas 2006a, p. 52). This is both an observation on the internal political dynamics of the European Union and a fairly realistic assessment of where the power engine of the Union still lies.

The place of conflict and consensus in European political identity

There is much that is attractive in the Habermasian position on European political identity. As we have seen, he rightly outlines the limits of those positions that underestimate the role that a shared sense of belonging may need to play at this stage of the integration process. Although not original, his argument for the necessity of a certain political identity in a community whose functions are increasingly political is compelling.[2] Such political identity cannot simply reflect unmediated and unreflective processes of identification. This is not so in the context of the nation-state, and, as Habermas suggests, it is even less likely to be so in a supranational context, where political identity will have to be more artificially constructed and mediated by legal and political experiences and institutions. But Habermas recognizes that political allegiance needs some kind of socio-psychological basis and cannot be just an abstract kind of attachment. In this respect, his position is much closer to the one defended by those who believe in Europe as a superstate, with the difference that Habermas is convinced that the kind of constitutional patriotism he advocates for Europe is a

---

[2] Habermas's argument here is part of a more general turn toward a normative discussion of the extent and rationale of European integration; for a list of works arguing along similar lines, see Bellamy and Castiglione 2003, fn. 2.

particularist reading of more universal principles and that, as we have seen, the "identification with the state mutates into an orientation to the constitution" (2006, p. 78). This, for Habermas, is the post-national core of modern political identity.

But there are limits and tensions in the way in which Habermas tries to reconcile particularism and universalism in his construction of European constitutional patriotism. There are two main objections against it:[3] First, there is the issue of the role and identification of the substantive values on which Europeans converge; and second, there is the question of the way in which the construction of political identity is related to the nature and conditions of the European polity. I shall discuss these two issues in this section and readdress the more general question of what lies at the core of a post-national conception of political identity in the concluding section of this chapter.

Political identity and European values

The position holding that European constitutional patriotism is founded on universal values is not an easy one to maintain with coherence. It requires a difficult balance between a justification of cosmopolitan values (universal in nature) and a more communitarian explanation (linked to particular features of the community) of how they have emerged, how they have become our own, and how they ultimately contribute to distinguishing us from others. There is no doubt that moral justification of attachments to particular communities, or of the ethics of citizenship in general, may require precisely such a reconciliation between these two tendencies (Appiah 2005; Bellamy and Castiglione 1998; Taylor 1989). But the Habermasian position seems still uneasily poised between a defense of universal values that is too "thin" to mobilize people's allegiance and loyalty, and a reconstruction of European values that may become too "thick" in the way in which Europeans use it as a form of identification.[4]

Habermas's position can sometimes be interpreted as purely cosmopolitan, so that adherence to liberal democratic principles on its own is sufficient to generate a patriotic allegiance to any just society. In other

---

[3] For criticisms of the Habermasian position along similar lines, see Balibar 2004, ch. 4; and particularly Laborde 2002.
[4] The following paragraph is indebted to Bellamy and Castiglione 2004.

instances, however, his attempt to present his argument as a distinctively "European" account risks transforming it into a form of supra-nationalism. In his reconstruction of the historical roots of European values, Habermas greatly exaggerates both the degree of system and value convergence within the EU, and the extent to which political and national values can be separated.

In fact, Europe is far more diverse, and the sense of Europeanness among its peoples far shallower than Habermas allows. He also underestimates both the elements of negative identification discussed in the chapter's second part, and the eclectic (and sometimes contradictory) way in which collective identities emerge. As a consequence, his vision of European values and value convergence is both overoptimistic and overconfident, despite his own reference to the reflexive and self-critical way in which Europeans deal with their unmastered past. Moreover, his political insistence on the need for a "core" Europe to force the pace of political unification and identity construction underestimates the tendencies toward administrative centralization implicit in the European project as it has developed so far, while underplaying the dangers of the exercise of hegemonic power by a small number of elites or the possibility of domination of certain territorial coalitions.

Habermas seems strangely uninterested in the multiplicity of cleavages that traverse the European Union. His construction of constitutional patriotism fails to confront the more contingent aspects from which political identity emerges. In this respect, his is an overly idealized picture of Europe's geopolitical role, one that fails to perceive the importance that both the post-Maastricht developments and Enlargement have played in forming the still confused self-understanding of the European polity (see Case and Kaelble in this volume).

Habermas also seems oblivious to the potential difficulties presented by the project of constructing a value-based identity that is not exclusionary. To the extent that the European values are presented as "our" values, there is always a tendency to construct them in opposition to those of others and therefore to exclude the others. In the reality of an increasingly multicultural and diverse Europe – where mobility and immigration play a much larger role than in the near past – such an insistence on values, even on universal values, risks being socially and culturally divisive rather than unifying. Moreover, in some cases, it is difficult to see what makes certain values specifically our own, if not a selective reconstruction of the historical evidence.

Take, for instance, Habermas's explicit reference to the "social pri-
vatization of faith" as something that divides Europe from the United
States: "a president who begins his official functions every day with a
public prayer and connects his momentous political decisions with a
divine mission is difficult to imagine" (2006, p. 46). Although the public
show of religious zeal may be alien to most political cultures in Europe,
religion's public role is probably as much a matter of contention in
the United States as across Europe, and crucially, within each of the
European countries. Arguably, the role of religion within European
public cultures has recently become, if anything, more prominent, not
least as a result of Enlargement (cf. Byrnes and Katzenstein 2006).

The tendency in Habermas's analysis of value convergence to show a
common European political culture tends to constrain the diversity of
Europe. Unwittingly, his proposal promotes the very talk of an ethnic
Europe he seeks to avoid, offering the idea of Europe as a superstate, or
Fortress Europe, a spurious legitimacy in order to retain an allegiance to
putatively common constitutional values. In other words, Habermas
fails to see both the inevitable dangers (i.e. the exclusionary side) of any
construction of political identity, and the deeply ingrained divisions of
European political culture, which cannot easily be reconciled by a broad
Enlightenment view of European identity.

The constructive role of democratic conflict

The failure, in my view, of Habermas's attempt to construct European
political identity mainly on abstract values is that his conception of
democratic politics is over-reliant on the idea of consensus, downplay-
ing the important role of political conflict. Although he views value
convergence and the rights that follow from it as the result of communicative processes within the public sphere, the difficulty with his theory
is that beyond the most abstract level, and sometimes even there, there is
considerable disagreement about how values translate into particular
policies and institutional arrangements, and on the foundations and
character of rights and their application to particular issues. Debates
and conflicts over values and rights not only provide the substance of
many political debates, they also produce different accounts of the
nature of the political (Bellamy and Castiglione 2008). The same goes
for political identity and its effect on the practice of citizenship. Neither
is simply constructed on a set of political values and political rights.

Rather, political identity is partly expressed in how we, as citizens, go about claiming rights or participating in politics at different institutional levels.

A different way to see the formation of political identity in Europe, one more attuned to the issue of democratic disagreement and conflict rather than consensus, is to emphasize the structural as opposed to the value and legal mechanisms as the key factor of European constitutionalism – most particularly, the balance and separation of powers produced by the EU's unique mix of intergovernmental, supranational, and transnational decision-making mechanisms. Hence, European political identity needs to be adapted to the plurality of political and legal systems that have both legitimated and fostered European integration. The involvement of different peoples and nations is also an important factor in ensuring a flexibility of approach that takes into account the very different economic and social circumstances of the member states – a factor that has become all the more important with Enlargement. From this perspective, the appeal to constitutional patriotism risks being a purely rhetorical exercise and may occasionally stifle the ongoing constitutional dialogue that has so far led to an increasing sense of mutual respect and recognition, combining both diversity and an ever closer Union of peoples rather than a nationalistic creation of a European people.

Although multilevel governance undermines the sense of unity and purpose that characterizes traditional forms of democratic power, it does not necessarily exclude the introduction of other forms of more diffuse democratic participation and deliberation, thereby giving the citizens input on what matters in their lives. In the practice of common deliberation on common problems, European citizens can develop a sense of sharing a common identity and of solidarity. In terms of democratic participation, Europe offers gains as well as apparent losses. European politics is undeniably often characterized by log-rolling and horse-trading between national governments in defense of sectoral interests of various degrees of legitimacy. However, it also offers fora for a more deliberative style of politics – one that is partly detached from the constraints imposed by modern-day party politics and sometimes better able to combine individual and democratic perspectives with those advanced by expert bodies. But the reverse also holds true: intergovernmentalism has also allowed particular interests to be successfully defended against the force of simple majoritarianism within a given national community. It is arguably the very diversity and mutually balancing character of the various policy-making polities and regimes comprising the European Union that places it in a better position to represent the variety of rights, interests, and identities that characterize citizenship in modern societies. In this respect, European political identity needs to reflect the institutional plurality that characterizes political Europe.

Conclusion: the ties that bind a community of strangers

The more conflictual and divided image of political identity that I have suggested here takes us back to the question from which this chapter started. Has the relationship between political identification and political allegiance changed as a result of the growing internationalization of politics, of which the European integration process is part? Part of the answer, as Habermas correctly identifies, is already inscribed in the experience of the nation-state.

The ties that bind a political community can be seen as a form of "social cement" but also as a form of "political allegiance," a distinction that runs along similar lines to Ulrich Preuss's "Transaktions-Wir" (we-transactions) and "Solidaritäts-Wir" (we-solidarity) (2005). Although these elements are often confused because the historical experience of the nation-state has linked them in an inextricable knot, they are separate and are somewhat captured by the paradox expressed by the idea of a "community of strangers." Such an idea is somewhat counterintuitive, if we adhere to Tönnies's famous distinction between "community" (*Gemeinschaft*) and "society" (*Gesellschaft*): "all kinds of social co-existence that are familiar, comfortable and exclusive are to be understood as belonging to *Gemeinschaft* ... In *Gemeinschaft* we are united from the moment of our birth with our own folk for better or for worse. We go into *Gesellschaft* as if into a foreign land" (Tönnies 2001, p. 18).

When we speak of a "political community," we do not mean the cozy and intimate relationships that exist in small groups. Our life in a political community is mostly conducted as a series of relationships in a *Gesellschaft*, in the sense meant by Tönnies. But we do not treat our political community as a "foreign land," nor do we view the other members as "strangers." Modern political and sociological discourse has therefore been careful to suggest that, although our life in large modern societies is a life among strangers – characterized by anonymous relationships in the public sphere, mediated by the market, the law, institutions of public and private administration, and various forms of associations – our destiny as members of a political community remains linked to that of others, with whom we live in an *inclusive* relationship of relative familiarity and identity and on whose solidarity we rely. The question then becomes, in what sense can the European Union be a society of strangers (even more so than a nation-state would be) and at the same time a "political community"? And how is this possible without entering into direct conflict with nation-states' claim to a very similar status and loyalty from its citizens?

One way of answering this question is perhaps to take a step back and look at the connexion between the modern conception of political allegiance and the conception of the modern state. In discussing the nature of the "modern" form of political community, Weber (1968) emphasizes three elements characterizing the organization of a collectivity of people: (1) a territorial space; (2) the availability (and virtual monopoly) of physical force; and (3) the wide scope of the community's social action (beyond that of the satisfaction of common economic needs, or of other specialized functions). The crucial point for our discussion is the second one. Force is available for external or, more routinely, for internal use. Such use of force is crucial in defining the relationship between the community and the individual, since it defines the extent of the obligations of the member toward the community itself. With regard to the internal use, physical force is functional to backing up the member's obligations, while excluding the private use of force except in narrowly defined circumstances. With regard to external use, the community requires that the individual participate in the defense of its interests. Weber talks of this "common political struggle of life and death" as the political community's "particular pathos," requiring "enduring emotional foundations." According to Weber, such emotional foundations come from the ties of memory, even more than from those of cultural, linguistic, and ethnic identities (1968).

If Weber is right about the modern form of political community, it is easy to conclude that the European Union is not a political community, nor is it likely to become one soon. However, as we have already seen, our conception of the political community has changed somewhat. Indeed, Weber himself notes that the type of "discipline" required of members of a political community finds its roots in more military kinds of organization, in which citizens are directly involved in the defense of the community. This raises the interesting point of whether, in our modern political societies where nation-states have largely abandoned the practice of national conscription for professional armies, the ordinary citizen is indeed required to commit what Weber calls the "ultimate" sacrifice in defense of the community. Of course, one may envisage exceptional circumstances in which the entire population may need mobilizing; but this could indeed be true of natural cataclysms or other situations where people may need no particular motivation to participate in rescue operations at the risk of their own lives. There may still be some important sense in which the political community needs the allegiance of its members, and we may not like the way in which the arrangements for war and security have been privatized; but the close connexion between the idea of a political community and the expectation that its members may "ultimately face death in the group interest" is not as obvious nowadays as it was in Weber's time. From this point of view, the recognized inability of the European Union to inspire such extreme forms of sacrifice does not exclude it from performing other functions of a political community, as long as it can mobilize people's solidarity in other respects.

But there is more. As Hegel, for one, perceptively noted, it is mistaken to think of patriotism mainly as a "readiness for exceptional sacrifices and actions" (1952, p. 164). Hegel describes patriotism as a more ordinary and banal sentiment about how our own life depends on the operations of the political community. It is a form of trust, or, as he put it, "the consciousness that my interest, both substantive and particular, is contained and preserved in another's (i.e. in the state) interest and end." It is from the daily exertion (and self-conscious realization) of this form of trust that "arises the readiness for extraordinary exertions." The point here is not about the nature of patriotism but about the way in which the individual may relate to the community – for if a sense of obligation can be cultivated through more ordinary acts and exertions, we may have no need to find deep "emotional" roots, but merely a mixture of rational self-interest, habituation, and cultivation of a sense of the collective interest.

This point is closely linked with another made by Hegel in his comment to the same passage on patriotism, in which he remarks that "commonplace thinking often has the impression that force holds the state together, but in fact its only bond is the fundamental sense of order which everybody possesses" (1952, p. 282). If this interpretation is convincing, the European Union must cultivate its political identity neither in the heroic form of the "ultimate sacrifice," nor in high-principled forms of constitutional patriotism, but in the more banal sense of citizens' growing perception that the Union contributes to a fundamental (though multilayered) institutional and legal order within which they can exercise their liberty.

Finally, the internalization of politics, and the form of "open state-hood" that increasingly characterizes the relationship among states (particularly within the European Union), is changing the state of affairs that Weber seems to presuppose in his analysis of the role of force as a constitutive element of the modern state. Nowadays, it is indeed less clear whether the emotional and imaginary rootedness of national patriotism is what is required to sustain political communities in the twenty-first century. It is possible to imagine a more variegated pattern, something that is not unknown in history. In his dialogue *On the Laws*, for instance, Cicero (1999) distinguishes one's affection toward one's "fatherland" (based on memories and the idea of custom and tradition) from one's feelings toward the "commonwealth" (based more on the importance of laws and republican institutions): ultimately, the latter should prevail over the former.

Cicero's was a more "republican" interpretation (in the classical, historical sense) of the demands of the political community, and it may be as inadequate today, if applied to the EU, as the invention (or rediscovery) of common European memories. But it also suggests that open statehood may mean more fragmented identities and allegiances and the possibility that they will enter into conflict with each other. However, there is no reason to believe that such conflict should be unmanageable. Of course, there will always be a danger that conflicts and disagreement may degenerate into a deadlock or even into vio-lence. But the solution may lie more in imagining how an interlocking political space may need interlocking systems of trust, solidarity, and allegiances – none of which may need to be absolute – than in the assumption that we can reproduce the absolute demands of national citizenship at a European level.

3 | *Experimental identities (after Maastricht)*

DOUGLAS R. HOLMES

The imperatives of European integration are inciting identity experiments, often involving dissonant and unstable forms of consciousness, that defy or exceed familiar categories of analysis. Rather than a mere shift in identity from, say, being German, Irish or Latvian to being European, a fundamental change in the underlying dynamics of identity formation is underway. Identities are coalescing on the level of intimate encounters, expressed in obscure and arcane cultural vernaculars, by which experience gains highly pluralist articulations posing unusual analytical challenges. Perhaps the most important challenge is to candidly acknowledge that "identity" has become, to a greater or lesser degree, an ambiguous and, at times, vexatious issue not just for us as observers, but also for our subjects (Boyer 2005). The people of Europe are at the outset of the twenty-first century negotiating among liberal and illiberal registers of consciousness, and these shifting configurations typically do not succumb to a single, stable, and unambiguous expression (see introduction to this volume).

I suggest in this chapter that what we awkwardly and imprecisely term "identity" has acquired a twofold nature. On the one hand, it is not merely or solely contingent on convention, tradition, and the past, but has assumed a future-oriented purview and experimental dynamic. On the other, citizens of the EU as they pursue these experiments are continually parsing the nature of cultural affinity and difference as they participate in the creation of a vast, multiracial and multicultural Europe. Neither of these characteristics is entirely new, but after the ratification of the Maastricht Treaty the nature and the temporal trajectory of identity projects have shifted decisively. After the completion of the great identity project of the second half of the twentieth century – the integration of Germany within Europe – and under the sway of a comprehensive and far-reaching liberalism, a new and very different project of identity has been delineated (Katzenstein 1997). After Maastricht, the EU imparts to its citizens the distinctive challenge and the ambiguous burden to negotiate continually the cognitive meanings and political exigencies of a pluralist Europe.

I start with a paradigmatic moment – an address delivered by Jean-Marie Le Pen to an audience in Budapest – that marks a decisive shift in the scale and the reach of identity based politics. The event is significant because of the curious manner in which his message, designed to speak to a very particular community of French nationalists, resonated with a Hungarian public. I then turn to two related though very different intellectual fields – Catholic social doctrine and European Monetary Union – and examine how they are establishing the communicative space within which emerging identity projects are articulated and contextualized. This discussion is followed by the examination of a series of identity experiments drawn from a selection of ethnographic studies of "communities of practice" among Alpine farmers; "ethical citizenship" among urban Catholics; the predicaments of identity experienced by Turkish lobbyists living and working in Brussels; and the stylistic innovations of youth cultures in Croatia and inner London as they inspire experimentation with incendiary forms of political consciousness. The final case focusses on a speech by Tony Blair – delivered under duress – in which he sought to formulate a political and ethical framework that could speak to the racial and cultural exigencies increasingly defining Britain and Europe. Each of these experiments is thus aligned with a very particular problematic of Europe that emerged after Maastricht, addressing the shifting nature of society as a moral framework, analytical construct, and empirical fact. I begin, however, with a prelude to the current era of European activism spawned by a fateful American intercession at the close of World War I.

1919

Woodrow Wilson's ill-fated interventions in the aftermath of World War I and in the wake of the collapse of the Romanoff, Turkish, and Hapsburg empires sanctioned a precarious era of cultural innovation (see Case in this volume). By inscribing in the Versailles Treaty the right of "self-determination" and conferring this right on loosely constituted collectivities – nations, peoples, and minorities – radical experiments with cultural identities were set in motion. The Treaty legitimized various collective ideals – enshrined in fraught historical claims of loss

and injury – inspiring communal aspirations and political activisms that
were played out across new and contested borderlands (Cowan 2003a,
2003b, 2006a, 2007a, 2007b).

The Wilsonian formula – particularly V–VI and IX–XIV of his
fourteen points – was crafted from an admixture of illiberal ideas
drawn from the Romantic tradition, together with liberal notions of
self-determination to establish legally enforceable rights and protections.
The result was a tragic reification of "culture" and "history" by which
peoples and nations could be constituted or reconstituted in relationship
to what were believed to be fundamental affinities and irreconcilable
differences (Berlin 1976, 1979, 1990, 1997; Herzfeld 1987; Holmes
2000; Skowronek 2006). Theorists of fascism and National Socialism
refined these principles of collective belonging during the interwar
years, aligning their respective projects with an ardent orientation to
the future and thereby creating an *illiberal* modernism (Mazower
1998; Sternhell 1996).

Typically, the disturbing consequences of the Versailles Treaty are
ascribed to tragic errors, miscalculations, parochial disputes, and political intoxication with the idea of reparations. Recent Wilsonian scholarship by Stephen Skowronek, however, suggests deeper resonances.
The American president, raised in the South, brought to Paris his own
fraught liberal and illiberal dispositions forged in the aftermath of the
Civil War and Reconstruction. These compelled him, on the one hand,
to overrule a majority vote that would have "inserted into the preamble
of the League of Nations charter the principle of racial equality" while,
on the other, allowing him to argue for democratic self-determination of
and for nations and peoples (Skowronek 2006, p. 389). Skowronek's
analysis not only anticipates the dissonant pluralisms that are emerging
in Europe at the opening of the twenty-first century; it also and, perhaps
more importantly, suggests discordant cultural configurations inherent
within and entirely inseparable from liberal projects of globalization.[1]

As we know too well, the violent enthusiasms spawned by the
Versailles agreements contributed to the most blighted episodes in the
history of twentieth-century Europe. This earlier era of experimentation
with collective aspirations is, however, linked inextricably to the current

---

[1] The study of these dissonant pluralisms and discordant cultural configurations
that imbue liberal projects of globalization can provide a critical area for scholarly
collaborations between political scientists and anthropologists.

situation insofar as the project of European integration has sought explicitly and implicitly to extinguish or otherwise circumvent the legacy of 1919. Much as the Treaty of Versailles impelled an era of experimentation, the European Treaties are framing "new" identity projects – projects that infuse Europe with diverse and at times contradictory political significance (Judt 2005; Lipgens 1984).

As a young man, Jean Monnet served as Chief of Staff to the General Secretary of the League of Nations, a position that afforded him an unusually intimate purview on this ill-fated project of supranationalism (Monnet 1978). After World War II, he and the other architects of the European Union designed an institutional practice in which liberal strategies of technocratic reform were designed to circumvent the tragic legacies of ethnic and national identity. The overriding historical agenda sought, as we know, to circumvent the traditional antagonisms between and among the nation-states of Europe – notably those between France and Germany – and substituted, ideally, a pragmatic institutional practice in the service of a particular expression of liberal governmentality (Ferguson 1990; Haas 1964, 1968).

The history of the EU has of course been punctuated by numerous episodes in which these old antagonisms reasserted themselves; however, by the adoption of the Maastricht Treaty in the early 1990s, the main goal of this agenda had been accomplished. Germany was fully integrated in Europe, and this was achieved by means of an emphatic constitutionalism inscribed in diplomatic treaties and informed by liberal principles of political reform and economic restructuring (Moravcsik 1998, 2007; Weiler 1999). The grasp of a blighted history was renounced as pragmatic technocratic reforms and progressive institutional narratives were embraced.[2]

European integralism

In the spring of 2007, Jean-Marie Le Pen placed fourth in the first round of the French presidential election. Despite this dismal showing, Le Pen had in a profound way won the election. He had succeeded in reshaping the political debate in France around a key set of issues that he first

---

[2] Much, if not all, of the analysis that follows in this chapter can and should be read in productive counterpoint with Neil Fligstein's contribution in this volume as well as that of Adrian Favell.

articulated in the 1970s, issues preeminently concerned with identity. His opponents had skillfully appropriated these ideas to inform their discourse and to underwrite their own electoral success (Berezin 2006a, 2007; Bowen 2007).

More significantly, his ardently French cultural agenda had by the first decade of the new century spawned political movements across every member state of the EU, led by figures who explicitly or implicitly modeled themselves on Le Pen's insurgency. Le Pen, more than any other figure, "re-functioned" the nature of European identity, imparting to it an experimental ethos and an illiberal dynamic. I have cast Le Pen as a "European integralist" – rather than merely a French nationalist – to emphasize what I believe are his remarkable political innovations.[3] Le Pen is the most conspicuous, but by no means the only agent actively recasting identity as a subject of political practice (see Castiglione in this volume). That said, he stands out as the individual who first diagnosed how fundamental aspects of integration were inseparable from questions of identity (Le Pen 1984, 1989).

Le Pen conjured a wide-ranging discourse on Europe that was ardently opposed to the basic assumption of integration and, significantly, he formulated this agenda while serving as an elected member of the European Parliament. From his vantage point within a major European institution, he discovered that his message, designed to address a tiny conservative, if not reactionary, French public could be re-crafted, giving it wide currency that could inspire activism beyond the borders of France. Le Pen distilled a conceptual architecture for integralism around postu-lates that speak to what he contends are the essence of human nature and the character of cultural affinity and difference. By so doing, he provided analytical purchase on the shifting nature of collective life, transforma-tions of the public sphere, and realignments of human intimacy (Betz 2002; Bowen 2007; Hannerz 2006; Gaillard-Starzmann 2006; Banks and Gingrich 2006; MacDonald 2006).

In my writing on integralism, I increasingly use "Le Pen" *figuratively* to stand for a series of innovations that Le Pen, the person, initially worked out, but which now operate beyond his control in all twenty-seven member states of the EU in the hands of other agile and typically

---

[3] For a comprehensive ethnographic overview of European integralism, see Holmes (2000). For the earliest example of anthropological work on European integration and its relationship to issues of identity, see Wilson and Smith (1993).

younger political actors. The key point here is that "identity" emerges in the twenty-first century, not as an idiosyncratic psychological reflex or residual collective sensibility, but as a phenomenon that can (or must) be framed in reference to contemporary institutional realities after Maastricht.

By its nature, integralism is an unstable phenomenon that is continually being reinvented, defying easy definitions by blending what appear to be incompatible elements drawn from the political traditions of the Left and the Right. That said, Le Pen endowed this field of ideas and practices with a distinctive political configuration and dynamic trajectory; thus, I have chosen to personify my conceptualization of integralism in relation to this mercurial figure, rather than defining it systematically. Furthermore, my aim here is to demonstrate how by virtue of "ideological drift," just about every mainstream political grouping in Europe has assimilated elements of the "inner truths" that animate this kind of politics (Skowronek 2006, p. 387). Thus, for the purposes of this chapter, I am emphasizing the range and spread of these political innovations as a macro-level phenomenon and, hence, highlighting what Susan Gal (2007) refers to as the "interdiscursivity" of these ideas – rather than typologizing them within discrete and neatly circumscribed political groups or grouplets.[4]

Though the account that follows is notional, it was provoked by an actual event: the appearance of Le Pen at a public rally in Budapest earlier in this decade, a rally at which he was enthusiastically greeted and where the form and content of his message had deep resonances.[5] His appearance posed for me a key question: Why would Le Pen's message, formulated to appeal to an ardently French audience, have appeal in Central Europe, to a Hungarian audience organized by the

---

[4] Gal comments on this communicative phenomenon as follows:

Let's elaborate the notion of "interdiscursvity" – a concept meant to capture "semiosis across encounters" – and one on which there is already important work in linguistic anthropology. This way, we develop the tools of linguistic anthropology so that it can provide a better grasp of the **communicative and semiotic** aspects of contemporary interconnection ... I argue that *arenas* of action – culturally created and demarcated – are linked to each other through various interdiscursive devices. These constitute what is usually called circulation, and allow us to see how practices seem to spread and with what effect. (2007, pp. 1–2; emphasis and italics in the original)

[5] I am indebted to Endre Fischer, who attended the rally with a group of friends and provided a provocative account.

Hungarian Justice and Life Party (MIÉP)? Or put slightly differently, how is a political message gaining articulation that can speak directly to the emerging predicaments of local audiences in a way that acknowledges the old divisions of East and West and yet can also transcend them?

Audience

In my earliest observation of Le Pen almost two decades ago, I recognized that his political practice embraced far more than fidelity to the idea of "nation"; rather, it drew authority from a wide range of collective sensibilities. Specifically, he understood that a dynamic pluralism could be cast in opposition to the EU's supranational exigencies, revealing the potential of integralism to join, fuse, merge, and synthesize what might appear to be incompatible principles of association. Moreover, simple distinctions between Left and Right no longer served as a reliable guide within the communicative space defined by Le Pen, in which "socialism" can be reconstituted in relation to illiberal cultural values. I begin this discussion with an examination of the audience for this politics and the perils of reductive and oversimplified representation of the identities and sensibilities of its members (Holmes 1993, 2006).[6]

If early in the twenty-first century one were to walk through the crowd at a public rally for Le Pen in France, or for one of the many political figures who model themselves on Le Pen elsewhere in Europe, one would see the embodiment of integralism, particularly its pluralist character. As one surveyed the audience – whether on the outskirts of Budapest, Antwerp, Lisbon, Prague, or Rome – one could identify by dress, demeanor, dialect, or other overt characteristics the distinct groups and identities that constitute this notional audience. The remnants of the great constituencies that animated the era of the modern nation-state seem to be recruited to this politics of disaffection and loss. Though not wrong per se, this is an oversimplified and incomplete understanding of the groups that are drawn to this identity inspired politics.

One would likely find: farmers, conservative Catholics, pensioners and military veterans, schoolteachers and other low and mid-level government employees, factory workers, owners of small shops and businesses, university students and members of other often religiously

---

[6] An earlier version of this account appears in Holmes (2006).

sponsored youth organizations, a coterie of skinheads and, at the margins, the police, who participate alternately as a security contingent and as attentive listeners. The speaker typically acknowledges these groupings and addresses them on their terms: members of the audience need not divest themselves of their idiosyncratic identities; on the contrary, the only way their participation makes sense is from the standpoint of their own particular sensibilities and consciousness. Neither are they addressed as abstract subjects of a nation-state or as citizens of a European Union; and they certainly are not addressed as "consumers" to be sold a political message.

These groupings are equally hostile to the rule of the market and to the logic of technocracy. For them, political meaning can only be socially mediated through idioms of family, town and country, ethnic and linguistic assemblages, religious communities, occupational statuses, social classes, and so on. Their faith and loyalty reside in *experience* reconciled through these collective entities, and thus through forms of solidarity that are simultaneously prosaic and radical. Again, the keen irony, which Le Pen so carefully configured, is that only from the perspective of these collective groupings is the "true" meaning of the new Europe revealed: only from these vantage points can the supranational project be critically appraised and its meaning apprehended.

Members of these groups appear to share a sense of encroachment that threatens the integrity of their diverse communities, providing the common thread that weaves their distinctive agendas together. Le Pen observed that one can experience intense estrangement and alienation, not as a result of exile per se, but in one's homeland, in one's rural parish, urban neighborhood and just about everywhere in between. He recognized that integration is paradoxically creating new domains of alienation in which discordant identities can establish the terms of struggle. He mobilized complex emotional sensibilities to animate his insurgency, in which sublime longings and desires are crosscut by acute fears and anxieties. These are the manifold human predicaments gaining political articulation as integralism, an integralism that resonates across a supranational Europe. Le Pen substitutes the authority of "experience," shared experience, as the basis of legitimacy, credibility, and truth. He recognizes that a particular kind of message – an integralist message – can be communicated in ways that are not susceptible to the forms of rational scrutiny and intellectual mediation that characterized the era of the nation-state, but can enter the lifeworlds of a new European public and be accepted, as it were, on "faith" (Habermas 1987).

There is, however, something fundamentally misleading about this political tableau. There are other incongruities operating within this audience that are deep and profound, disrupting demarcations between, for example, emerging and eclipsed groups in contemporary Europe. The same people – and their children, friends, and relatives – who drift in and out of these rallies are often the most agile and adroit agents exploiting new opportunities unfolding across the EU. These figures avail themselves of the new freedom to traverse Europe (typically from East to West), establishing perhaps the most important and little understood axis of contemporary identity formation. They are paradigmatically seen or identified, at least at the moment, as "Polish workers-cum-entrepreneurs" who move into Western European cities and quickly establish themselves socially and economically. These sojourners appear to have a subtle understanding of the nature of risk and opportunities created by integration and are equipped to pursue and exploit them with great speed and shrewdness. One thing is clear: a simple calculus of advantaged and disadvantaged does not capture the complexities and contradictions of their experiences and their political aspirations. These people are searching for a politics that speaks to their experience and captures their inchoate struggles – a politics that can alternately appear liberal and illiberal.

An experimental ethos becomes plausible only in the wake of a prior institutional transformation in the nature and scope of communicative action. I have drawn on the work of David Westbrook (2004) to address how the project of integration yields a discursive field of supranationalism as an alternative to the communicative space afforded historically by the nation-state. Two intellectual traditions give form and structure to this emerging communicative field: social Catholicism and French technocratic modernism. Both traditions guided the specific design of a supranational polity and the daily management of its institutions. The interleaving of these two traditions creates a discursive field in which a multicultural and multiracial Europe gains expression, if not coherence.

Monetary problematic

In my current research in Frankfurt, I am examining the communicative imperatives operating within the European Central Bank (ECB), the main institutional project after Maastricht. On the face of it, the assertion that a central bank might be an agent of identity formation seems curious. The role of the Deutsche Bundesbank, upon which the ECB is modeled, is instructive. The Bundesbank's overt commitment to price stability is not merely an expression of prudential monetary policy but is informed by the searing historical experience – the interwar period – when episodes of inflation proved destructive to the social and the political order, inflaming various extreme identity projects in Germany – most notably, but by no means exclusively, National Socialism. The ECB's commitment to consistent, balanced growth without inflation, inherited from the German Federal Bank, is thus a means not only for mediating the value of the euro, but also for framing the contingencies of identity formation (McNamara 1998). Officials of the ECB must continually address two implicit political challenges: Can the European project be held together through the operation of a common currency? Can the euro create the basis of a *shared* economic fate and hence promote a European identity (Berezin 2006b; Shore 2000)?

Jean-Claude Trichet, President of the ECB, is charged with implementing what is arguably the most radical agenda of integration, the project of monetary union (EMU). He noted recently, "All in all, the art of central banking involves finding a fine balance between action and words" (Trichet 2005, p. 12). When President Trichet speaks, he is not merely expressing an interpretative account or commentary on financial matters; he is creating the economy itself as a communicative field and as an empirical fact. An integrated, European economy is thus being configured and reconfigured discursively in the obscure patois of monetary theory.

Trichet is a legatee of the French technocratic tradition that since the early nineteenth century designed and managed the operation of the modern French society and economy. He and his predecessors – notably Jean Monnet and Jacques Delors – transferred this institutional practice from Paris to Brussels, from the French nation-state to the supranational space of Europe. Trichet must in this new century answer the key intellectual preoccupation that has animated the French administrative movement since the 1830s: Can *solidarity* be orchestrated through technocratic interventions? More precisely, can money anchor mechanisms of solidarity consistent with an emerging multiculturalism and the multiracial architecture of Europe (Rabinow 1999; see Castiglione in this volume)?

David Westbrook argues acutely that under the EU's technocratic regime, supranational markets serve as constitutional devices – by which he means that

to understand the way we now live rests therefore, on a restatement of politics
as it appears in the context of supranational capital, legitimated through our
faith in the institutions of money and property, as opposed to the modern
nation state, legitimized through the familiar mechanisms of the liberal republic. (2004, p. 12)

Restated, if the conditions of social and so political life are undergoing
profound change, then supranational markets are decisive mechanisms
of such change and transformation. With the arrangement of social
affairs through markets, however, comes an attenuation of political
meaning:

The market's grammar, the dialectic between property and money, does not
express many things important to being human. Capitalism is therefore
radically impoverished as a system of politics. Insofar as we long for community, we necessarily experience life in capitalism as a sort of exile. (Westbrook
2004, p. 164)

The constitution of a polity in this manner will frustrate continually the
articulation of an overt politics that can unambiguously espouse and
align a single configuration of solidarity.

   Again, this predicament of meaning was, in the early 1990s, given a
far-reaching interpretation by a very unlikely figure – Le Pen – from the
vantage point of one of Monnet's supranational institutions. He recognized that the impoverishment of meaning of which the EU is inces-
santly accused is itself a template of identity. His integralist rejoinder to
the monetary problematic posed implicitly by Trichet is that under the
thrall of liberal supranationalism, diverse expressions of an illiberal
pluralism can attain political articulation, thus addressing the multicultural and multiracial realities of Europe. He understood that within
the expanding communicative space of supranationalism, identity projects can proliferate, independent, if not defiant, of the EU's regulatory
influence and control.

Catholicism within

The founders of the EU – notably Robert Schuman, Konrad Adenauer,
and Alcide de Gaspari – were social Catholics and drew on Catholic
doctrine, particularly as expressed in neo-Thomist philosophy, to impart
an intellectual architecture to the project (Amato 1975; Hellman 1981;
Maritain 1950). For them, identity was a key concern on a number of

different philosophical and instrumental levels. They designed a framework in which a commitment to pluralist identities was fundamental, a commitment that went beyond any particular confessional or secular stance. After Maastricht, Catholic social doctrine was widely embraced – encompassed by the principle of subsidiarity – to guide intellectually and regulate institutionally the cognitive meanings and political exigencies of a pluralist Europe (MacDonald 1996; Millon-Delsol 1992; Ross 1995; Zorgbibe 1993). The Catholic problematic can be stated in deceptively simple terms: Can the philosophical ideas that inform the principle of subsidiarity underwrite constitutionally a European social order predicated on multiple registers of faith and values?

Based on its ability to sustain pluralism and diversity across an integrated Europe, the Catholic configuration of identity has since the 1990s had broad political appeal (Katzenstein 2006). Yet, as the following excerpts, drafted in the 1940s, attest, it is plagued with an arcane and at times cloying philosophical language that frustrates its articulation as a wide-ranging political rhetoric addressed to a mass audience.

Different "spiritual families," in a common French phrase – Catholic, Protestant, Marxists, humanists, or whoever they may be – should ... be permitted and enabled to follow their own way of life, even when they are in a minority in a nation or group as a whole ... [Ideological pluralism] reduces conflict since it allows everyone, without discrimination ... to build up a set of associations, which fits his own ideals. (Fogarty 1957, p. 42)

By maintaining diversity of ideological perspectives, the terms of political engagement are established within the Catholic framework. And, though it seems counterintuitive, the doctrine holds that it is precisely in the clash of these diverse orientations and their vigorous expression that solidarity is engendered.

Since, in an imperfect world, some conflicts of ideals and loyalties are inevitable, the essential thing is that they should be fought out in a way which lets the truth eventually emerge and form the basis for a settlement. But this is likely to happen only if the parties in conflict hold firm, clear, views which provide a solid basis for argument, and yet are open and sensitive to the views of others ... everyone must sail "under his own flag" ... And organizations have a right and duty to "sail under their own flag" in the same way as individuals; for association with others is needed even to reach a full understanding of one's own ideals, let alone to express them effectively in action. "Tolerance" is hardly the word for this attitude ... There is ... a warmth of common humanity and common responsibility before God. But "the rigor of the game" is also part of its essence. (Fogarty 1957, pp. 42–3)

Political discourse, under the terms of Catholic social theory, operates in such a way that issues are contextualized constantly within a wider interplay of interests and remedies. It is this concern for the "totality" that creates a shifting consensus that can embrace and transform a broad spectrum of beliefs and interests. It is an approach that is intended to restrain partisanship. The aim is to achieve a "common good" in which shifting and unequal societal interests are linked through ties of cooperation and mutual aid to achieve social justice. The powerful sociological consequence of the political practice of "subsidiarity" is the promotion of a diversely constituted European social order. It provides an administrative model for aiding diverse collective groups – with distinctive liberal and illiberal identities – and drawing them into a common political process. Promoting these collective groupings with their distinctive cultural aspirations creates a broad political field, outside the ambit of the nation-state, for political innovation (Byrnes 2001; Katzenstein and Byrnes 2006).

Catholic political influence is manifest in the current composition of the European Parliament, where the European Peoples Party, the European wide Christian Democratic organization, has been the largest parliamentary group since 1999 and currently controls 277 of the 785 seats. The shrewd orchestration of Catholic political affiliations among diverse identity projects has also been instrumental in underwriting the project of EU enlargement in East and Central Europe over the last two decades. Within the parliament, the transnational and the supranational expressions of Catholic political and intellectual practice thus meet. Despite its electoral power and institutional authority, the Christian Democratic movement continues to operate as an elite project in which its theoretical ideas and its philosophical doctrines circulate primarily within a highly circumscribed community of adherents.

Communities of practice

Cristina Grasseni (2003, 2007) examined ethnographically the consequences of EU directives on the lives of herders in the alpine valleys of Lombardy. The generation of EU laws and directives has a very distinctive and often a very disruptive influence that differs in important ways from the administrative practices of state bureaucracies. The regulatory interventions described by Grasseni were simultaneously being applied in literally thousands of upland valleys from the Pyrenees to the Carpathians by local communities of practice that interpreted and adapted these laws and directives to their own local traditions, environmental conditions, and economic needs. The aim was not to institute a uniform regime that sought to regularize grazing practices in every rural locale; rather, it was understood that people within their *own* communities would gradually embrace the new institutional incentives and disincentives, complying over time with the rules on terms that endow them with very particular meanings. These administrative arrangements provide room – substantial room – for citizens to accommodate, interpret, and adapt this regulatory framework to their own immediate circumstances within a diversely constituted federal system. By so doing, a European identity is imparted to the lives of citizens through the operation of their *own* communities of practice, articulated in their own cultural idioms and social vernaculars.

In the classical bureaucratic tradition, laws were propagated in national capitals and transmitted to various administrative levels and jurisdictions of the state where they were enforced (more or less) uniformly and (more or less) to the letter. Often, various categories of officialdom were physically present in local settings to oversee and insure accountability with these legal standards and administrative provisions (Crozier 1973). By contrast, the EU interventions are perhaps more ambitious, aimed at recasting incentives and accountabilities across various social, economic, environmental, political, cultural, and educational spheres and not merely at compelling conformity to particular rules and regulations.

In this micro-level example, EU regulation disrupts traditional social practices in an Alpine community, creating what the outside observer and the people themselves would characterize as "havoc." I use this case to demonstrate how this chaotic condition is, in fact, instrumental insofar as it establishes the terms by which the people themselves mediate this process of identity formation. The responses of these people to the disruptions introduced by the EU regulatory regime – its program of discipline and punishment – become the means by which these Alpine herders assimilate over time the sentiments and expectations that constitute the basis of a European identity.

The "chaos" incited by these directives is assumed to be resolved over time by the citizens themselves as they are recruited to perform the labor of integration. Rather than being compelled or coerced to follow new sets of rules and regulations, people will instead embrace the incentives and disincentives inherent in these directives, adapting them to countless situations and contexts. EU citizens in innumerable settings will thus accomplish the social and cultural labor of integration themselves; over the medium term the chaos – as Grasseni points out – will be mastered in relationship to local practices as a European consciousness of sorts is ingrained in the lives of these citizens through a gradual and almost imperceptible process (Ferguson 1990).

Grasseni illustrates how the intricate networks of traditional relations and tenant payments that govern the movement of herds of cattle each year from lowland to upland pastures and back were dislocated by new incentives. The annual cycle of summer grazing, called *alpeggio*, had clear advantages for these communities of herders.

Feeding costs drop for as long as a third of the year. Secondly, cheese produced on the pastures is highly valued and may be sold for a high price. In the long run, a natural diet and outdoor lifestyle make the cows fit, resilient to infectious disease and visibly happier. The practice of *alpeggio* has been recently reconsidered also as a fire-prevention measure, in that the practice of grazing avoids bush and grass overgrowth. Self-ignited fires (but also arsons) are often headline news in the Italian summers, and especially in mountain areas they contribute to irreversible erosion, putting the territory at risk of landslides. (Grasseni 2007, p. 442)

EU aid distributed in the summer of 2000 sought to encourage these practices with bonus payments of up to 40,000 euros.

As a result of these incentives, farmers who never practised *alpeggio* before were spurred to take part in tendering competitions (*gare d'appalto*) for the high pastures. Likewise, the pasture-owners … were motivated to increase pasture rents, which were previously almost symbolic. This created havoc among established patterns of pasture allocation, which in recent decades, because of massive farmers' migration, had happened in the virtual absence of competition. This caused conflicts that revealed how sensitive local contexts may be to external incentives. (Grasseni 2007, p. 443)

Tensions, conflicts, and litigations ensued between the established herders and the newcomers, many of whom had never practiced *alpeggio* before. Rents were bid up, and herders with traditional claims refused to relinquish their access to pasturage secured by newcomers under the reformed tender system. New competition was also stimulated from sheep- and goat-herders who were further viewed by the cattle herders as a threat to ecological balance and likely to overgraze the Alpine pastures. Hence, the "introduction of artificial incentives in a very delicately balanced network of communal rents and local tenders, intensified competition to the point of disrupting the network" (Grasseni 2007, p. 444).

And, as Grasseni argues, "competition and conflict can lead to the dismantling of the very local networks, the *communities of practice* of peers, administrators and technical advisors, who guarantee the survival of the [local] context" (2006). The introduction of EU law and administrative directives are understood to be antagonistic and may, in fact, be intentionally antagonistic to pre-existing cultural norms, values, and social practices. They seem alien to the citizens who are subjected to them because they operate outside the realm of familiar contextualizing traditions and histories. This is, as Grasseni notes, a very incomplete reading of what actually unfolds in this and countless other settings. In fact, she demonstrates that within a relatively short time – a matter of two or three years – the community had begun to adapt to these new incentives, incorporating them within their own local framework of expectations and sentiments.

My point here is that similar processes are unfolding in communities of practice encompassing virtually all those industries, professions, government bureaus, and nongovernmental organizations that are in one way or another subject to EU regulatory standards. These diverse communities of practice serve as the milieus within which identity assumes a future-oriented purview and experimental dynamic impelled by the evolving regulatory regime of the EU itself. Chaotic conditions like those described above impel people themselves – operating within their own variously constituted communities of practice – to resolve the processes of identity formation. Again, the micro-level disruptions introduced by the EU regulatory regime become the means by which these varied groups of people negotiate over time the common sentiments and expectations that constitute a very broadly based European identity.

Ethical citizenship

Andrea Muehlebach's ethnographic study of "ethical citizenship" examines experimentation with Catholic identity gaining expression within programs of voluntary service in Lombardy and Italy more generally. These projects seek in part to fill the functions relinquished by the welfare state with an alternative activism, by which cadres of volunteers operate in a public service that is imagined to be separate from the influence of market forces and the conventional (secular) political preoccupations of the state. Rather, an ethically and spiritually defined duty binding the individual and society impels this volunteerism. The aim of this activism is the promotion of a human fulfillment espoused by the Church that can reanimate Catholic identity.

Muehlebach examines how a "new" ethical framework for Catholic identity and voluntary practice is institutionalized in Milan through formal training classes and the contractual instruments that define volunteerism in relationship to Italian law. She demonstrates how this identity project realigns human sentiments with social action in a manner that circumvents conventional, secular assumptions, creating a very distinctive space of a "soulful" and "virtuous" identity that can underpin a new framework of "freedom" and "citizenship."

Gratuità (translated as "free-gifting" or "free-giving" on the Vatican's webpage and considered essential to the Biblical revelation) is a theological virtue often mobilized by members of the Italian public who question the nature of contemporary capitalism. The late Pope John Paul II was only one particularly prominent voice in this debate when he insisted during his last years that "society needs to convert to the idea of unselfish giving." As he said in a speech on Ash Wednesday in 2002, "today's society has a deep need to rediscover the positive value of free giving (*gratuità*), especially because in our world what often prevails is a logic motivated exclusively by the pursuit of profit and gain at any price." (Muehlebach 2007, p. 201)

This overtly illiberal identity project defines itself in opposition to the market's preoccupations with material values, establishing an alternative ethical foundation for social life. Identity is thus implicated in an "epochal struggle" that seeks to mobilize a potentially large and idealistic collective following.

The pope had made it one of his priorities to argue that Christianity was the antidote to free marketeering because it proposed "the idea of free giving, founded on the intelligent freedom of human beings inspired by authentic love" ... In Catholic theology, the spirit of free giving is instantiated in activities like charity. Individuals engaging in charitable actions are considered to be directly animated by divine grace, their souls infused with the holy spirit. With his promotion of the virtue of free giving, the pope had evoked an epochal struggle between divine love and the weakness of human beings for material things. (Muehlebach 2007, pp. 201–2)

This project is contingent on a "hybrid legal-theological context" that rests on reforms of welfare policies as well as a radical rethinking of strategies for intervention. The aim is to cultivate emotions that can mediate between identity and action.

[N]ew legal regimes and state institutions aim to produce the public figure of "the volunteer," and to create a symbolic and material infrastructure around a sphere imagined to be saturated with the sacrality of the gift. As thousands of members of "the volunteer sector" are schooled in training courses every year, the state marshals what it imagines as the affective, empathetic, and "caring" stances of citizens. (Muehlebach 2007, pp. 203–4)

Muehlebach demonstrates how "emotions" are transformed by this movement into "conventionalized, stabilized, and qualified sensibilities" that can be put to work within a new framework of citizenship.

[T]he Ministry of Welfare is gearing parts of its organizational architecture around the soliciting of empathetic responses to social problems within its citizen-volunteers. In its education of desire, state practice aims to produce a normative moral citizen-subject propelled not by a rational, but by an affective will, not by reason, but by desire. The summoning of ethical citizens relies on the dissemination of a standardized account of "the volunteer," and of what it means to provide volunteer "service" in the emerging service sector of which volunteering is a crucial part. (Muehlebach 2007, p. 204)

Most brilliantly, Muehlebach captures how identity projects become aligned with very specific "inner-truths" and how these projects can assume an overt institutional reality and political expression.

Through an analysis of several volunteer training classes that I attended, I explore how ethical citizenship is promoted through multiple registers, all of which share a particular persuasive form. I show that techniques of citizen-moralization rely on the cultivation of an ethic of self-reflection amongst trainees. Built around self-knowledge and (depending on the register used, the feeling of empathy or empowerment) these interior states are said to only come to full, meaningful fruition once they are translated by citizens into pragmatic ethical action – action which, in turn, is imagined to produce public, conspicuous virtue. Through the externalization of a caring self, the neoliberal public that is emerging here is propelled by moral sentiments; a public peopled by citizens desiring to become co-responsible for the common good by actively contributing to it through empathetic action. Ethical citizenship is built around the metaphysic of care. It not only helps recast modernist state welfare and the kinds of social citizenship it entailed, but the meaning of "the human" as such. (Muehlebach 2007, pp. 204–5)

This elaborate identity project described by Muehlebach, rooted in the metaphysics of caring, informs distinctive configurations of consciousness and very particular ethical configurations of citizenship. Catholic values become in this case a powerful idiom for negotiating the relationship between ethics and action: articulations of identity thus respond to the exigencies of European integration, creating spheres of politics that are reciprocal to these initiatives. In this case, liberal reform of welfare animates illiberal identity experiments focussed on public service and the metaphysics of caring.

Bad faith

Bilge Firat is studying the daily interchanges among lobbyists seeking to influence the terms and conditions of Turkish accession to the EU. Broadly, she is examining the incremental progress as well as the impediments and outright obstructions to Turkey's European aspirations (Firat 2007).

The project illuminates the specific issues of market liberalization, labor laws, civil and corporation law, environmental standards, transportation, civil and human rights questions, taxation structures, banking and finance, food safety, education, pension benefits, healthcare, electoral rules, public works, border controls, agricultural subsidies and so on, that constitute the accession process. Each of these questions is framed and crosscut on a daily basis by complex issues of history, religion, secularism, nationalism, and sovereignty from the perspectives of Turkish lobbyists and EU officials.

Against this formal analysis of the integration process, Firat creates a parallel ethnographic inquiry, following her Turkish subjects as they move through a series of ethnographic settings in Brussels. She examines how Turkish diplomats and lobbyists and, crucially, their families have become and are becoming ineluctably "Europeanized" by virtue of their residence in Brussels. She examines how these Turkish expatriates respond to and evaluate critically the complexities of life in a city in which European identity is an overriding preoccupation, if not an obsession (Borneman and Fowler 1997).

Firat's subjects representing government and industry groups are perhaps Adrian Favell's (contribution in this volume) "Eurostars" in the making. Their work deals on a daily basis with the *acquis communautaire*, the technocratic issues at stake in integration; in their daily lives they confront the intimate realities of European identity. These figures reside in the prosperous districts of Brussels alongside EU officialdom. Each morning they drop off their children at a neighborhood crèche, where French-, Flemish-, and English-speaking teachers care for their children. During their workdays they meet with officials of the European Commission, the Council of Ministers, and the Parliament, arguing from the "outside" the case for Turkish accession. In the evening they attend embassy receptions where they meet Turkish representatives fully integrated into the social and political fabric of NATO, or Bulgarian members of the European Parliament representing Turkish-speaking communities. On a daily basis, Firat's subjects also come into contact with the significant Turkish community in the city, stimulating interactions with individuals with whom – for various, class, ethnic, and religious reasons – these lobbyists would in all likelihood not associate in their homeland. Fully European representatives of these Turkish communities hold elective office in Brussels municipal government and the Belgian state, and their distinctive outlooks are publicly voiced in the press and the media.

The routine encounters of these figures thus demonstrate the social *fact* of an ongoing process linking Turkish and European identities that significantly pre-dates the formal process of Turkey's accession to the EU, reaching back at least to the mid-twentieth century. Immigrant and increasingly European-born Turkish populations are present in major European cities, and each of these communities encompasses diverse groups of individuals experimenting with secular and Islamic identities and with differently constituted European identities. As these lobbyists negotiate daily life in Brussels, the peculiar contradictions of Turkey's relationship to Europe are exposed. On the one hand, these actors are constantly reminded of the degree to which Turkish communities are already fully within Europe. On the other, they see how the arguments opposing Turkish accession to the EU are couched in bad faith, incandescent bad faith. They also understand fully that the identity projects unfolding in Europe reach back to the politics of their homeland.

Encrypted identities

In the 1990s I examined in detail a case that demonstrated how identity – among a tiny group of activists – could oscillate between fashion and politics, yielding a mass European audience for various stylistic expressions of a marginal political project. I interviewed members of the British National Party (the BNP) who have experimented with identity as far back as the 1960s, provoking innovations that were inadvertent and unanticipated. As one of these figures put it:

I remember skinheads from years ago: burly sort of thugs, shaven heads and wore swastika badges. They looked fine, didn't they? ... Yes, the early 60s. I remember, because I had just left school and it was just starting then; 1961 or 1962. Yeah. It's all over Europe now but it did start in the East End. But, when it started it wasn't political at all, it was just a little cult. Now, it's really political. You just have to say "skinhead" now you immediately think "nationalist." (Holmes 2000, pp. 135–6)

In their view, British nationalists had to act tough because the newspapers ignored them. They tried "to kick their way into the headlines." Denied access to networks of the conventional media, their experiments took on a radically different symbolic form, one that was communicable over an alternative, perhaps more powerful, global circuitry. The fashion accessories of skinheads, spawned and nurtured in the East End of London, penetrated taste across Europe. Leather clothing, shaved heads, pierced body parts, macabre talismans, extravagant alcohol and drug consumption, football hooliganism, reckless street-fighting, racist invectives, and assaults came to be associated overtly with a brutal nationalist politics of the young; yet, re-coded as fashion, much of this repellant political stance gained a different and far broader currency. In other words, the "unspeakable" messages contrived in urban Britain found expression in defiant styles of self-presentation, taste, and appearance. Instilled as fashion, these astringent messages moved – uncensored – onto the bodies and into the imaginations of a generation (Holmes 2000).

At the opening of the twenty-first century, we also know that these kinds of local stylistic messages can move easily across various global retail and electronic circuits. Though they remain largely latent and relatively harmless as unorthodox or offensive expressions of "taste," the prospect that these elusive messages can be read and deciphered politically is disturbing. Croatian rock star Marko Perkovic is a good example of a current manifestation of this phenomenon.

In the journalistic account by Nicholas Wood (2007), the ease by which emphatic representations of a distasteful and shameful politics can gain expression as dissonant style is observed. Wood also captures the intergenerational slippages and convergences of these symbolic messages as ratified by the Balkan wars of the 1990s:

On a hot Sunday evening last month, thousands did just that in a packed soccer stadium here in the Croatian capital. Photographs from the concert show youths wearing the black caps of the Nazi-backed Ustasha regime that ruled Croatia, and which was responsible for sending tens of thousands of Serbs, gypsies and Jews to their deaths in concentration camps ... Perkovic's popularity is nothing new in Croatia. It dates back to the Balkan wars in which he fought in the Croatian Army. His patriotic and sometimes violently nationalist songs made him an instant hit. Most Croats know him better by his stage name, Thompson, which was given to him during the war, when he carried the vintage British-made submachine gun of the same name.

And, more significantly, the indifference to the political message on the part of those who recognize fully the nature of its meaning is also registered:

But now Thompson's growing success – among a new generation of Croats, many of them apparently oblivious to the history of the Holocaust – has prompted concern and condemnation from minority groups in Croatia and Jewish groups abroad. The concert last month was his biggest to date, with at least 40,000 people in attendance ... What has shocked those groups more, though, is that in the ensuing debate, many senior politicians and the members of the media have not seen a problem with the imagery or salutes.

Experiments like this with localized and highly stylized expressions of alienation emerge as if awaiting the arrival of a new generation of young, charismatic leaders who can rearticulate their implicit messages as an emphatic politics, leaders who can exploit the ambiguous spaces between and among style, fashion, identity, and politics. As these accounts suggest, the circuitry for this kind of message is in place, the preliminary labor has been accomplished, and the politics is imminent.

Duty to integrate

In a speech entitled, "Our nation's future: Multiculturalism and integration," delivered on December 8, 2006, Tony Blair addressed the dilemmas posed by a new British and European pluralism. The speech is a highly personal statement – though, no doubt, drafted with the aid of speechwriters and advisors – by a skilled politician as he seeks to come to terms with the predicaments posed by extremist identity projects operating beyond the institutional reach of the nation-state: predicaments that can compromise the ethos underwriting newly defined British and European identities (Stolcke 1995; Modood and Werbner 1997). The solution he proposes is drawn from a philosophical tradition of shared values reconciled implicitly by the principle of subsidiarity.

As Blair reminded his audience, the bombings of 7/7/05 followed the day after the awarding of the bid for the 2012 Olympics to London (Blair 2006, from which all extracts in this section are taken). London's winning of the Olympic bid had been viewed at the time as a ratification of the successful racial and cultural experimentations that had fundamentally transformed British society over the prior three decades. The counterpoint of events unfolding within a mere twenty-four hours revealed the stark vulnerability of a regime of values upon which Blair had staked his career.

We should begin by celebrating something. When we won the Olympic Bid to host the 2012 Games, we presented a compelling, modern vision of Britain; a country at ease with different races, religions and cultures…

We now have more ethnic minority MPs, peers and Ministers though not enough. We have had the first black Cabinet minister. The media are generally more sensitive, and include ethnic minority reporters and columnists. Racism has, for the most part, been kicked out of sport. Offensive remarks and stupid stereotypes have been driven out of public conversation. The basic courtesies, in other words, have been extended to all people.

Events intervened that challenged this celebratory view, a challenge orchestrated by a tiny, murderous group of committed activists:

The day after we won the Olympic bid came the terrorist attacks in London. These murders were carried out by British-born suicide bombers who had lived and been brought up in this country, who had received all its many advantages and yet who ultimately took their own lives and the lives of the wholly innocent, in the name of an ideology alien to everything this country stands for. Everything the Olympic bid symbolized was everything they hated.

Their emphasis was not on shared values but separate ones, values based on a warped distortion of the faith of Islam.

Native-born and yet alien protagonists posed a deep affront to the ideals underwriting Blair's political philosophy. Most outrageous from his standpoint is that precisely the diversity and openness that enlivens this new societal ethos can feed radical aspirations committed to injuring the innocent.

[I]t has thrown into sharp relief, the nature of what we have called, with approval, "multicultural Britain." We like our diversity. But how do we react when that "difference" leads to separation and alienation from the values that define what we hold common? For the first time in a generation there is an unease, an anxiety, even at points a resentment that our very openness, our willingness to welcome difference, our pride in being home to many cultures, is being used against us; abused, indeed, in order to harm us.

Against this backdrop, Blair sought to resurrect the values of and for British society as well as the accountabilities its government must require of its citizens. His remedy is framed in the idiom of "values." He alludes to the Westphalian prerogatives of the nation-state to define and to mediate – coercively if necessary – public values and private consciousness; yet he acknowledges that contemporary circumstances make this difficult. Notably, the liberal reforms that he so ardently pursued during his tenure have freed various domains of "culture" and "lifestyle," allowing them to develop increasingly beyond the reach of governmental surveillance and political control.

Blair – a sophisticated social Catholic – invokes a European solution in order to address the predicaments of British pluralism. He invokes subsidiarity as a formula for legitimizing pluralism, but he adds a series of new and subtle elements to address the current threat:

Christians, Jews, Muslims, Hindus, Sikhs and other faiths have a perfect right to their own identity and religion, to practise their faith and to conform to their culture. This is what multicultural, multi-faith Britain is about. That is what is legitimately distinctive ... But when it comes to our essential values – belief in democracy, the value of law, tolerance, equal treatment for all, respect for this country and its shared heritage then that is where we come together, it is what we hold in common; it is what gives us the right to call ourselves British. At that point no distinctive culture or religion supersedes our duty to be part of an integrated United Kingdom.

Blair concedes that he was counseled to avoid broaching the ethical distinctions upon which multiculturalism absolutely depends, but he defied this advice. Indeed, his optimistic analysis draws on familiar ethical ideas to address circumstances of diversity that are for many difficult to parse. He reasserts notions of tolerance, duty, dialogue, and solidarity. And, perhaps most interesting, he recasts the complexities of British pluralism as a problem of the integration of a particular minority, in fact, a minority of a minority of Muslims.

But actually what should give us optimism in dealing with this issue, is precisely that point. It is true there are extremists in other communities. But the reason we are having this debate is not generalized extremism. It is a new and virulent form of ideology associated with a minority of our Muslim community. It is not a problem with Britons of Hindu, Afro-Caribbean, Chinese or Polish origin. Nor is it a problem with the majority of the Muslim community. Most Muslims are proud to be British and Muslim and are thoroughly decent law-abiding citizens. But it is a problem with a minority of that community, particularly originating from certain countries. The reason I say that this is grounds for optimism, is that what the above proves, is that integrating people whilst preserving their distinctive cultures, is not a function of a flawed theory of a multicultural society. It is a function of a particular ideology that arises within one religion at this one time.

Blair contends that it is a theory of society that must be defended; *pluralism is under threat* and policy needs to be articulated that acknowledges that reality. This is difficult for Blair, who took the ideals of solidarity as a matter of faith, and who must now publicly articulate them as a matter of duty. Blair takes not a secular theory, but a confessional theory with deep European intellectual roots, and he transforms it in manner that can address contemporary predicaments. He invokes a formula that sets out principles for negotiating the nature of cultural affinity and difference, thereby challenging a highly problematic, Islamic consciousness by recasting it within a broader political discourse:

Yet, because this challenge has arisen in this way, it is necessary to go back to what a multicultural Britain is all about. The whole point is that multicultural Britain was never supposed to be a celebration of division; but diversity. The purpose was to allow people to live harmoniously together, despite their difference; not to make their difference an encouragement to discord. The values that nurtured it were those of solidarity, of coming together, of peaceful co-existence. The right to be in a multicultural society was always, always implicitly balanced by a duty to integrate, to be part of Britain, to be British and Asian, British and black, British and white. Those whites who support the BNP's policy of separate races and those Muslims who shun integrations into British society both contradict the fundamental values that define Britain today; tolerance, solidarity across the racial and religious divide, equality for all and between all.

It is only in response to an overt challenge that the largely implicit assumptions of pluralism achieve public articulation:

So it is not that we need to dispense with multicultural Britain. On the contrary we should continue celebrating it. But we need – in the face of the challenge to our values – to re-assert also the duty to integrate, to stress what we hold in common and to say: these are the shared boundaries within which we all are obliged to live precisely in order to preserve our right to our own different faiths, races and creeds … We must respect both our right to differ and the duty to express any difference in a way fully consistent with the values that bind us together.

Blair's political message seeks to persuade the circles of supporters who may be in one way or another sympathetic to the "Jihadist" sensibilities of the suicide bombers. They are within reach of his multicultural theory and his pluralist rhetoric. But he concedes that the 7/7 bombers, like the BNP activists, operate beyond the reach of this kind of political message.

Blair's uplifting analysis and energetic prose cannot account for the motives, the consciousness of those British-born individuals who orchestrated the 7/7 attacks. The identity experiments of these young men are inaccessible and inscrutable from the standpoint of conventional political analyses. These individuals are engaged in a politics of identity that operates in an alternative public sphere under a jurisdiction of style, as communicative action that moves across an alternative circuitry and enters the lifeworlds of adherents and is accepted emphatically on faith.

Unstated and yet implicit in this remarkable speech is the suspicion that the political traditions of Britain and the institutional practices and consensual politics of the EU are poorly adapted or entirely incapable of addressing the vexatious political issues posed after Maastricht. The monumental frustration is, of course, that Blair and his cohort of politicians in Europe have played a decisive role in giving life to these proliferating identity projects. He understands how illiberal identity projects pose implicitly and explicitly an emphatic taunt or challenge. Can liberal principles that have been so brilliantly deployed instrumentally to achieve the political aims of the European project now be redeployed to address new cultural predicaments? Can liberalism – as a system of values, beliefs and technocratic practices – orchestrate the solidarity necessary for its own perpetuation, for retaining or expanding public support for an evolving and still ill-defined European project? In the interplay of these taunts and rhetorical questions, Blair's vision of Europe converges with that of Jean-Marie Le Pen.

After Maastricht

The premise of this chapter is that there are now countless experiments with identity unfolding across Europe, almost all of them in some way related to European integration, though *not* necessarily the outcome of any EU policy initiative per se. Many of these experiments are idiosyncratic and self-limiting; some are totally irrelevant. That said, my contention here is that a few of these identity projects are absolutely essential for understanding the future course and political dynamics of European integration.

I have followed over the last two decades what I believe to be the most important identity project unfolding in contemporary Europe, a project that covers wide-ranging experiments aimed at defining a fully elaborated, supranational political program: an agenda that addresses the distinctive features of a multiracial and multicultural polity. This project – encompassed by what I have termed integralism – captures *macro*-level configurations of identity coalescing in all twenty-seven member states of the EU. I have argued that the innovative work of Jean-Marie Le Pen established integralism as the model for illiberal experiments gaining expression – not merely in France – but across the EU as a fully and forcefully articulated politics of Europe.

Thus, in this chapter I have developed analytical perspectives on European identity rather than providing an exhaustive survey of all the groups, movements, and parties engaged in this kind of political activism. Hence, each case that I have discussed frames paradigmatically a very particular problematic of Europe that emerged in the aftermath of Maastricht, configuring specific experiments with the form and substance of identity. I have been particularly interested in developing examples that demonstrate how highly localized circumstances can enliven forms of activism with a broad European reach. The key analytical aim of the piece has been to trace out the links between micro-level experiments with identity and various path-dependent macro-level politics. Though this yields at times jarring shifts in perspectives, it none-theless provides glimpses of a volatile and a still rather occult political landscape taking shape across all of the member states of the EU.

Numerous questions remain. Will identity projects continue to proliferate, yielding ever more diverse groups, factions, parties, and movements? Or, as appears to be a tendency at the moment, will these experiments be stabilized intellectually and mediated politically around integralist configurations of activism? Or will some other forms of meta-politics, like social Catholicism, assume the role of regulating and mana-ging the accretion of diverse pluralist agendas? The answers to these questions are, as we have seen repeatedly, dependent on reciprocal ques-tions about the institutional nature of the EU itself and its political agility in articulating the substance and the meanings of liberalism.

Finally, the reader may have noticed in this piece a peculiar metho-dological conundrum: the subjects of this study – notably the political activists themselves – are engaged in intellectual labors that resemble, approximate, or are entirely indistinguishable from the analytical prac-tices of an ethnographer. To pursue their insurgency, these figures employ intellectual modalities to inform their politics that continually draw on what are essentially ethnographic insights. To align their message with the at times strident experience of their audience, they must craft ethnographically informed discourses. These activists are acutely sensitive to cultural idioms, dialects, and patois in defining the messages by which they seek to mobilize the sensibilities and the aspirations of an inchoate European public (Holmes and Marcus 2006; Holmes *et al.* 2006). In other words, the identity experiments that have proliferated after Maastricht expose how elements of an ethnographic "method," broadly conceived, have been assimilated to enliven a dis-tinctive and, perhaps, decisive politics that speaks to the cultural pre-dicaments of our time. The key predicament, as I have argued in this chapter, is that in the post-Maastricht era, the EU confers on its citizens the abiding challenge to negotiate among those liberal and illiberal imperatives that can inform and underwrite a pluralist Europe.

Acknowledgment

I would like to thank Jeff Checkel and Peter Katzenstein for inviting me to contribute to this volume, for their meticulous comments on earlier drafts of this manuscript, and for their skill and generosity in promoting at every stage of this project a stimulating interdisciplinary environment. The acute comments of participants in the Ithaca and Oslo workshops provoked me to think about the issues at stake in this chapter in new and productive ways. Iver B. Neumann, in particular, provided detailed comments and suggestions that were invaluable in the final revisions. Sarah Tarrow performed a very careful copyediting that helped clarify the arguments and insights presented herein. Any errors, omissions, and failures of interpretation and of analysis are, of course, entirely my responsibility. The project upon which this chapter is based was supported by funding from the National Science Foundation and the Wenner-Gren Foundation for Anthropological Research.

4 | *The public sphere and the European Union's political identity*

JUAN DÍEZ MEDRANO

Since the early 1990s, two factors have had a significant impact on the pace and character of European integration. The first factor is the end of the permissive consensus that had prevailed until then. The main symptoms of this change have been a steady decline, to historically low levels, in the level of popular EU support; and episodes such as the rejection of the European Constitution by a majority of French and Dutch voters. The second factor is division among European leaders concerning future institutional developments in a twenty-seven-member Union.

The two factors converged in the 2005 constitutional crisis, not because cleavages among the elites mimic those among the population, but rather because popular discontent helped to undo the fragile consensus that had been achieved by European Union elites around the constitutional project. At stake is disagreement between political elites and a significant segment of the population on the values that should sustain the European project (see Hooghe 2003) and also among the different national elites on the limits of supranationalism. In the context of the politicization of the European Union in the 1990s, triggered by the increasingly political character of the EU and signaled among other things by the repeated organization of referenda on new EU treaties, the permissive consensus prevailing until then has broken down (see Katzenstein and Checkel in this volume) and deep disagreement among elites has surfaced.

With regard to the sensible distinction of the three meanings of identity (Brubaker and Cooper 2000), I narrow my focus on political identity as political self-understanding, that is, on the project dimension of political identity (see Checkel and Katzenstein in this volume). The concept of political self-understanding, however, is itself multidimensional. There is the political self-understanding reflected in the documents that shape a polity (e.g. treaties, laws, decrees). There is also the political self-understanding reflected in the actual behavior of those interpreting and implementing the content of those documents. Finally, there is the political self-understanding that transpires in public discourse. These three dimensions of political identity as project are equally real, equally interesting from a scientific point of view. The latter becomes especially relevant, however, when examining how the citizens conceive the polity and their attitudes toward it. It is the interface between elites and citizens that interests me, and this is why I focus on political identity-as-project from a public discourse perspective. Through content analysis of debates in the public sphere, I argue that there is currently an unbridgeable mismatch between the national leaders' conceptions of the EU and those of a significant minority of citizens and, at the same time, a strong disagreement among the elites about Europe's political identity.

The data come from two databases. The first is the Europub.com database, which includes data on seven European countries for the 1990–2002 period (on the content analysis method, see Koopmans *et al.* 2005; Koopmans and Statham 1999). The second is a database collected for Poland for the 2000–2004 period.[1] The analysis shows that in the past decade or so, political elites in Europe have emphasized a republican rather than a cultural political identity for Europe, and they have remained relatively silent about the EU's social dimension. They have thus triggered resistance to European integration efforts among alienated segments of the population that are fearful of growing cultural diversity in Europe and sensitive to the negative impact that globalization may have on their wages, job prospects, and working conditions. Furthermore, the analysis demonstrates that while political elites agree on the desirability of strengthening the EU's political dimension and on a multilevel distribution of competences, they disagree on the further transfer of sovereignty to the

---

[1] The source of the Europub.com data are a sample of newspaper articles from Left, Right, regional, and "yellow" press newspapers from Germany, France, Italy, the Netherlands, the United Kingdom, and Switzerland, covering the 1990–2002 period (Vth Framework Programme of the European Commission. Contract Number HPSE-CT2000-00046). An extra sample of 129 newspaper articles from the Polish newspaper *Gazeta Wyborcza* was collected and analyzed specifically for this chapter (for codebooks, see Koopmans 2002). I thank Joanna Jasiewicz for selecting and coding the newspaper articles. The unit of analysis is the political claim, defined as an act of strategic communication in the public sphere, entailing the expression of a political opinion or demand through physical or verbal action, which may take various forms (verbal statements, judicial rulings, political decisions, violent or non-violent public demonstrations, and so on) and be made by various actors (governments, MPs, political parties, interest groups, social movements, NGOs, and so on) (Koopmans 2002).

EU (especially in the areas falling under the second pillar) and on the division of power among the various EU institutions.

A full understanding of the EU's loss of legitimacy in the 1990s and of the constitutional crisis requires more, however, than a systematic analysis of the public sphere, for the public sphere is only one factor shaping the citizens' attitudes toward the European Union. In particular, its role in explaining the EU's loss of legitimacy and the constitutional crisis becomes clearer if examined in conjunction with the analysis of the mobilization of an important set of actors, relatively invisible in public debate about European integration, which has worked to amplify both the lack of synch between elites and segments of the citizenry and intra-elite conflict. Far-right political parties and movements, Euro-skeptic social movements, and anti-globalization groups, examined by Doug Holmes in this volume, have indeed played a key role in aligning frames and in strengthening the camp of those who call for a more organic or a more social Europe, and thus oppose the dominant model of European integration (see also Berezin, in press).

The chapter begins with a synthetic discussion of the parameters of the 2005 referendum outcomes and the political confusion that followed. This discussion challenges prevalent views and proposes an alternative interpretation that stresses the role played by the elites. The section that follows focusses on the characterization of national public spheres, where debates on the EU's political identity take place. I summarize the state of the art in research on the Europeanization of national public spheres and justify the analysis of the public sphere to uncover the EU's political identity project. The next two sections examine public frames about the European Union. The goal of this analysis is to examine the public actors' conceptualizations of what the EU is and should be. Finally, the last section focusses on the architectural designs for the EU displayed in the public sphere. This section shows that competing models form a more complex set of alternatives than seen in the binary distinction between supranational ("cosmopolitan") and nationalist ones often discussed in the media.

The European Union's constitutional crisis

In the aftermath of the French and Dutch "No" votes, explanations that emphasized the roles of nationalism and national identity were frequent (although there were others). For instance, one could read in an editorial

published in the *New York Times* ("The French Non," June 1, 2005) that
the "fear of losing the French identity, the fear of 'Anglo-Saxon'
(read British and American) economic reforms" underlay the French
results. William Pfaff, commenting on the French and Dutch referenda
in the *New York Review of Books*, conveyed a very similar message:

The rejection surely demonstrated the current gap of comprehension between
European political elites and the European public, but was mainly evidence of the
consistently underestimated forces of national identity and ambition in each of
the twenty-five nations. The French were enthusiastically seconded by another
highly nationalistic and individualistic European society, the Netherlands – also
one of the founding Fathers of the European Union. ("What's left of the Union,"
July 14, 2005)

North American explanations were echoed on the other side of the
Atlantic. In the Netherlands, for instance, Sophie Vanhoonacker,
Director of the Center for European Studies of the University of
Maastricht, explained the Dutch results as follows: "everything that is
not Dutch is taken as a menace to identity" (English translation from
"Le non à la Constitution reflète la crise identitaire des Néerlandais,"
Agence France Presse, June 1, 2005). Across the Channel, the *Daily Mail*
rejoiced at the outcome of the French Referendum, which it interpreted as
a reflection of the fact that "there is still no such thing as a common
European identity. The sense of national interest that Europeans have
always had has not been eliminated: and it exploded in France on
Sunday" (Simon Heffer, "Why can't the arrogant elite see ... enough is
enough," May 31, 2005).
   Identity has partly determined the recent twists and turns of the goal-
less road that is European integration and the constitutional crisis, but it
does not tell the whole story. Growing ethnic diversity resulting from
increased migration since the mid-1980s, and the prospect of yet more
immigration as new states join the European Union, have met with
resistance in host countries by citizens unwilling or unable to cope
with bearers of different cultural traditions. As Favell comments in
this volume, "issues of multiculturalism or inter-ethnic conflict that
were most familiar to former colonial powers like Britain and France
are now raised in every country in Western Europe, and increasingly
East and Central Europe too." Electoral support for xenophobic far-
right parties all across Europe testifies to this unrest. For Holmes (this
volume), electoral support for Le Pen in fact represents the most overt

political expression of what he defines as the "integralist" macro-project, "a project that covers wide-ranging experiments aimed at defining a fully elaborated, supranational political program: an agenda that addresses the distinctive features of a multiracial and multicultural polity."

Some commentators' reduction of the EU crisis to a problem of identity, or the *Daily Mail's* extension of the identity argument to encompass the population's weak sense of identification with Europe, however, considerably simplify the problems faced by the populations of the enlarged European Union. Furthermore, explanations solely focussed on the French and Dutch "No" minimize the extent and complexity of the EU crisis: First, because they do not contextualize it within the parameters of historically low levels of support for the EU since the mid-1990s and the crisis of national democracies; second, because they do not answer the question of why the two referenda outcomes were sufficient to derail the ratification process; and third, because they implicitly assume that the themes that motivated a major-ity of French and Dutch voters to vote "No" on the Constitution are the same as those that pitted leaders of the EU member states against each other for two years as they debated how to reform EU institutions.

The identity argument for the constitutional crisis exaggerates the role of national and European identification in the European integration process. Europeans have strong national or subnational identities and a weakly developed sense of being European. This is partly because, as Fligstein emphasizes in "Deutschian" manner, the development of a European identity hinges on frequent interaction between nationals of different EU states (see Fligstein in this volume). They feel comfortable with membership in the EU, however, and support European integration. This observation has been repeatedly confirmed by Eurobarometer sur-veys, even as support waned in the 1990s and never returned to earlier levels. There is certainly significant variation across countries; but suppor-ters outweigh opponents even in "Euro-skeptic" countries like Sweden, Finland, Austria, and the United Kingdom. In fact, citizens, including the French and the Dutch, support integration in the areas of foreign policy more than the political leaders of their countries do (83% of French citizens and 82% of Dutch citizens support it, compared to an average of 77% for the European Union as a whole[2]) (see also Cerrutti 2006).

---

[2] Source: Eurobarometer 64 (2005).

Thus, European citizens in many ways approach European integration as what Habermas would call constitutional patriots (with a small "p"). That is, they support the EU because they largely agree with the goals and principles that it embodies, even though their sense of who they are remains anchored at the national or local levels. To simply focus on the small number of integration proposals that a majority of citizens in some countries have occasionally opposed, including the constitutional project, risks overlooking all the EU institutional developments that European citizens have accepted in the last fifty years and the success that the EU has had in enroling new members. Consequently, relatively low levels of support for the EU, low turnout in European elections and referenda, and "No" votes in referenda ought to be interpreted not as a sign of a poorly developed sense of membership in Europe or as a lack of constitutional patriotism, but rather as normal political outcomes in a democratic polity.

In other words, one should not conclude that when European citizens oppose an EU initiative, regardless of its scope, they are expressing their opposition to the European integration project. The EU is already a polity. New treaties reconstitute this polity or make it evolve. Therefore, when a new reform treaty is subjected to a popular vote, citizens are not presented with a plebiscite on the existence of the EU. They are simply presented with alternative political projects among which to choose. One need only connect the public lack of enthusiasm toward the EU and its proposals with parallel developments at the national and regional levels to draw the logical conclusion that principled opposition to the EU does not underlie the current crisis. It may well be that similar processes and structural factors explain why European citizens are less and less involved in both national and European politics.

European citizens have reasons to be disappointed with their lack of influence on national and European politics. As Eurobarometer 62.0 (2004) shows, only about 38 percent of the EU-25 respondents believe that they personally have a voice on European affairs. Analysis of the 2004 Eurobarometer data also shows statistically significant relationships between perceptions of personal efficacy and support of membership in the EU (e.g. Berezin and Díez Medrano, forthcoming). There is, in fact, plenty of evidence supporting the claim that citizens are offered scant opportunity to shape the political process, and this applies especially to the EU. The Europub.com project on the European public sphere, for instance, demonstrates that state and party elites monopolize public debate on the EU (see Koopmans 2004a). Reports on the Convention proceedings also reveal that despite the talk of openness to citizen participation, this was more marketing than reality (Cerrutti 2006). More generally, in the last decade, Europe's political elites have often pursued major policies against their constituencies' wishes: they introduced the euro despite deep-seated opposition in countries like Germany, and they proceeded with Enlargement from fifteen to twenty-seven members despite the opposition of about two-thirds of the population in many EU member states. Interestingly, one of these countries was France, where in 2004 only 31 percent of the population supported Enlargement. The referendum on the European Constitution in May 2005 offered the French population a unique opportunity to express this rejection indirectly.

Efforts to understand the two moments of the constitutional crisis of the EU must thus take into account that the majority of the population supports the integration process despite identifying primarily as members of their nation-states. Furthermore, these efforts must consider that the citizens have been largely excluded from the European integration process and consequently come to resent the technocratic character of decision-making in the EU. The "No" votes in the French and Dutch referenda certainly involved a national identity component but had little to do with an insufficiently developed sense of membership in a European political community. In fact, the absence of a strong identification with Europe among French and Dutch citizens removed the possibility of some political elites' "Euro-nationalist" appeals confounding the citizens' electoral choices, allowing for national identity, social, and political concerns to be the decisive factors. The French and Dutch referenda provided large segments of the French and Dutch citizenry a rare opportunity to vent their frustrations on a variety of issues, including past EU decisions (i.e. the euro and Enlargement) that exacerbated their fears of ethnic diversity and declining living standards. The pre-referendum televised question-and-answer debate between Chirac and a group of young French citizens, where an impatient Chirac complained that the questions and comments addressed to him had nothing to do with the content of the Constitution, clearly supports this view.

The constitutional crisis, however, did not begin and end with the outcomes of the French and Dutch referenda. It also included the long period of post-referenda uncertainty in the EU, as European political leaders debated how to proceed after these negative outcomes. EU leaders certainly saw through nationalist discourse to read what the referenda outcomes said about the citizens' wishes. Within a year, they watered down the Bolkenstein directive on services, to reduce fears of social dumping among French and German workers, and they made clear that despite the beginning of accession negotiations, Turkey's membership would not happen anytime soon (provided, of course, that no other international development – i.e. Russia's rediscovered military assertiveness – led to reassessment of the costs and benefits of having Turkey in the EU). Their response to the citizens' fears ended here, however. Enlargement from twenty-five to twenty-seven proceeded as planned, and the proposal that emerged from the June 2007 European Council Summit showed instead that the outcome of the referenda had increased the assertiveness of the intergovernmental and neoliberal camps (e.g. the United Kingdom, Poland). Thus confronted, the majority of the EU governments appeared to prioritize the efficient functioning of the EU over citizens' rights in the EU (e.g. the Charter of Fundamental Rights).

The description and interpretation of the EU crisis above leaves only limited room for national identity and certainly no room at all for weak levels of identification with Europe among the population. Yet, when one reviews the recent literature on European integration, one is surprised by the scholarly community's interest in these topics. For many years, intellectuals have predicted that further European integration is unthinkable beyond a certain stage, unless Europeans do not develop a strong sense of identification with Europe (e.g., unless they come to consider people born in EU countries other than their own as belonging to the same community that they themselves feel part of [see Hoffman 1966; Checkel and Katzenstein in this volume; Herrmann *et al.* 2004; Habermas 2006b]). The rejection of Turkey is, in turn, interpreted as revealing of an ethnic conception of what it means to be European.

These interpretations of the constitutional crisis have fed the growth of an already existing industry of research on the so-called European identity deficit (Cerutti 2006; Habermas 2006b; Herrmann *et al.* 2004; Risse 2003; Viehoff and Segers 1999). This industry has dealt with a myriad of questions: How developed is the sense of identification with Europe? Is there a need for a European identity? How far can European integration proceed without a well-developed sense of European identity? What is the nature – civic or ethnic – of European identity? What needs to be done in order to develop a sense of community among Europeans? The most ambitious scholars even offer advice to the European Commission on the nature of the symbols to promote a collective European identity: Do we go for the Holocaust (Giesen 2003), or do we leave it to marketing professionals who work with images and sounds rather than with words? (Eder 1999). Here I am not concerned with judging the value of this discussion – "De gustibus non est disputandum." I take issue, however, with those who – aligning themselves with the political elites – emphasize identity factors when explaining the last decade's relatively low levels of support for the European Union and the French and Dutch referenda outcomes.

Instead of focussing on the citizens' degree of identification with Europe, in this chapter I follow the argument developed above to explain the constitutional crisis. This argument stresses the lack of fit between the political elites' European identity project and the diversity of citizens' current political, social, and cultural concerns, and divisions over Europe's political project among the elites themselves. The European public sphere is a key setting for the examination of the elites' European political identity projects and for the development of an interpretation of the EU's current hesitations.

The European public sphere

The public sphere is well suited for the examination of political identity projects because, contrary to treaties like the European Constitution, it offers access to the diversity of elite viewpoints on which these treaties rest. In addition, contrary to the information that one would obtain through interviews with the elites, discourse in the public sphere is the actual interface between elite views and citizen reactions to these views, thus allowing for a better interpretation of phenomena such as the French and Dutch "No" votes to the European Constitution and the crisis that followed.

The emergence and characteristics of a European public sphere have concentrated scholars' attention in the last fifteen years almost as much as the topic of Europe's identity. In fact, for authors like Habermas (1991 [1962]), Eder (1999), and Risse (2003), the public sphere is not only a prerequisite in an EU that wants to be democratic, but also a key institution for the development, through communication, of a shared sense of belonging to a European community. Most research efforts until now have been geared toward determining the existence or even the possibility of a European public sphere. Some authors have given a negative or pessimistic diagnosis (Schlesinger 1999; Pérez-Díaz 1998). Authors like Grimm (1995a), Kielmansegg (1996), and Calhoun (2003) invoke linguistic heterogeneity when accounting for this presumed absence of a European public sphere. Other authors refer to the absence of media with a European scope (Calhoun 2003; Scharpf 1998). Meanwhile, Gerhards uses empirical data to conclude that, in Germany, the presence of European themes in the quality press between 1951 and 1995 represents a much smaller percentage of news content than that of national or international, non-European themes (2000). He also notes that newspapers lack a European perspective when reporting on the EU (see also Jochen and De Vreese 2003; Schlesinger 1999).

As of late, a consensus is emerging that the EU's problem is not the lack of a European public sphere but rather its small scale. Most authors accept Gerhards's distinction between a pan-European public sphere, for which they see few prospects, and the Europeanization of national public spheres (1993), which they deem a reality. Authors disagree, however, with respect to the criteria to define a public sphere as Europeanized (e.g. Sifft *et al.* 2007; Trenz 2004; Steeg 2004; Dereje *et al.* 2003; Kantner 2002; Díez Medrano 2001; Eder and Kantner 2000; Gerhards 2000, 1993; Schlesinger 1999). Empirical research aimed at determining whether the national public spheres are Europeanized concludes that information on the EU is infrequent compared to coverage of national news (Machill *et al.* 2006; Trenz 2002; Díaz Nosty 1997). Furthermore, authors often note the irregular character of the coverage of EU affairs and make the criticism that the EU is generally faceless (Machill *et al.* 2006; Le Torrec *et al.* 2001). Even more relevant for this chapter's content, because of its potential contribution to explain the citizens' disengagement, is the fact that the European public sphere is closed to civil society actors (Marx Ferree *et al.* 2002).

Although rich pools of information are slowly becoming available, the theoretical and analytical debate on the European public sphere is getting increasingly confusing. Authors develop ad hoc criteria to define the Europeanization of public spheres; the term "European" tends to be used in a rather loose way; data seem to dictate how one analyzes the public sphere, and there is a tendency to attach the same weight to empirical studies with different geographic and temporal scopes. In order to refocus this research tradition, it is worth going back to the reasons that motivated studying the public sphere in the first place.

The public sphere is a deliberative political space in which both government and civil society participate. It provides political information to the citizens and a channel of communication that citizens can use to influence government. In contemporary societies, a public sphere exists when a minimum of free speech allows for political debate through the media. The geographic scope of this public sphere corresponds to the space covered by political or government institutions, be they municipal, regional, national, European, and so on. The EU is a peculiar form of polity, with multiple levels of governance and encompassing the citizens of twenty-seven democratic states. Therefore, political debate at any level of governance should be seen as constitutive of the European public sphere, and research should simply determine whether the relative presence of the local, the national, and the European correspond to the role each level of governance plays in the lives of individuals.[3]

There is a normative aspect of the public sphere that deserves elaboration in our search for an interpretation of the constitutional crisis and of the relatively low levels of support for the EU in the last decade: the degree to which the EU's public sphere meets basic democratic requirements. The main requirements are (1) transparency at all levels of governance and in all policy areas, and (2) access to all groups in society. The latter, in particular, is emphasized in the Habermasian (Marx Ferree *et al.* 2002; Habermas 1991), liberal participatory (Curran 1991; Barber 1984), and constructionist traditions (Fraser 1997; Young 1996; Benhabib 1992). The enrichment of the deliberative process, the empowerment of participants, and the assertion of non-hegemonic identities are some of the justifications that authors in these

---

[3] The literature discusses other criteria that one should take into account when examining the European public sphere. These discussions approach the public sphere normatively, focussing on traits that public spheres should ideally have. These criteria include the requirement that EU topics be discussed under the same criteria of relevance (Steeg 2006), through a common European – rather than domestic – perspective (Schlesinger 1999; Gerhards 1993), in a way that would serve to singularize it with respect to public spheres beyond the EU (Steeg 2004). Treating nationals and non-nationals as legitimate debating partners (Risse 2003) falls in the former category. Empirically examining the European public sphere from these perspectives is legitimate, for it provides us with valuable information on the degree of homogeneity of the EU's political culture and on whether a European collective identity exists; but it is not necessary when determining whether or not there is a European public sphere.

traditions provide for an inclusive public sphere. In contrast, the liberal representation tradition does not make social inclusion a prerequisite for a democratic public sphere (Mill 1991 [1861]; Burke 1993 [1790]; Schumpeter 1942; Downs 1957; Kornhauser 1960). For this tradition, the citizens' role is to elect representatives among contending political parties, and a democratic public sphere is one where the voices of the various contenders for power can be heard and understood by the citizenry. The Europub.com project, coordinated by Ruud Koopmans, has demonstrated that the actual European public sphere conforms more to this liberal representative view of the public sphere than to the liberal participatory, the Habermasian, and the constructionist perspectives: Non-political actors are virtually absent in this public sphere, even when one goes beyond print media into new media such as the Internet. Further, when non-political actors are present, they are usually interest groups such as trade unions or employers' associations (Europub.com 2004; see Koopmans 2004a).

Identity is another aspect that could underlie the 2005 constitutional crisis and that is relevant in the study of the public sphere. Research on the public sphere has very frequently revealed a preoccupation with the emergence of a European culture and identity. Niedhardt *et al.* (2000) even go as far as to assert that a European public sphere requires that participants display a minimum level of identification with Europe. Many of the criteria authors focus on when analyzing the European public sphere are also indirect indicators of the degree of homogeneity of the EU's political culture and the degree of collective identification with Europe. To share values, beliefs, cognitive frames across national public spheres is a sign of sharing the same political culture. Meanwhile, to treat political actors in other countries as legitimate partners, the use of a European perspective when reporting or evaluating a particular topic, and the amount of information on EU countries other than one's own are signs of a sense of membership in a European community.

In what follows, I examine the content of political debates in the European public sphere with the restrictive goal of revealing the political project for the EU underlying these debates. This analysis affords us a unique opportunity to assess to what extent public actors are driven by short-term or long-term political goals, to map the range of projects that are debated, and to measure the degree of consensus and main cleavages characterizing this debate. This examination is relevant because future developments in the EU depend on the views of actors in the public sphere, because citizens' social representations of the stakes in the European integration process are shaped by debate in the public sphere, and because the European Union's degree of legitimacy depends to some extent on agreement between the political elites' goals and those given priority by the citizens. As the sections below show, political elites are currently divided over further transfers of sovereignty, and their discourse deviates from the political, social, and cultural concerns of a significant segment of the European citizenry.

Is there a European project?

We take for granted that European leaders are driven by long-term political identity projects for Europe. Judging from what one finds in the public sphere, however, this is not the case. After almost sixty years of institutionalization, most public debate about the EU concerns "mundane" policy-related issues and bargaining between states, where it is uncommon for claimants to express their subjectively held images of the EU and coherent political identity projects. Thus, only one-third of the subset of claims in the Europub.com database that deal directly with European integration or have a European scope contain statements concerned with questions such as what the EU is or should be, and where the EU leads or should lead. In Poland, the percentage is slightly higher (39%); but this reflects the fact that the Polish sample only includes articles directly related to European integration, whereas the Europub.com sample also includes articles with a European scope (issue, main actor raising the claim, or addressee of a claim) in seven policy fields. Also, only about 19% and 14% of all Europub.com and Polish claims, respectively, directly related to European integration address the EU's architectural design. If one adds to the claims in the Europub.com sample the 17% concerned with Enlargement, one is left with about two-thirds addressing day-to-day politics in the EU. This is of course not the case in Poland, where almost three out of four claims in the 2000–2004 period dealt with entry negotiations. There was thus no room in Poland for public discussion of either routine politics or a well-defined project for Europe. Meanwhile, examples of routine politics in the Europub.com countries were the relative power of different EU members, the Haider affair, or proclamations about the need to "strengthen" the EU. As the former figures demonstrate, however, public debate on the architecture of Europe has generally been shallow, with more posturing than substance. If one wants to determine what Europe's political elites want, one might do better to read and interpret the project for a European Constitution than to listen to the "empty" words and posturing expressed in public. The European Constitution, however, like any other European Treaty, reflects a bargain between different approaches rather than a unified political vision for Europe. Furthermore, it is the projects outlined in the public sphere, if any, that reach the citizens, which is one good reason to examine them.

The self-presentation of the European Union in everyday life

The findings above have implications for political actors' ability to sell previous EU accomplishments and reform packages to the population. Not knowing what their leaders are up to when it comes to further European integration, the population is hardly in a position to develop a firm commitment to the EU. In the worst case scenario, they can become easy prey for social movements that manipulate frames to align citizen grievances with EU policies. This is partly what transpired from pre-referendum debates in France and the Netherlands, as citizens linked the constitutional draft to issues that had little to do with the document on which they had to vote (e.g. Turkey's "imminent" entry into the EU).

Political elites fail not only to discuss an identity project for Europe, but even more to provide information on the EU's political contours. This section focusses on the ways in which social and political actors characterize the EU when making claims in the public sphere. Intentionally or not, these descriptive and evaluative characterizations frame the claims and thus shape their meaning to the audience. The analysis below shows that the elites' project, sketchy as it may be, emphasizes values that can alienate a significant segment of the population. The Europub.com project coded up to three frames per claim. The quantitative content analysis of these frames reveals an identity that is more economic and politico-cultural than political proper (see Table 4.1). A focus on the seven Europub.com countries shows that one in five claims containing at least one frame, or 20 percent of these, portrays the EU as a big market, needed for competition in a global economy and consequential for economic growth, inflation, and unemployment. The EU is portrayed in cultural terms too, but much less frequently. When it is, a republican rather than an ethnic cultural identity emerges, with democracy trumping religious or ethnic images.

Thirteen percent of claims refer to democracy or citizenship in some way. Occasionally, the EU's values or institutions, or those of the member states, are invoked. This was particularly the case during the well-known and thoroughly analyzed Haider Affair, which prompted many European politicians to justify EU interference in Austrian politics by invoking the need to insure that the resulting government would be democratic. At other times, especially during the drafting or reforming of EU treaties or during the Enlargement negotiations, the EU has been criticized for its democratic deficit. Members of the European Parliament, for instance, made repeated calls for democratization before Enlargement (for example, Jo Leinen in *Süddeutsche Zeitung*, February 12, 2000; Elizabeth Guigou and Elmar Brok in *Le Figaro*, June 5, 1995). Generally, however, positive democracy frames are four times more frequent than are negative frames. On the whole, these results mean that public actors situate democratic values and institutions at the center of current thinking about the EU. At least in the 1990–2002 period considered in the Europub.com project, ethnic cultural traits failed to gain as much visibility in the public sphere as democracy did. Furthermore, while 6 percent of claims display an ethno-cultural conception of the EU articulated around the concept of a "community of values," there is no elite consensus on what those values are. Often, public actors simply refer to this community of values without further specifying what it consists of. In many other instances, however, public actors refer to either Enlightenment or Christian values. During the Convention debates, for instance, Christian Democrats and leading Church representatives backed the inclusion of a reference to Christian values in the Constitution's preamble, by stressing with Pope John Paul II that "Christendom's decisive contribution to the history and culture of the different countries is part of a common treasure and it would thus make sense to inscribe this in the constitutional project" (*Le Monde*, November 8, 2002). Meanwhile, other political actors emphasized shared human rights, democratic and tolerance values, and attached priority to the inclusion of the Charter of Fundamental Rights in a future EU Constitution (for example, Walter Schwimmer in *Frankfurter Allgemeine Zeitung*, September 25, 2000; Eduardo Ferro Rodrigues in *Le Temps*, February 12, 2000).

The de-ethnicized view of the EU described above is certainly welcome from a normative viewpoint, but it does not speak to segments of the population who have proven unable to cope with the ethnic diversity that surrounds them; this may undermine the EU's legitimacy among these segments. A shift in public discourse toward a more ethnic cultural identity in the public sphere may be taking place, however, as a result of 9/11, EU-enlargement from fifteen to twenty-seven members (see Favell in this volume), and the debate over Turkey's accession. Byrnes and Katzenstein, for instance, discuss the increasing salience of Europe's religious definition (2006). Although the Europub.com data stop in 2002 and do not allow the possibility of examining changes in some of the old EU member-states, Poland's data for the 2002–2004 period support this impression. In pre-accession Poland, economic frames are certainly dominant, just as they are in the Europub.com countries between 1990 and 2002. Contrary to what happens in the latter, however, public debate in Poland hardly ever refers to the European Union's democratic values. Only 6 percent of the claims use a democracy or citizenship frame. Ethno-cultural frames, on the other hand, are much more frequent in Poland than in the Europub.com countries (14.4% versus 6.1%). Indeed, the 2000–2004 Polish public debate contains abundant references to Europe's Christian roots, especially during the early stages of the constitutional debate. What predominates then in Poland is an ethno-religious instead of a republican conception of Europe.

Economic and cultural conceptualizations of the EU predominate in public debates. In addition to this, however, content analysis of claims in the European public sphere reveals that the EU is also conceived as a polity with specific structural and functional characteristics over which public actors often disagree. The surrender of sovereignty, the transfer of competences to supranational levels of government, and the subsidiarity principle are the three major traits of this polity about which public actors seem most concerned. One in ten claims in the Europub.com countries and 16 percent of them in Poland depict the EU in terms of its impact on its members' sovereignty. In Poland, ethno-cultural conceptions of Europe often converge with concerns over sovereignty, as when Poland's Bishop Piotr Libera, Secretary of the Polish Episcopate, criticized the European Parliament for pronouncing itself on abortion, thus "interfering" with national prerogatives on the "defense of unborn children" (*Gazeta Wyborcza*, March 7, 2002).

Detailed statistical analysis of the frames discussed above shows that one can safely generalize to all actors and countries in the European public sphere. There are certainly subtle contrasts among types of actors. For instance, civil society actors emphasize the political and cultural aspects of the EU less frequently than do political actors; British public actors perceive the EU as an economic and political club slightly more frequently than do other European actors, thus neglecting to discuss commonly shared values. These particular contrasts are very small, however, and pale in comparison with the commonly shared characterization of the EU as a market, a democracy, and a polity.

The European Union as political identity project

The data collected by the Europub.com project allow us to shift the analysis from a global consideration of how people conceive of the EU to an examination of the subset of frames regarding what the EU *should be* and *where it should lead* (see Table 4.1). These conceptions most clearly convey the broad contours of the elites' political identity projects for Europe and prevailing elite–civil society cleavages. A comparison between the two columns of Table 4.1 reveals that this project, sketchy as it is, coincides to a very large extent with the political elites' general representations of the EU. The predominance of themes such as economic prosperity and democracy over institutional issues like the transfer of sovereignty reveal again that the elites' project evolves more around economic goals and broad politico-cultural values than around a particular political architecture for Europe, which is the subject of the EU's paralysis. This is not the case in Poland, however, where few frames contain normative prescriptions regarding the future of the EU, and where most of these deal with the future of national sovereignty and cultural diversity in Europe (five and three frames respectively, of a total of only nine frames concerned with what the EU should or should not be and where the EU should and should not lead).

Most relevant for this chapter's interpretation of the EU's crisis is the finding that the achievement of social equality and cohesion is the fourth most salient identity project among the Europub.com countries, but one that is given greater priority by trade unions than by politicians. Among the statements that enter this category of frames are references to the structural funds, to European social rights, and to the fight against unemployment. We heard the UK's Minister for Europe say that "at a time when the Left has suffered defeats in Europe, we will continue to press for a social Europe" (*The Times*, September 11, 2002), or French National Assembly member Elizabeth Guigou say that "one needs to build a social Europe that is not simply a free-trade

Table 4.1 *Descriptive and projected frames about the European Union (1990, 1995, 2000, 2001, 2002), for Europub.com countries, and for Poland (2000–2004).*

	Total number of frames about EU (%)		Subset of frames about *projected* EU (What the EU *should/should not be* / Where *should it/should it not lead to*) (%)	
	Europub.com countries	Poland	Europub.com countries	Poland
Functioning of the economy (total, including neutral statements)	19.8	14.5	6.0	0.0
Democracy, rights, and citizenship	12.8	6.0	8.1	0.0
Sovereignty related issues (e.g. transfer/no transfer)	10.9	15.7	5.6	6.0
Security and peace	8.8	10.8	3.2	1.2
Equality and cohesion	8.2	2.4	4.9	0.0
Strong economic and political bloc	7.3	0.0	3.0	0.0
Efficiency	6.2	0.0	2.6	0.0
Community of values	6.1	14.4	1.2	3.6
Ethnic exclusion	4.0	0.0	1.1	0.0
A bloc organized around neoliberal and free trade principles	2.6	0.0	1.1	0.0
National identity (erosion/maintenance)	2.5	2.4	1.0	0.0
N	3654	83	3654	83

Sources: (1) Koopmans, Ruud. *The Transformation of Political Mobilization and Communication in European Public Spheres.* Vth Framework Programme of the European Commission. Contract Number HPSE-CT2000-00046.

N refers to the total number of claims by actors in the public sphere for which the presence of frames was ascertained. Frames were coded only for claims referring to European integration, either because the topic was European integration or because it linked European integration to issues in the following policy fields: Education, Monetary Policy, Pensions, Agriculture, Immigration, Troop Deployment. The table includes only the most salient frame categories. For each claim, we coded up to a maximum of three frames. Because of this and because of the fact that the table includes only the most frequent frames, the percentages should not add up to a hundred. The first two columns encompass the second and, in addition, include frames as to what the European union is/is not and leads/does not lead to.

Europub.com countries: France, Germany, Italy, Spain, Netherlands, United Kingdom, Switzerland.

(2) Data collected for Poland by the author, with the assistance of Joanna Jasiewicz (a sample of 129 newspaper articles referred to European integration from the Polish newspaper *Gazeta Wyborcza* for the 2000–2004 period). N refers to the total number of claims for which the presence of frames was ascertained. The sample includes only articles whose main topic was European integration.

area" (*Le Monde*, December 4, 2002). In even more concrete terms, Gerhard Schröder warns in an *El Mundo* article against an East–West social divide (*El Mundo*, December 22, 2000), and European Parliament president Klaus Hänsch criticizes the fact that while monetary policy has been transferred to Europe, employment policy has only been partly Europeanized, and economic policy remains anchored at the national level (*Le Figaro*, December 16, 1995). Politicians are much less prone, however, to speak for a social Europe than are trade unions. Whereas 28% of the claims by trade unions use this frame, the overall percentage is 4.9%. This is actually the only statistically significant contrast between civil society's and political actors' European identity projects (on this contrast, see Hooghe 2003). The fact that trade unions often criticize politicians for making insufficient progress toward strengthening Europe's social dimension bears directly on the interpretation of the citizens' opposition to the enlargement process and for the "No" vote in the French referendum on the European Constitution (empirical analyses of the Dutch referendum point to other explanations, such as political alienation and xenophobia). Indeed, the inconsistency that one reads in the public sphere between politicians' proclamations in favor of a social Europe and trade unions' frequent criticism of the EU's neoliberal bent may have raised skepticism and insecurity among French working-class citizens as to the politicians' real motivations, moving many to vote "No" in the 2005 referendum.

Whereas politicians and trade unions differ in the extent to which they emphasize the social dimension in their political project for Europe, contrasts among European states in this and other dimensions are minor. Statistical analysis indicates, indeed, that the thirteen most prevalent frames explain only about 9 percent of the variance in the country where the frames originate. It also shows that three clusters of frames discriminate best among the frames in various countries. The first is dominated by egalitarian/cohesion and democracy frames, the second by non-economic frames, and the third by anti-exclusion and consumer protection frames. It is difficult to discern clear cultural or geographical patterns in these results. The French and Spanish public spheres, for instance, display more non-economic frames and a greater concern with equality and cohesion than do other countries. The lack of emphasis on these topics in Italy, however, prevents us from speaking of a Southern European pattern. Also, the statistical analysis reveals that Northern European states, especially the Netherlands, are more focussed on growth and less on equality. Here, however, Germany spoils the geographic pattern, for the frames in this country express a triple concern for democracy, economic growth, and social equality/cohesion. The ambiguity of the contrasts described here thus recommends a focus on patterns observed for the entire group of states in the sample rather than on cross-country contrasts.

The European Union's architectural design

It should surprise nobody if citizens do not vote in EU elections and stay home when summoned to vote on the EU Constitution. Debates in the public sphere rarely concern key political decisions like transfers of competences, transfers of sovereignty, or even the balance among the various pillars of the Union. Of 2,593 coded claims, only 495, or 19%, spoke to any of these issues.[4] In Poland for the period 2000–2004, the figure is even lower, 15%, which reflects the fact that most of public debate in this country centered on the membership negotiations. In line with an approach that I used in my book *Framing Europe* (2003), I distinguish claims about the EU's architecture along the sovereignty and competence transfer dimensions, to which I add a third: the degree of support for a political Europe. This classification of constitutional models is only adequate when characterizing public debate, where concrete projects are seldom discussed and ideas tend to remain vague. Were one to systematically characterize the constitutional designs defended by those actually involved in building the EU, one would need a much more detailed typology, as developed by Jachtenfuchs (2002). It is those rough and vague ideas, however, that reach and impact on ordinary citizens, while at the same time shaping their perceptions of the extent to which elites listen to their preferences. As the following analysis demonstrates, public debates on the EU's architecture display a gap between elites and the citizens and the divisions between the political elites on the EU's political identity that have led to the current institutional standoff.

   Before discussing the relative preferences for various European political projects, it is worth stressing another empirical finding: Claims related to the architecture of the EU are almost exclusively made by political elites and, perhaps more striking, by political elites in Germany, France, and the United Kingdom (320 or 65% of all claims that speak to any of the

---

[4] This analysis only includes claims whose main topic is European integration. Therefore, the total number of claims is 2,593 and not 3,654 as in Table 4.1.

three institutional design issues in the Europub.com countries – 60% if we add the Polish claims). In the remaining countries, participants in the public sphere refrain from taking active part in the "high politics" debate over the architecture of the EU, tacitly recognizing the big three's leadership role. In Poland, in fact, issues such as the construction of a political Europe or the number of competences in the EU were off the public debate. The only issue pertaining to the EU's architecture that was discussed in Poland during the pre-accession years was the sovereignty issue. Because of this finding and the fact that the Polish sample does not cover the same years as that of the remaining six countries, the following discussion, except when noted, refers to the Europub.com countries only.

Claimants in this sample almost unanimously favor a political Europe (85% of the claims that address the political EU/non-political EU issue), with Britons as the only exception (44% only). There is no information in the claims, however, to substantiate the conclusion that support for a political Europe means that actors in the public sphere are willing to surrender sovereignty in foreign affairs or security issues. The content of the Constitution for Europe itself leaves little doubt that European political actors still see the second pillar of the EU as an intergovernmental sphere.

There is also a great deal of support for the general transfer of competences to EU institutions and, more specifically, for increases in these competences. In only one-third of the claims addressing the EU's competences do actors call for a reduction in their number or for strict application of the principle of subsidiarity. In most cases, debate over the EU's competences focusses on social issues. Whereas support is relatively high in countries like Spain, the Netherlands, and France (100%, 80%, and 74.5%, respectively), it is relatively low in countries like Italy and the United Kingdom (36.8% and 21.7% respectively). More significantly, however, those advocating a social Europe are predominantly union leaders, as I previously noted when discussing frames about European integration. The percentage of claims that express support for a social Europe thus drop significantly when one excludes union leaders from the picture, even though support still trumps opposition.

Finally, public actors remain most divided with respect to the transfer of sovereignty to EU institutions.[5] They lean toward supranationalism

---

[5] The vagueness with which public actors discuss the topic of sovereignty prevents making subtle distinctions between absolute transfers and partial pooling of sovereignty.

in only a slight majority of claims dealing with this issue (58%). Spanish, German, and Dutch public actors are the most consistent supporters of transfers of sovereignty (100%, 100%, and 75% respectively for all claims speaking to the sovereignty issue), whereas French, Italian, Polish, and British public actors favor these transfers the least (53.6%, 57.9%, 24%, and 17% respectively).

Since German, French, and British actors are the most vocal on issues of institutional architecture, it is legitimate to talk of Germany and France/UK as the two poles of this debate. Beyond this point, however, a subtle reading of the claims involved must complement cold statistics. The contrast between Germany and France largely concerns the question of a federal Europe. In the years that comprise this sample, German proposals for a federal Europe (i.e. German Foreign Minister Joschka Fischer's speech at the European Parliament) were strongly rejected by segments of the French political elite on the grounds that Germany was trying to force its own political system into Europe. Opposition to a federal Europe among French political actors mainly expresses a rejection of the specifically parliamentarian supranational structure proposed by the Germans.[6] This federal structure pivots around a strong parliament (with or without a second chamber composed of one delegate per member-state) and a strong Commission, acting as the parliament's executive branch. Instead, the institutional model of French political actors pivots around the Council of Ministers, where the bulk of decisions would be reached through qualified majority voting (this was the traditional Gaullist consensus, only recently broken by anti-Europeans and French federalists – see Goulard 2002).

It is indeed the case that French claims concerned with the sovereignty issue invoke more frequently the extension of qualified majority vote than do corresponding German claims. One should thus be careful when concluding that the French opposition to a supranational Europe is significantly greater than the German. What French and German elites are defending are different models of supranationalism, anchored in their respective political traditions – presidentialist and parliamentarian, respectively. Without taking into account the

---

[6] The view that German political elites see Europe as an extension of their own institutional arrangements is also discussed in Jachtenfuchs 2002, p. 286; see also Katzenstein 1997 for a discussion of the institutional similarities between Europe's and Germany's systems of governance.

competences that French and Germans want to transfer to the European level, or how these competences would be allocated across different levels of government, it is problematic to attribute a greater nationalist bias to French political actors than to Germans. For one, German political actors have often stressed strict application of the subsidiarity principle. Also, the German federal system is one where competences are not allocated as strictly between the federal and the state levels as they are in the US. Instead, competences tend to be shared, with the federal government providing the main legislative or policy framework and states implementing it with a great deal of autonomy. Finally, in a critical domain such as foreign affairs and defense policy, the EU's second pillar, German public actors have rarely expressed a willingness to decisively move toward qualified majority making or to the creation of a European army. In sum, one cannot exclude the possibility that a presidentialist approach to Europe-making in which the Council of Ministers, adopting decisions through qualified majority voting, might develop into a model at least as supranational in its effects as the architecture that German political actors propose.

The description above refers to competing architectural designs for Europe, *as they appear to the citizens in the public sphere.* The architectural designs proposed in actual parliamentary debate or in negotiations at meetings of the European Council may of course differ from those outlined above. Most citizens would not know it, however, and their views on the EU will develop mainly in dialogue with the messages they get from the public sphere, a public sphere in which the media are the main stage for communication. Content analysis of claims in this public sphere allows for the distinction of various competing models for Europe. Political identity projects are either intergovernmental or dual supranational/intergovernmental, where the latter indicates that nowadays few political actors defend a centralized version of supranationality, in which sovereignty would be strictly divided between various levels of government or in which the subsidiarity principle would not reign. This second project is also dual because public actors have rarely supported the abandonment of the intergovernmental approach in the EU's second and third pillars.

Of the countries examined here, the United Kingdom's and Poland's projects qualify as intergovernmental (see Table 4.2). Within the dual supranational/intergovernmental projects, we can distinguish the federal parliamentarian one often supported in Germany, Spain, and the

Table 4.2 *Publicized political identity projects in the EU (examples)*

	Dual supranational/intergovernmental		Intergovernmental
	Federal parliamentarian	Presidentialist	
Non-Social*	German political elites	French political elites	British political elites
	Netherlands political elites		Polish political elites
Social	Spanish public actors, both political and civil		
	Trade unions in all countries		

* Those which do not openly call for a social Europe in public discourse and stress economic growth instead.

Netherlands from the presidentialist one supported by French public actors. Finally, cutting across the distinctions between the intergovernmental and the dual supranational/intergovernmental projects, we may distinguish between the non-social one, focussed on economic growth, and the social one, which emphasizes equality and cohesion. In this sample, the latter is only advocated by trade unions and by Spanish political actors. This does not mean that political actors in other countries oppose a social Europe; but Spain is the country where those political actors who support a social Europe have been featured most prominently.

The classification of political identity projects above delineates three major issues of contention that help to explain the paralysis in today's EU. The first concerns the limits of supranationalization. This contentious issue pits intergovernmentalists against supporters of the supranational/intergovernmental model. The Europub.com dataset does not show clear trends in support for transfers of sovereignty to the EU in the period considered here. This may be partly due to the paucity of data points considered and to the small number of claims that deal with institutional design in the EU. My qualitative examination of a large number of newspaper editorials between 1990 and 1997 (Díez Medrano 2003) suggested, however, that the debate on European Monetary Union was the first symptom of an emerging elite split between those still wanting a greater transfer of sovereignty to the EU and those content with leaving things as they currently stand. I thus demonstrated that in Britain, Germany, and Spain, conservative newspapers were significantly more reluctant to abandon the national currency than were more progressive ones. Lack of or limited progress since then in a number of issues where sovereignty cannot be shared by different levels of governance, whether taxes or armies, suggest that the EMU episode was not a random one. European elites are perhaps still ready to transfer to the EU competences that can be shared between levels of government (for example, energy policy or environment), but they have not shown interest in the transfer of those that cannot be shared, especially in areas like foreign policy and defense where a majority of citizens are favorable to this transfer.

The second issue of contention in today's EU concerns its parliamentarian or presidentialist design. Again, the Europub.com data show no distinctive trend between 1990 and 2002. The European Constitution, however, expressed a slight shift toward the former but stopped short of the federal model advocated by political leaders such as Joschka Fischer. One can easily envisage that this issue will continue to divide France and Germany in years to come.

Finally, the third issue of contention in today's EU concerns the neo-liberal or social spirit that guides both institution-building and policy. The Europub.com data show quite clearly that trade unions are much more vocal than political elites in supporting the maintenance of a strong social dimension in Europe. I would argue that this split between political elites more concerned with gross economic performance and trade unions still attached to the European social model reflects a broader split between political elites and citizens, which underlies the latter's lack of enthusiasm for the euro, Enlargement, and the European Constitution. In other words, I would argue that the lack of a clear commitment to the European social model by political elites favors the channeling of frustration by Europe's have-nots toward both national and European institutions (see Holmes in this volume). This frustration takes the form of abstention in electoral contests or of opposition to European developments such as the euro, the Enlargement process, and the European Constitution. The Europub.com data do not provide enough information to test the hypotheses outlined here in a more systematic fashion.

Conclusion

Political elites like to invoke citizens when justifying their positions on European integration, and they tend to blame them when explaining crises in the integration process. Citizens are rarely invited to participate in the integration process; and when they are, political elites tend to interpret what they say with a great deal of discretion. The previous pages have shifted attention to the political elites' responsibility for the constitutional crisis and relativized the role of the citizens' degree of identification with Europe in explanations of their diminishing faith in the European project. The empirical analysis of debates in the public sphere on which this chapter rests suggests that the EU's constitutional crisis has pivoted on a mismatch between elite consensus and citizen divisions on its cultural and social agenda, as well as on divisions between national political elites regarding the transfer of sovereignty to the EU. This is probably what one should expect as the EU transforms itself from a market into a multilevel system of governance.

This chapter demonstrates that until the latest EU-enlargement process, there was a great degree of consensus across Europe on the conceptualization of Europe-as-polity and on the architectural features of the EU. The EU was conceived as a political entity, as a democracy, as focussed on economic performance, and, at least among unions, as a social and solidarity project. Ethnic or religious issues played a much smaller role in the definition of this political project during the 1990s and early 2000s, although the Polish data described above suggests that Europe may be at a crossroads, where ethno-political and republican views of Europe increasingly conflict with each other and bring the EU to a standstill.

In a sense, this consensus is good, because it allows the EU to speak with one voice. Problems currently faced by the EU, such as the accession of Muslim countries and the rise of far-right mobilization and violence, can only be addressed effectively under a broad consensus among its members. Across Europe, however, the citizens are split regarding its cultural identity and social model. The rise of the far right and the anti-globalization movements testify to this split. This means that in the short run, a European political leadership that clearly sides with one of the poles of the citizens' preferences must pay a price, and the price is the potential loss of legitimacy and the prospect that some of its proposals will be defeated in referenda. In this context, the EU leaders' temptation to depoliticize the EU again is likely to be strong. In fact, the way in which the constitutional crisis has been resolved, mainly through backdoor bargains, suggests that, sad as it may be, this is the main lesson that the EU political elite drew from the French and Dutch "No" votes.

The prospect of a depoliticized EU should not lead to the expectation that further reforms will proceed smoothly. Whereas the mismatch between the elites' high degree of consensus on cultural and social issues and the growing cleavages on these issues among the population risks derailing some of the EU's projects, dissent among national political elites on the desirability of further transfers of sovereignty to the EU slow down the resolution of crises and the design of the EU's architecture. The dominant architectural design projected for Europe is dual supranational/intergovernmental, with strong emphasis on subsidiarity, politics, and a tendency to move away from Europe's traditional social model. This complexity supports Katzenstein and Checkel's criticism of simplistic polarities (nationalism/cosmopolitanism) prevailing in the literature on European identity. In a context in which routine politics and policy bargaining dominate public debate in the EU, both the neoliberal/social and the federal parliamentarian/presidentialist debates, together with the debate on Turkey's accession, may be the main institutional issues of contention in coming years, and the ones whose resolution will determine the EU's degree of legitimation.

PART II

European identity as process

5 | *Being European: East and West*

HOLLY CASE

This essay traces events and ideas that have blurred the boundary between supranational and national conceptions of European identity, starting with the French Revolution and its ideological and geopolitical progeny. The essay is organized thematically, so following a section on "Foreground and background" are "Revolution and counter-revolution," "Nation and supra-nation," and "Remembering and forgetting." Although the themes are paired opposites, the analysis shows how readily the oppositional character of the words breaks down under the pressure of historical contextualization. This notion of opposites in name only – a perception of difference that masks a profound similarity – is one that extends to the pair of opposites that appear in the title of this chapter; namely "East and West."

Modern conceptions of European identity formed during the course of wars, revolutions, and utopian political projects that both "halves" of Europe experienced and interpreted in very localized ways, increasingly within national historical frameworks. This evolution made for disagreements regarding the nature of "universal" European values and projects between "East" and "West." But if we pull back the curtain of false oppositions, we begin to see the outlines of a structural similarity in the way "Europeanness" is understood. The similarity rests on the premise that being "European" is not only compatible with being "national," but is a constituent element of national identity. The oppositions themselves, I argue, are thus manifestations of national elites' desire to associate or disassociate their nation's course with/from that of their near or more distant neighbors in order to achieve localized, generally "national" goals. Historically, attempts to conceptualize a European identity are rooted in these localized – one might say

I would like to extend special thanks to the volume editors, Jeffrey Checkel and Peter Katzenstein, as well as to my colleague at Cornell, Valerie Bunce, for their very helpful comments and feedback on this piece.

"neighborhood" – experiences and initiatives which national elites cast in universalist terms, starting with the French Revolution. Thus, when the editors of this volume argue that Europe's ambivalence over its sense of community is due to politics, the statement holds for both the past as well as the present, for historically the politics of national elites – from Danton to Derrida, and from Kościuszko to Kaczyński – have converged around the question of what it means to be European.

Foreground and background

In early 2003, on the eve of the US invasion of Iraq, Donald Rumsfeld was asked what he made of the fact that 70 percent of Europeans were opposed to the Iraq invasion. His answer was: "You're thinking of Europe as Germany and France. I don't. I think that's old Europe" (quoted in "Outrage at 'old Europe' remarks" 2003). With that, he implied the existence of a "new Europe" – namely the countries of East-Central Europe – which thought and acted differently from those of the "old Europe," most notably by supporting the war in Iraq.

Shortly thereafter, Jürgen Habermas and Jacques Derrida – two well-known European intellectuals from Germany and France respectively – countered Rumsfeld's neologism with one of their own: "Core" Europe. On February 15, 2003, mass demonstrations protesting the impending US-led war in Iraq took place in London, Rome, Madrid, Barcelona, Berlin, and Paris. These demonstrations signaled what Habermas called "the birth of a European public sphere." "Europe has to throw its weight on the scales to counterbalance the hegemonic unilateralism of the United States," he wrote, and in the construction of this new European identity, the "Old Europe," namely France and Germany, would lead the way (Habermas and Derrida 2005, p. 6).[1]

There were many responses to the Habermas/Derrida idea of "Core" Europe, among them the following from Hungarian writer Péter Esterházy:

Once I was an Eastern European; then I was promoted to the rank of Central European ... Then a few months ago, I became a New European. But before I had the chance to get used to this status – even before I could have refused it – I have now become a non-core European. [W]hile I see no serious reason for

[1] It should be noted that the text itself was written by Habermas and only signed by Derrida (p. 3).

not translating this new division (core/non-core) with the terms "first class" and "second-class," still, I'd rather not speak in that habitual Eastern European, forever insulted way. (Esterházy 2005, pp. 74–5)

Like Rumsfeld and Habermas/Derrida, writers on European identity have often sought to make decisions for Eastern Europeans about who they are and where they fit into the going version of "Europe." Before the mostly Western European Orientalists constructed "the Orient," luminaries of the Enlightenment had first flexed their encyclopedic zeal on the Eastern neighbors (Todorova 1997; Wolff 1994). And advocates for the region have bemoaned the devastating effects of Western attempts to create and later "solve" the "Eastern Question" and its successors. Partitions, buffer states, the "cordon sanitaire," the 14 Points, Munich, *Lebensraum*, the "iron curtain," European expansion: all bear testament to Great Powers' attempts to neutralize, parcel off, or make useful the so-called "lands between" of East-Central Europe (Walters 1987, p. 117; Palmer 1970, p. 405).

But for every narrative of Great Power manipulation, there is one of injured faith. This was a "powder keg," an ungrateful beneficiary of Western civilization, a territory outside Great Power jurisdiction – not "Core Europe's" problem, about which Neville Chamberlain opined in September of 1938, "How horrible, fantastic it is that we should be digging trenches and trying on gas-masks here because of a quarrel in a far away country between people of whom we know nothing" (California University Committee on International Relations 1939, p. 184). The 1848 revolutions met a bitter end here, the two most devastating global conflagrations of all time began here, national self-determination went haywire here, the ideal of a socialist utopia was forever tainted by what happened here, and now the most optimistic project of the twentieth century, the European Union, is being tested here. Marx wrote that "all great world-historic facts and personages appear, so to speak, twice ... the first time as tragedy, the second time as farce" (Marx and De Leon 1907, p. 5). He might have been speaking of East-Central Europe, always a step behind, always taking a good idea and getting it all wrong, ruining it for the rest of us, so to speak.

Of course, the countries and peoples of East-Central Europe have had their own stories about what it means to be European, no less packed with drama and accusations. The "true" Europe is Latin Christianity, or simply Christianity, and this region has taken countless beatings from Eastern infidels of various stripes (Mongols, Turks, Soviets) so that

"Core" Europe could sit back and enjoy the fruits of overseas trade networks and the Industrial Revolution. States and peoples on Europe's Eastern periphery repeatedly sacrificed themselves on the altar of Europe, serving as the "last bastion of Western civilisation." But they did so at the expense of their own development, focussing on resistance above all else, becoming proud, poor, and stubborn, while Western Europeans became enlightened, rich, and tolerant (Berindei 1991, p. 3).[2]

Another version of the story goes that East-Central Europe has always been European. It had medieval kingdoms with lavish courts, it had a Reformation and a Renaissance, it took the French Revolution seriously, and it shared in a "common European culture" (Kosáry 2003, p. 7) from start to finish, even if it did not always seem like it.[3] Furthermore, the manic economic growth of Western Europe was the aberration, the exception where East-Central Europe was the norm (Brenner 1989).

These stories may have relatively short historical pedigrees (most of them eighteenth- and nineteenth-century creations, as in fact were idea-of-Europe stories more generally); but they also have breathtaking geographical sweep, extending into Turkey, Ukraine, Russia, Armenia, even Kazakhstan. In fact, throughout the past three centuries, Russia has arguably more consistently considered itself – and been considered – "European" than has Great Britain.[4] Clearly, today's Russia is not as invested in the "common European home" as Gorbachev's USSR (or maybe just Gorbachev) was;[5] but the fact that further expansion of the European Union is still likely suggests that

---

[2] A version of this narrative of self-sacrifice can be found in the pages of J.R.R. Tolkien's *Lord of the Rings* trilogy, in which the peace-loving hobbits can be read as English, the swift and beautiful elves as Scandinavians, and the men as Slavs – fierce warriors who have a hard time controlling their pride and passion and seeing the big picture (the most prominent in this regard being the character of Boromir, who even has a Slavic-sounding name). This stereotype is replicated in *Harry Potter*, with the Slavs playing the dumb but benign wizard school of Durmstrang, whose featured characters are Viktor Krum and Igor Karkaroff. See also Wolff, "The Rise and Fall of Morlacchismo" (2003, pp. 37–52).

[3] This is the central premise of Czech author Milan Kundera's famous essay "The Tragedy of Central Europe" (Kundera 1984).

[4] Russia played a prominent role in the Holy Alliance of the post-Napoleonic period, whereas Great Britain sat out the alliance. Great Britain was also not part of the interwar "Pan-Europe" project as conceptualized by Richard Coudenhove-Kalergi (Coudenhove-Kalergi 1926, p. 39).

[5] In Mikhail Gorbachev's speech before the Parliamentary Assembly of the Council of Europe on July 6, 1989, he outlined the notion of a "common home" shared by Western Europe and the USSR together with its satellites (Council of Europe 1997).

European identity is but loosely tied to geography, and stories about what it means to be European and how different states and peoples fit (or do not fit) that mold will continue to abound both within and beyond the boundaries of the EU.

But for the time being, the stories "Core" Europe must take most seriously are those of the new member states of East-Central Europe, stories of always having belonged to, protected, defended, preserved, represented European culture and values. These stories have the tenor of gentle criticisms but were crafted as appeals: We gave life and limb for your safety and prosperity, now how about letting us have Macedonia or Transylvania or Volhynia or, better yet, our own state. And these appeals were competitive between the states and nations of East-Central Europe. Hence the term Balkanization, meaning the parcelling up of land, the most recent manifestation of which is the newly won independence of Montenegro. Such pleas often seemed incomprehensible in their pettiness and frustrating in their persistence to "Core" European statesmen, who forever lamented what they perceived as the lack of transcendent ideals and insistence on particularist goals they saw in East-Central European interpretations – or perversions – of Europe's "universalist" projects. Conflict between states in the region was seen as counterproductive, retrograde, and typical.[6] But these tensions were also useful to the Great Powers of Europe – Croat antagonism with Hungarians was useful to Austria, Polish aspirations for recovering their state and the Little Entente were useful to France, interwar Hungarian and Bulgarian revisionism were useful to Nazi Germany.

Overlooking or belittling the East-Central European perspective on what it means to be European is thus not an error of snobbery alone, it is a form of denial about the links between cause and effect and, as such, a political move. When an international commission went to gather information on the Balkan Wars, its report spoke of how "all these countries, not far from us ... are still unlike Europe, more widely separated from her than Europe from America." It went on to disclose "an excess of horrors

---

[6] George Kennan thus compared the First and Second Balkan Wars of 1912–1913 to the Wars of Yugoslav Succession of the 1990s, both typified by a variety of nationalism "inherited ... from a distant tribal past: a tendency to view the outsider, generally, with dark suspicion, and the political-military opponent, in particular, as a fearful and implacable enemy to be rendered harmless only by total and unpitying destruction. And so," he concludes, "it remains today" – nothing for it but to watch and shake one's head disapprovingly (International Commission 1993, p. 11).

that we can scarcely realize in our own systematized countries," and concluded with a grateful sigh that "the Great Powers are manifestly unwilling to make war. Each one of them ... has discovered the obvious truth that the richest country has the most to lose by war, and each country wishes for peace above all things" (International Commission 1914, pp. 3, 13, 17). The report was published in 1914, on the eve of World War I.

Efforts to slough off undesirable elements of the European experience have allowed both "East" and "West" to remain at least partially blind to what truly connects the two. At the core of this experience is the slippage between universalist and particularist European utopian visions, a confusion that is largely of late-eighteenth-century vintage. In fact, the "Core" Europe thesis of Habermas and Derrida is itself a product of this slippage, for the two men's act of coming together to make a positive political statement about Europe's trajectory makes sense only in the context of the "neighborhood" problem of German-French historical rapprochement. Yet, in the essay, the resolution of that interstate problem is cast as the ultimate manifestation of "European" goals and values. Little wonder others who like to consider themselves European are inclined to bring their own "neighborhood" problems to bear on formulations of European identity.

Revolution and counter-revolution

Although we newcomers like to point out that we, too, have always been Europeans, we still march to a different tempo, so to speak ... and we use words differently. (Esterházy 2005, p. 75)

In the wake of the failed 1848 revolutions in different parts of Europe – East and West – Friedrich Engels wrote that

the "European brotherhood of peoples" will come to pass not through mere phrases and pious wishes but only as a result of thorough revolutions and bloody struggles; ... it is not a matter of fraternization between all European peoples underneath a republican flag, but of the alliance of revolutionary peoples against counter-revolutionary peoples, an alliance which does not happen on *paper* but on the *field of battle*. (Engels 1973, p. 227)

The Slavs of Russia and Austria were the "counter-revolutionaries" who had betrayed the revolution by blocking German and Magyar revolutionaries with their narrow self-interest. "[W]e shall fight 'an implacable life-and-death struggle' with Slavdom, which has betrayed the revolution; a war of annihilation and ruthless terrorism, not in the interests of Germany but in the interests of the revolution!" (p. 245). Engels's version of the revolution was thus to be one between peoples perhaps more than between classes, since some peoples were "revolutionary," while others were "counter-revolutionary."

For Engels, the Russian-born anarchist/pan-Slavist Mikhail Bakunin, who called for a "European brotherhood of peoples," was ignorant of "the utterly different levels of civilization of the individual peoples and the equally different political needs conditioned by those levels. The word 'freedom' replaces all of this [for Bakunin]" (pp. 227–8). Engels also felt uncomfortable when Bakunin employed the catch phrases of the French Revolution: "liberty, equality, fraternity." Uttered by a Slav, these words sounded naive and outdated, even perverse, because they were used to call for the dissolution of the Austro-Hungarian Empire, rather than in the true spirit of the (German) revolution.

The French Revolution has always had a mixed legacy throughout Europe. From the beginning there were strong feelings about when, how, and whether it "went wrong" and which bits of it – the rights of man, the Terror, the *Code Napoléon* – bore preservation, in what form, and where. There is no question, however, that it reverberated well beyond France and set the tone for revolutionary activity in Europe and beyond. Its reverberations in East-Central Europe were myriad, but consistently powerful. In the northeast it meant the partial resurrection of the Polish state, for anachronistic "Illyria" it meant elementary education in the Slovene and Croatian languages, for Hungary it was a model on which they would in part base their own 1848 revolution.

The French revolutionary slogan of "liberty, equality, fraternity" was picked up by anarchists, nationalists, and romantic poets as a motto for everything from socialism to pan-Slavism (Petőfi 1974; Bakunin 1971; Levine 1914). Italian nationalist Giuseppe Mazzini used the phrase as a cornerstone of his 1834 "Pact of Fraternity of Young Europe," among the first efforts at conceptualizing a European project by uniting the nationalist elites of different peoples working toward national independence and unification (Mazzini 1872, pp. 151–91). Furthermore, myriad groups sought to establish themselves as the torch-bearers of the ongoing revolution.[7]

---

[7] Leader of the 1848 Hungarian revolution, Lajos Kossuth, said in a speech to the US Congress in 1852 that "every disappointed hope with which Europe looked toward France is a degree more added to the importance of Hungary to the world"

But the Revolution was paradox-ridden from the beginning: how could something so French also be universal? If entire groups demand liberty for themselves, what becomes of equality and fraternity? (If the Hungarians are having a revolution to throw off Austrian rule, and at the same time the Romanians in Hungary are having a revolution to throw off Hungarian rule, does that make the Romanians counter-revolutionary? Or if the Polish nobility rises up to throw off Habsburg rule, and the Polish peasantry rises up to protest the oppression of the Polish nobility, who is the "true" revolutionary?) All of this related to the question of whether the "rights of man" could be expanded meaningfully to nations. Did a nation (nationality) have the same rights as an individual, to "liberty, property, security, and resistance to oppression"?[8] And if so, which had trump status, the individual or the nation? This conundrum seemed to take two divergent paths into the twentieth century – pitting "democracy" against "fascism" or "totalitarianism." In the former, the individual forms the main unit of consideration for rights, in the latter the nation or state. Herein lies the tension between what Castiglione (this volume) terms the liberal and communitarian models for citizenship as "citizenship-as-rights" and "citizenship-as-belonging," respectively.

Revolution is at the core of both branches. Fascism, communism, and liberalism all share a utopian strain,[9] and responses to them also sought to mimic their revolutionary components.[10] Hence the distinction between revolution and counter-revolution was never an easy one to make, which is perhaps why Germans have a fuzzy collective memory of the 1918–1919 revolutions across Germany and why Hungarians

(de Puy 1852, p. 396). Bakunin wrote to his "brother Slavs" that "the eyes of all are fixed upon you with breathless anxiety. What you decide will determine the realization of the hopes and destinies of the world – to arrive soon or to drift away to a remote and uncertain future" (Bakunin 1971).

[8] See Article 2 of the *Declaration of the Rights of Man* (1789). It is worth noting that Article 3 outlines how "The principle of all sovereignty resides essentially in the nation. No body nor individual may exercise any authority which does not proceed directly from the nation."

[9] This phenomenon was brilliantly described in the doctoral thesis of the young poet/historian Peter Viereck (1941).

[10] Slovene-American writer and political thinker Louis Adamic tapped the wellspring of revolution-as-reaction when, in 1941, he called for an American-style revolution to take place in Europe to counter the forces of Nazism and fascism. He wrote, "We must never forget that revolution in Europe means revolution against the misleaders of the past, who made Hitler's road easy, as well as revolution against Hitler" (Adamic 1941, p. 259).

literally buried the Hungarian revolution of 1919.[11] The Cold War, despite ushering in an era of ideological witch-hunts, did little to clarify the ambiguity between revolution and reaction. In 1956, for example, following Nikita Khrushchev's "Secret Speech" – in which he denounced Stalinism as overly harsh and called for a new course – Poles initiated strikes and demonstrations, calling for the creation of workers' councils. The councils were later allowed to convene following a tense standoff with the Soviet leadership, but thereafter they were slowly stripped of their power and then eliminated completely. In solidarity with the Poles, many Hungarians demonstrated, calling for a reform communist, Imre Nagy, to resume leadership of the Communist Party. The concession was granted, but when state security forces fired on demonstrators, the demonstrators started to fire back. Within a short time, Soviet tanks came in to put down the uprising – or was it a revolution? The post-1956 communist regime in Hungary called the events a "counter-revolution," since the "real" revolution had been initiated by the Bolsheviks and had served as the model for state socialism in Hungary and other countries in the Eastern Bloc. To the West and many of those who participated directly in those events, what took place that autumn was a *revolution*, and its participants were freedom fighters drawing on the ideals of the French Revolution and 1848. The year 1956 also posed a problem in "Core" Europe for socialists, who were forced to recognize that not every deed undertaken in the name of socialism matched the platonic ideal.[12] They scoured the Left for a "nouvelle alternative," a "third way" out of the problem that East-Central Europe represented for the European Left.[13] Their vanguardism was not without condescension toward dissidents living in the region, seen by the Western leftists as "opposed to the very idea of socialism" and therefore suspect (Kenney 2002, p. 93).

---

[11] On memory of the 1919 revolution in Hungary, see Rev (2005, ch. 3).

[12] See, for example, Italian Communist Party Secretary Palmiro Togliatti's telegram from October 30, 1956, in which he declares that "Hungarian events have created a heavy situation inside the Italian labor movement, and in our Party, too" ("Togliatti on Nagy," p. 357).

[13] The French journal *La Nouvelle Alternative*, for example, was founded in 1986 in part to support "third-way" movements like Polish Solidarity. That objective is echoed, however faintly, in the present mission of the journal *Présentation* (2007).

It was clear that many of the dissidents had their own ideas about revolution. In 1989, a youngster named Viktor Orbán gave a speech on the occasion of the reburial of Imre Nagy, who had been executed in 1958 for his role in the Hungarian "counter-revolution" of 1956. In the speech, Orbán linked 1848 to 1956 to 1989, calling the latter the fulfillment of "the will of the revolution" (Orbán 1989, p. 26). In 2006, the legacy of 1956 was hotly contested in a Hungary now governed by a socialist coalition. Was the revolution of 1956 a leftist/ liberal revolution? Or was it a national one? The question applied as much to 1848 and 1989 as to 1956. Demonstrators led by Orbán, by then former prime minister and leader of Hungary's conservative opposition, packed the square in front of the Hungarian parliament building for weeks. During a protestors' raid on the television building, participants took down the EU flag, mimicking the removal of the communist red star from buildings during the 1956 events. Was the EU just one more foreign oppressor – like Austria in 1848, or the Soviet Union in 1956? Or would the youngsters who lobbed Molotov cock- tails at tanks and security police in 1956 perhaps now be termed "terrorists" (a term that was in fact used at the time by some communist commentators)?[14]

Since the French Revolution, revolutionary activity lies close to the heart of what is considered "European"; yet there is nothing like a consensus regarding what counts as revolutionary and what is good and bad about revolutions.

Nation and supra-nation

In the competition of new ideas about the new European self-consciousness, I have the odd feeling that we wanted a new giant national state, feelings of identity, a common enemy, and, instead of national character traits, Euronational character traits. (Esterházy 2005, p. 78)

World War I made many people wonder what being a European meant in its aftermath. The works of Virginia Woolf, Siegfried Sassoon, Robert Graves, Erich Maria Remarque, and Paul Valéry all said "Good-bye to All That," to the way things were before the war; a recent

---

[14] Hungarian communists referred to the "terror" perpetrated by the "counterrevolutionaries" of 1956. See Granville (2004, p. 87).

French novel/film proposes that the hero being shell-shocked into complete amnesia is the only possible happy ending to a story about World War I.[15] Paul Valéry wrote in 1919 that during the war, Europe "felt in every nucleus of her mind that she was no longer the same, that she was no longer herself, that she was about to lose consciousness" (Valéry 1919). History seemed to have run its course, and Europeans were strumming the lyre to their own demise.

But new voices sprang up to counter the pessimism hanging over the continent, among them that of Richard Coudenhove-Kalergi. His 1923 book called for the creation of a Pan-Europe, or "self-help through the consolidation of Europe into an ad hoc politico-economic federation" that would stretch from France to the border with the USSR, from Sweden to Africa, restoring Europe to her former glory as a world player and a truly Great Power (Coudenhove-Kalergi 1926, p. xv). Coudenhove-Kalergi agreed with those like Valéry for whom "the World War destroyed the bridges leading to the past, and [e]very man who goes across them will fall into the abyss," but optimistically concluded that "the only way to safety, the way upwards and forwards, is the steep way to Pan-Europe" (p. 211).

Ideas about European unity have nevertheless tended to come at awkward times for East-Central Europe. It is true that Mazzini's nineteenth-century "Young Europe" had a Polish chapter, and some elites from the Little Entente states found Coudenhove-Kalergi's ideas attractive. Yet while World War I had been devastating for many in the region, it had not resulted in the loss of empires or a humbling of national hubris – quite the reverse. In 1915, the soon-to-be president of the new state of Czechoslovakia, Tomas Masaryk, declared in a memorandum for the British government that the aim of the war was the "regeneration of Europe" (Masaryk 1915, p. 117). This idea, espoused earlier by a number of British statesmen and diplomats, later informed the tone of the postwar treaty conferences. In the wake of World War I, a "New Europe" was born, one that was supposed to correct the injustices of the old by breaking up empires (most notably that "prison of nations," the Dual Monarchy/Austria-Hungary) and allowing for the self-determination of peoples. New states appeared – or in the case of Poland, reappeared – on the map, and old ones were resized or reshaped.

---

[15] The film is *A Very Long Engagement*, directed by Jean-Pierre Jeunet and released in 2004. It is based on a 1993 novel of the same title by Sebastien Japrisot.

Czechoslovakia, Yugoslavia, Bulgaria, Romania, Hungary, Poland, and Albania replaced the sprawling Habsburg Empire and created a land wedge between Germany and the Soviet Union.

Thus the interwar period was one of trying to make new states work, rather than about joining another European empire (espoused by an Austrian, no less, in the person of Coudenhove-Kalergi). For although Coudenhove-Kalergi saw the seed of Pan-Europe in the Little Entente and argued that in a new Pan-Europe "the greatest advantage would be enjoyed by the states of eastern Europe" (Coudenhove-Kalergi 1926, pp. 128–9, 177), his movement posed little threat to the nation-state during the interwar period. For one thing, the advocates of "Pan-Europe" still felt that "every nation is a sanctuary – as the hearth and home of culture, as the point of crystallization for morality and progress." Thus, "Pan-Europe" would arise out of the "deepening and broadening of national cultures," rather than their negation (p. 161). Coudenhove-Kalergi himself perceived interwar Europe as "twenty-six human beings [living] within a narrow space," thereby conflating nations with individuals such that Pan-Europe could only be conceptualized as a conglomeration of discrete national units (p. 105). Furthermore, political union was a pipe dream in a Europe where fascism and Nazism – the other ways to make Great Powers out of insecure or devastated states – were prevailing over liberal nationalism and beached democracy. Fascism revived the question of the primacy of the individual vs. the primacy of the nation/state, strongly favoring the latter.[16] Making the move to a United States of Europe, by contrast, was not so high on the list of priorities at that point. In the words of one Bulgarian professor writing in 1937, "every nation must concern itself with its own preservation, because if it does not, no one else will" (Genov *et al.* 1941a, p. 9).[17]

This is not to suggest that supranationalism disappeared during the dark years of World War II. On the contrary, Hitler had a supranational vision of a New European Order (Martin 2006). Furthermore, that vision

---

[16] In Mussolini's 1932 "The Doctrine of Fascism," he writes, "Anti-individualistic, the Fascist conception of life stresses the importance of the State and accepts the individual only in so far as his interests coincide with those of the State." See Mussolini (1935).

[17] This quote was taken from the program of the All-Bulgarian Union, established in 1937.

had its advocates in all parts of the continent, from France to Romania: individuals who imagined the future of their state in a Europe reordered by Nazi Germany.[18] In 1941, for example, Georgi Genov, the same Bulgarian professor who declared that the golden rule of European diplomacy should be every nation for itself, wrote of the interwar period that, "the idea ... of a so called Pan-Europe, that [Europe] should turn into a single federation, stressing the solidarity of European nations [is] precisely what Germany is calling for today" (Genov 1941b, pp. 7–8).

Indeed, World War II had many Europeans – most notably Hitler and his allies – talking again about a "new" Europe, one that would correct the injustices of the interwar period. Hitler's New European Order was itself to be a kind of "Pan-Europe" with a decidedly German "Core." Nevertheless, it maintained a fierce dedication to the principle of self-determination (for Germany), minority rights (for Germans), and European unity (under Germany), usurping the role the League of Nations had so ineptly played. In so doing, it won a following among the states and sub-states whose "revolutions" had proven incomplete. Slovaks stuck in a state with Czechs were given their own state, Ukrainians stuck with Poles, and Croats stuck with Serbs were similarly let loose, and Bulgaria and Hungary were allowed to stretch their borders back to correct some of the over-self-determination of the post-World War I treaties. There was great excitement about the New European Order in these places, and much projection as to what it should look like.

Hence, it is not even the case that World War II was two conceptions of Europe battling for preeminence – instead, some on Hitler's side had much in common with their counterparts on the Allied side and vice versa (was there widespread anti-Semitism in Allied countries? Yes. Was there concern with minority rights among Hitler's allies? Yes.) This problem is most starkly evident from Allied attempts to formulate concrete war aims rhetorically distinct from Germany's, much of which comes through in the pages of the journal *New Europe* of the time. In July of 1941, Felix Gross argued in its pages that "Just as Nazism prepared for the occupation from the ideological standpoint, so must we prepare for the moment of deliverance by creating ideological conditions for the dynamic

---

[18] My unpublished manuscript focusses on how Hungarian and Romanian leaders and spokespersons projected Hungary and Romania into the "New European Order" during the war (Case, forthcoming).

self-expression of the masses in Europe: an ideological dynamism." In
October of that year, John Wheeler-Bennett openly wondered, "What
have we to offer as an alternative" to the Nazi "New Order"? Answering,
"Frankly we cannot offer any blueprint ... Through the gloom of battle
and suffering – we grope toward the dawn" (Gross 1941, p. 202;
Wheeler-Bennett 1941, p. 278).[19]

In East-Central European states allied with the Axis, there was much
talk about "becoming more national" so we could be "more
European."[20] There was also speculation as to who would best represent
the interests of the New Order and whose dreams would be realized,
mimicking the revolutionary vanguardism of the previous century. These
discussions took place during the war but looked toward the peace,
trading loyalty to the Axis and sacrifices for the Axis war effort for
promises (even half-promises) of securing Transylvania, Macedonia,
Bessarabia, or an independent Croatia or Slovakia; again the concern
for territory and preoccupation with local squabbles, again the desire to
merge only so as to make a cleaner, fairer cut in the end. While Europe
was supposedly engaged in an ideological struggle of titanic proportions,
while the modern welfare state was being born, while "Core" Europe was
learning a lesson the hard way about isolationism and national chauvinism (again), while Bolshevism was getting a second wind, it may seem
that all the states of East-Central Europe could think about was advan-
cing the legitimacy of their national/territorial claims.

But, arguably, even "Core" European identity was driven by quite
national identity crises.[21] Just after the war had ended, in 1946,

---

[19] A similar idea is expressed in a 1941 book by Louis Adamic in which he laments that
"Since Hitler there haven't been any new ideas in Europe worth mentioning ... there
is as yet no idea beyond hatred of Hitler with which to challenge his 'New Order'"
(Adamic 1941, p. 257); second half of quote found in ("Books," p. 336).

[20] In a December 1941 speech, Hungarian prime minister László Bárdossy declared
that, in order to become part of the new European order, Hungarians had to
"emphasize their national uniqueness" (*Ellenzék* 1941, pp. 1–2). See also
Zathureczky (1943, pp. 7–8). For a comparable Romanian assertion, see
Porunca Vremii (1942).

[21] In his book *The European Rescue of the Nation-state*, the first edition of which
was published in 1992, Alan Milward sought to debunk the long-held
assumption "that [the European Community] is in antithesis to the nation-state."
He argued convincingly that "The European Community only evolved
[post-1945] as an aspect of ... national reassertion and without it the reassertion
might well have proved impossible. To supersede the nation-state would be to
destroy the Community" (Milward 1992, pp. 2–3).

Churchill called for European unity, while almost simultaneously dropping the Iron Curtain between "Eastern" and "Western" Europe (Churchill 1996, p. 46).[22] "Core" Europe emerged battered and worn, but ready to forget and eager to be supranational, cosmopolitan, and universalist – building again on one of the French Revolutionary legacies. At the root of the optimism and supranationalism of the postwar period, however, was the subtextual goal of "taming" Germany. Nor was postwar supranationalism necessarily cosmopolitan: in the 1960s Charles de Gaulle created a model for a *Europe d'États*, wherein the national interest would prevail over the "European" and France would lead the way for Europe. In a speech on April 19, 1963, he said:

[I]f the union of Western Europe ... is a capital aim in our action outside, we have no desire to be dissolved within it. Any system that would consist of handing over our sovereignty to august international assemblies would be incompatible with the rights and the duties of the French Republic. [I]t appears essential to us that Europe be Europe and that France be France ... our chief duty is to be strong and to be ourselves. (de Gaulle 1965, pp. 225–6)[23]

In his essay for this volume, Hartmut Kaelble notes that "the long history of debate by Europeans does not lead in a straight line to the modern, liberal identification with Europe." Similarly, Dario Castiglione points to the coexistent strains of cosmopolitan and communitarian ideas that – consciously or not – form the core of contemporary European political identity. Thus "Euroenthusiasm" and nationalism are not necessarily, or even commonly, manifest as polar opposites. Individuals like de Gaulle and Orbán have therefore viewed a united Europe as desirable, but not a trump to the national interest; rather, a constituent part of that interest.

---

[22] For Churchill's "Iron Curtain" speech, see Churchill (1995, pp. 298–302).
[23] In a speech from May 31, 1960, de Gaulle declared that France desired to

> contribute to building Western Europe into a political, economic, cultural and human group, organized for action, progress and defense ... the nations which are becoming associated must not cease to be themselves, and the path to be followed must be that of organized cooperation between States, while waiting to achieve, perhaps, an imposing confederation. But France, as far as she is concerned, has recognized the necessity of this Western Europe ... which appears today as the indispensable condition of the equilibrium of the world. (de Gaulle 1965, p. 78)

Joining the European Union thus was and is often celebrated by East-Central European politicians and commentators as a return to an important *national* project begun in the interwar and/or wartime periods that was aborted by the communist takeover. After 1989, again, as with Hitler's New European Order, there was talk of "building up our national character" so as to be "more European." In a Hungarian political commentary from 1990, the author declared, "we can only truly be Europeans if we are good Hungarians ... thus with the strengthening of our national essence we must knock on the doors of Europe so that we can get back in after a forty-year detour" (*Magyar Nemzet* 1990, p. 6).[24] The notion is echoed almost verbatim by Habermas and Derrida in their "Core Europe" piece, when they suggest that in Europe "The population must so to speak 'build up' their national identities, and add to them a European dimension" (Habermas and Derrida 2005, p. 6).

Remembering and forgetting

There was no 1968 here; there was no student movement and no reappraisal of the past. (Esterházy 2005, p. 75)

Tony Judt has argued in his recent history of Europe after 1945 that "Europe was able to rebuild itself politically and economically only by forgetting the past, but it was able to define itself morally and culturally only by remembering it" (quoted in Menand 2005, p. 168). Although the Europe Judt speaks of is again mostly "Core" Europe, East and West have much in common when it comes to the Cold War habit of selective memory and strategic forgetfulness.

The most notable convergence of selective memory was of wartime resistance, which both "halves" of Europe clung to in one form or another. The two extreme examples are France and Yugoslavia, where resistance to Nazism during the war was given cult status, and the heroes of the resistance became the postwar presidents of both countries, Charles de Gaulle and Josip Broz Tito. But other states, too, nursed their wounds with pride, most notably Italy and Slovakia with tales of belated self-liberation. Then there were the proud sufferers – Poland and Belgium, modern vanguard in the European hierarchy of undeserved obliteration.

---

[24] There were also more discussions about why "we" should be in and "they" should be out. See, for example "Németh..." (2004); *Adevărul Cluj* (1995, pp. 1, 4).

But heroes and victims alike were problematized, mostly following 1989, when the two Europes were forced to recognize that the new Cold War clothes that they had worn over their World War II pasts proved invisible. The perfect Polish victim became the anti-Semitic Jew killer. The Croat partisan became the man who welcomed the Nazi troops as they entered Zagreb. The evil Nazi perpetrator became the *volksdeutsche* victim of violence, internment, fire-bombing, and expulsion. The French national hero became a dictator who held the country back and down.

The problematic victim haunted postwar Europe. For the USSR and East-Central Europe, this meant the Jews, as privileged victims of Nazi and fascist violence when fascism was supposed to victimize everyone equally. Coming to terms with the extent to which the Holocaust was about killing Jews, rather than about fascists victimizing everyone, has proven a difficult challenge. It is inextricably tied to issues of collaboration and the wartime suffering of the population, most notably at the hands of the "liberating" Red Army soldiers, to whom countless statues and monuments were erected and who were regularly – if often insincerely – honored after the war. Rape, theft, expropriation, and expulsion are all components of that history (Polcz 2002, pp. 90–110; Temkin 1998, pp. 199–203).

Similarly difficult for "Core" Europe have been discussions around German suffering during the fire-bombings, forced expulsions, rape, and other abuses that took place late in the war or shortly thereafter. German novelist Günter Grass has placed grim episodes of German suffering at the epicenter of his literary work.[25] More recently, Grass has highlighted another area of memory and forgetting where East and West match neatly – specifically in dealing with the unsavory legacies of collaboration – when he admitted that he had joined the Waffen SS as a youth.[26] Germany's "unmasterable past"[27] renders it difficult to speak of German suffering without mention of German culpability and

---

[25] Most notably in his novel *Crabwalk*, about the sinking of the *Wilhelm Gustloff* on January 30, 1945, carrying many refugees fleeing the advance of the Red Army (Grass 2002).

[26] Nathan Thornburgh, "Günter Grass's Silence," *Time*, Monday, August 14, 2006, www.time.com/time/arts/article/0,8599,1226380,00.html (accessed March 16, 2007).

[27] This is a reference to a book by Charles Maier dealing with the memory of World War II and the Holocaust in Germany (Maier 1988).

collaboration. Such concerns reverberate in the states of East-Central Europe, as well, during the struggle to determine what aspects of their communist and World War II past should be spotlighted. Lustration laws in various countries, attempts at rapprochement with the past, have not diminished the drama of an opportunistic "outing" of former secret service informers. And in Poland (as in Turkey), there is a new law in place forbidding anyone to claim the Poles had any responsibility for Nazi or Soviet crimes.[28]

There was also another kind of forgetting the two halves of Europe shared, a forgetting induced by the magic of consumerism. Robert Paxton writes of a "New Europe" that emerged in the 1950s and 1960s in the West, one focussed on consumerism that would steer discussions away from difficult questions about the past (Paxton 2005, pp. 557–67). This was the time when Europe became a tourist destination for Americans who wanted to ski in the Alps, buy Italian leather and French perfume, and try their luck at Monte Carlo.[29] It was the Europe of James Bond, where history was decoupled from the present and served at best as a scenic backdrop for a car chase.

The 1960s were also the time when East-Central Europe was "bought" in exchange for forgetting the past, specifically the Stalinist, 1956, and later 1968 past. Kádár gave Hungary "goulash communism" in exchange for silence on the matter of the 1956 "counterrevolution." Czechoslovak and Yugoslav communists maintained power by providing consumer goods and offering market concessions, the ability to travel and buy a weekend house in the country or by the sea. This was the era that East-Central European intellectuals like Czesław Miłosz and Václav Havel felt brought East and West closer together into a modern malaise of consumerism and the lies it concealed.[30] The "buy-off" also produced generation gaps between those who benefited from it, and their children

---

[28] This law is Article 132a of the new Polish lustration law introduced in December of 2006 (Ustawa 2006). The corresponding Turkish legislation is Article 301 of the Turkish Penal Code, which took effect on June 1, 2005 (*Türk Ceza Kanunu* 2004).

[29] This is a reference to a 1970s board game created by the American Express company called "Money Card," which sets as its object precisely the acquisition of these consumer goods in the context of travel to Europe.

[30] Miłosz wrote that when the state "will supply its citizens with refrigerators and automobiles, with white bread and a handsome ration of butter, [m]aybe then, at last, they will be satisfied. Why won't the question work out as it should, when every step is logical? … What the devil does a man need?" (Miłosz 1990, p. 24).

and grandchildren to whom the bill was presented when the system could no longer sustain itself. In the caustic 1996 film *Pretty Village, Pretty Flame* on the Wars of Yugoslav Succession, Serbian director Srđan Dragojević includes a wrenching scene wherein a young Serbian militiaman stands up to his ex-partisan commander while both are trapped in a tunnel called "Brotherhood and Unity." The younger man asks the rhetorical question why it is so easy for Muslim, Croat, and Serb militias to burn down one another's houses – houses that had been built on borrowed money and inhabited on borrowed time.

In addition to the postwar buy-off, the long history of emigration, displacement, expulsion, labor migration – in short, of movement – is another aspect of especially the twentieth-century European experience shared by East and West. The memory of this movement was and remains highly politicized. The Holocaust, the expulsion of eleven million Germans from East-Central Europe, the population exchanges, the *Gastarbeiter* of the 1970s and after, and the refugees of the Wars of Yugoslav Succession all form a part of this genealogy of mass population displacement, as highlighted in the contribution (this volume) of Adrian Favell.

Conclusion

Following World War I, World War II, and 1989, when the reinvention of European identity was a top-priority issue, Europeanness was conceptualized not so much around what had worked, but as an evasion of what had not worked. National chauvinism, state socialism, Nazism – the list of failed "European" projects has grown over time, and it has become increasingly difficult to navigate the narrowing straits of viable alternatives.

Yet many aspects of self-identification that emerged from these "failed" models remain common among "Europeans," both East and West. There is, after all, a fine line between national chauvinism and the "building up" of national identities espoused by Habermas and

Václav Havel wrote, "It would appear that the traditional parliamentary democracies can offer no fundamental opposition to the automatism of technological civilization and the industrial-consumer society, for they, too, are being dragged helplessly along by it. People are being manipulated in ways that are infinitely more subtle and refined than the brutal methods used in the post-totalitarian societies." See Havel and Vladislav (1986, pp. 115–16).

Derrida. And the problem of relinquishing sovereignty that has doomed previous efforts to define and enforce Europeanness – in the form of the League of Nations system or Hitler's "New European Order" – now has a contemporary corollary: today's Europe allows for an expansion of states' effective influence and reach within the European Union. This means that states can *feel* bigger as part of a united Europe, can believe that they are achieving national unification, even a form of territorial expansion, by joining the EU; and many do feel that way.[31]

There is a broad consensus – both within and outside East-Central Europe – that integration and Europeanization are things that East-Central European states must do, implying that there is an already existing static entity called "Europe" that can be joined by assimilating to its ideals. But as discussed here and elsewhere in this volume, notions of what it means to be European have themselves been informed by localized and national experiences and struggles, for so-called "Core" European countries and peoples as much as for their East-Central European counterparts. Furthermore, a crisis of legitimacy looms among "old" EU member states as it becomes increasingly clear that elite European institutions neither attract the interest nor share the views of the majority of the population.[32] Just as European institutions are seeking to correct for this imbalance, a new group of countries has joined the EU. Thus, although change appears to be coming from many directions, conceptions of European identity will likely continue to be rooted in "neighborhood" problems and their resolution. The crucial difference is that there are now many more "neighborhoods" officially involved in the process.

Certain events, like February 15, 2003, but also 1968, highlight the localized and politicized nature of seemingly Europe-wide phenomena. One need only compare the slogans and graffiti of the demonstrators in Paris and Prague from forty years ago to glean what dissimilar universes the two groups inhabited and what disparate forces they opposed, despite

[31] Hungary's so-called "Renewed Nation Policy," as espoused by the country's Ministry of Foreign Affairs, further states that "Our diplomatic strategy is focussed on the reunification of the Hungarian nation in the framework of the European Union" ("Hungary's Renewed Nation Policy"). On a number of occasions in 2006, Romania's current president, Traian Băsescu, called for a similar reunification of Romania with Moldova. See "Muddled Amity."

[32] See, for example, the contributions of Helmut Kaelble and Juan Díez Medrano to this volume, as well as the introduction by Jeffrey Checkel and Peter Katzenstein.

occupying corners of the same Zeitgeist ("Civilian Resistance ..." 2007; *Bureau of Public Secrets* 1968; Vaculik 1968). The fallout of the Habermas/Derrida "Core" Europe essay reveals comparable divergences of opinion around the significance of February 15. Interpretations of these events are therefore rooted in politics that seek, reproduce, create, and propagate views of universality with particular – often very localized, or "national" – goals in mind. These goals are then cast in broadly "European" or otherwise universalizing terms that obscure the politicized nature and localized, "national" origins of European identity projects.

False oppositions, between cosmopolitan and communitarian, between top-down and bottom-up, between nation and supranation, are part of what many essays in this volume seek to undermine or refine. My own contribution has endeavored to complicate the false opposition between "East" and "West" by pointing to structural similarities in the way European identity has been formulated by invested national elites in both "halves" of Europe. In 1996, (formerly East) German writer Christa Wolf published a novel entitled *Medea: Stimmen* [Medea: Voices]. The work revisits the epic tale of Jason and Medea, evoking parallels with the relationship between West and East Germany following reunification. At the core of the narrative is a pair of crimes: the murder of two innocent children, heirs to the thrones of Corinth and Colchis. Using backhanded means, the two sides accuse each other of the crimes they themselves committed in an effort to mask the profound similarity between them. As only good fiction can, Wolf captures the tragedy of willful misunderstanding that defines the relationship between East and West.[33]

---

[33] Similar to her West German counterpart, Günter Grass, who joined the SS as a youth, in the 1990s it was revealed that Wolf worked for a short time as an informer for the Stasi.

6 | *Who are the Europeans and how does this matter for politics?*

NEIL FLIGSTEIN

The European Union has produced a remarkable set of agreements to guide the political interactions of countries across Europe in the past fifty years. These agreements have produced collective rules governing market transactions of all varieties, created a single currency, established a rule of law that includes a European court, and promoted increased interactions for people who live within the boundaries of Europe. Moreover, the EU has expanded from six to twenty-seven countries. The endpoint of the EU has been left intentionally vague and can be encapsulated by the ambiguous phrase "toward an ever closer union."

Much of the political criticism of the EU has focussed on the lack of transparency in its procedures and in its accountability to a larger democratic public (Baun 1996; Dinan 2002; McCormick 2002). Many of Europe's citizens have little knowledge about the workings of the EU (Gabel 1998). This lack of "connectedness" to the EU by ordinary citizens has caused scholars to try to understand why a European identity (equivalent to a "national" identity), a European "civil society," and a European politics have been so slow to emerge (Laffan *et al.* 2000). The main focus of these efforts is why, after fifty years of the integration project, there is so little evidence of public attitudes that reflect more feelings of solidarity across Europe. Even among those who work in Brussels, there are mixed feelings about being European (Hooghe 2005; Beyer 2005).

I argue that the literature has so far failed to understand how it is that some people across Europe are likely to adopt a European identity and

I would like to thank Svein Andersen, Jeff Checkel, Peter Katzenstein, Thomas Risse, and Ulf Sverdrup for comments. I would also like to thank the rest of the authors of this book, who participated in discussions of this paper at two separate meetings.

132

some are not. I propose that the main source of such an identity is the opportunity to positively interact on a regular basis with people from other European countries with whom one has a basis for solidarity. Since this opportunity is restricted to a certain part of the population, it follows that not everyone in Europe is likely to adopt a European identity. Moreover, those who have this opportunity tend to be the most privileged strata of society: managers, professionals, white-collar workers, educated people, and young people. This chapter provides evidence that it is precisely these groups who tend to think of themselves as Europeans, speak second languages, report having traveled to another member state in the past twelve months, and have joined European-wide organizations.

This unevenness of interaction with others in Europe has produced a counter effect. Those who have not benefited from travel and from the psychic and financial rewards of learning about and interacting with people from other countries have been less favorable toward the European project (see Holmes 2000 for a discussion of how some of these people have viewed what it means to be a "European" through the "Le Pen effect"). I will show that substantial numbers of people in Europe sometimes think of themselves as Europeans; but there remains a large group, somewhere around 45 percent, who are wedded to their national identity. This suggests several key dynamics for politics.

First, national political parties have responded to the pro-European position of middle- and upper-middle-class citizens by opting for a pro-European platform over time. I show that center-left/center-right parties in England, France, and Germany have all converged on a pro-European political agenda. This reflects their desire to avoid alienating core groups for whom European integration has been a good thing. In this way, the "Europeans" (that is, middle- and upper-middle-class people in each of the member states) have had an important effect on national politics. But parties on the far Left and far Right are full of people for whom Europe has not been a good thing. Right-wing parties worry about Europe undermining the nation, and they thrive on nationalist sentiment. Left-wing parties view the economic integration wrought by the single market as globalization and hence a capitalist plot to undermine the welfare state.

Second, the way in which particular political issues have played out across Europe depends on how the "situational Europeans" (that is, those who sometimes think of themselves as Europeans) come to favor or not favor a European solution to a particular political problem. Frequently, such groups examine these issues from the point of view of their own interest and that of the nation. They pressure their governments to respond to their interests and to undermine a broader possibility for European cooperation. But if those who sometimes think of themselves as Europeans recognize that a particular political issue should be resolved at the European level, they will support more European cooperation.

The chapter has the following structure. First, I consider the issue of how to think about European identity. I suggest a set of hypotheses about who are most likely to think of themselves as Europeans. Next, I provide data that are consistent with the hypotheses. I then show how the main political parties in the largest countries have sought out these voters by taking pro-European positions. In the conclusion, I discuss the issue of the "shallowness" of European identity and the problem this presents for the EU going forward.

Theoretical considerations

European economic integration has been good for jobs and employment across Europe. It has changed the patterns of social interaction around Europe. Over 100 million Europeans travel across national borders for business and pleasure every year, and at least 10–20 million go to school, retire, or work for extended periods across national borders (for an elaboration, see Fligstein 2008b; for a view of how working abroad changes one's identity, see Favell 2008a). This experience of citizens in other countries has been mostly positive. People have gotten to know their counterparts in other societies, appreciated their cultural traditions, and begun to see themselves as having more in common. These positive interactions have caused some of them to identify as "Europeans."

Sociologists, anthropologists, and political scientists have been interested in the formation of collective identities since the founding of their disciplines (for a critical review of the concept of identity in the postwar social science literature, see Brubaker and Cooper 2000). Collective identities refer to the idea that a group of people accepts a fundamental and consequential sameness that causes them to feel solidarity amongst themselves (Brubaker and Cooper 2000; Therborn 1995, ch. 12). This sense of collective identity is socially constructed, by which I mean that it emerges as the intentional or unintentional consequence of social interactions. Collective identity is also by definition about the construction of an "other." Our idea of who we are is usually framed as a response to some "other" group (Barth 1969). Collective identities are anchored in sets of conscious and unconscious meanings that people share. People grow up in families and communities, and they come to identify with the groups in which they are socially located. Gender, ethnicity, religion, nationality, social class, and age have all been the basis of people's main identities and their central relationships to various communities.[1]

National identity is one form of collective identity. Deutsch defined nationality as "a people striving to equip itself with power, with some machinery of compulsion strong enough to make the enforcement of its commands probable in order to aid in the spread of habits of voluntary compliance with them" (1953, p. 104). But in order to attain this, there has to be an alliance among the members of disparate social groups. "Nationality, then, means an alignment of large numbers of individuals from the lower and middle classes linked to regional centers and leading social groups by channels of social communication and economic discourse, both indirectly from link to link with the center" (1953, p. 101).

Deutsch's approach helps makes sense of one of the most obvious difficulties with a theory of nationality. In different times and places, the basis of an appeal to a common culture can include language, religion, race, ethnicity, or a common formative experience (for example, in the US, immigration). Deutsch makes us understand that any of these common cultures can form the pre-existing basis of a national identity; which one gets used in a particular society will depend on history. The historical "trick" to the rise of a nation-state will be to find a horizontal kind of solidarity that is appealing to a wide group of people of differing social strata, offering a sense of solidarity that justifies producing a state

---

[1] In this chapter, I lack the space to consider more adequately the problem of how people become socialized to identities. For a critical discussion of the use of the concept "identity" in the postwar era, see Brubaker and Cooper (2000). For a view from the social psychological literature, see Tajfel (1981) and Turner (1975). For a discussion of identity formation as socialization applied to the EU, see Checkel (2005). For a consideration of how people might hold conflicting multiple identities including national, regional and local identities, see Brewer and Gardner (1996), Brewer (1993, 1999), Risse (2004), Risse *et al.* (1999), Díez Medrano (2003), and Díez Medrano and Gutierrez (2001).

to protect the "nation." Nationalism can have any cultural root, as long as that culture can be used to forge a cross-class alliance around a nation-building project.

Deutsch recognized that not all forms of social interaction between groups were positive (1969). Groups who interacted could easily become conflictual if they came to view their interests and identities as competitive and antithetical. In this way, national identity could be a source of conflict for groups in a society who did not think of themselves as belonging to the nation and, if the patterns of interaction became conflictual, could result in some groups deciding to form a new or alternative nation. Thus, in order for a national identity to emerge, groups needed to come to a positive sense of solidarity based on the idea that they were all members of a single overarching group. National identities were also frequently imposed on unwilling groups through conquest or subordination (Tilly 1975; Gellner 1983). Subsequent attempts to theorize nationalism have focussed on understanding how these conflictual mechanisms might be institutionalized or overcome (Tilly 1975; Gellner 1983; Rokkan 1973; Breuilly 1993; Brubaker 1992).

Deutsch's theory helps us make sense of what has and has not happened in Europe in the past fifty years. If there is going to be a European national identity, it will arise from people who associate with each other across national boundaries and experience that association in a positive way. As European economic, social, and political fields have developed, they imply the routine interaction of people from different societies. It is the people involved in these routine interactions who are most likely to come to see themselves as Europeans and involved in a European national project. They will come to see that their counterparts in other countries are more like them than unlike them, and to relate to their counterparts as part of an overarching group in Europe, "Europeans."

Who are these people? My evidence suggests that these include the owners of businesses, managers, professionals, and other white-collar workers who are involved in various aspects of business and government. These people travel for business and live in other countries for short periods. They engage in long term social relationships with their counterparts who work for their firm, are their suppliers, customers, or in the case of people who work for governments, their colleagues in other governments. They speak second languages for work. Since 1986, they have created Europe-wide business and professional associations, where people gather yearly to discuss matters of mutual interest. Young people who travel across borders for schooling, tourism, and jobs (often for a few years after college) are also likely to be more European. Educated people who share common interests with educated people around Europe – such as similar professions, interests in charitable organizations, or social and cultural activities like opera or art – will be interested in travel and social interaction with people in other societies. People with higher incomes will travel more and participate in the diverse cultural life across Europe. They will have the money to spend time enjoying the good life in other places.

If these are the people who are most likely to interact in Europe-wide economic, social, and political arenas, then it follows that their opposites lack either the opportunity or the interest to interact with their counterparts across Europe. Most importantly, blue-collar and service workers are less likely than managers, professionals, and other white-collar workers to have their jobs take them to other countries. Older people will be less adventurous than younger people and less likely to know other languages. They are less likely to hold favorable views of their neighbors and more likely to remember who was on which side in World War II. They will be less likely to want to associate with or to have curiosity about people from neighboring countries. People who hold conservative political views that value the "nation" as the most important category will not want to travel, know, or interact with people who are "not like them." When they do, they will not be attracted to the "others" but instead will emphasize their cultural differences. Finally, less educated and less financially well-off people will lack the inclination to be attracted to the cultural diversity of Europe and be less able to afford to travel.

If I am right, this suggests that the basic conditions for a European national identity as posited by Deutsch have not been met. A cross-class alliance based on forms of shared culture and patterns of interaction has not emerged in Europe. Instead, the patterns of shared culture and interaction that have occurred across European borders have exactly followed social class lines. People who tend to think of themselves as European represent the more privileged members of society, while people who tend to think of themselves as mainly national in identity tend to be less privileged.

Sociologists tend to think that it is difficult to separate out the rational (that is, self-interested) from the affective component of identity (Brubaker and Cooper, 2000). Identities involve worldviews about who we are, what we want, what we think, and most important, how we interpret the actions and intentions of others. Implicit in this understanding of identity is that people often come to identify with a group of others because we share common interests (material and otherwise). In this way, an identity acts as a cultural frame that tells us who we are and how we ought to act. This view of identity embeds our sense of "what our interests are" in our sense of who we think we are in a particular situation. This conception of identity is as much cultural as it is normative.

Gabel (1998) demonstrates that people who have something to gain from the EU – professionals, managers, educated people, farmers, and the well off financially – are also more likely to be in favor of its activities. I produce results that support Gabel's view. My goal is to broaden his view of why these privileged groups are Europeans and why they support the EU. It is certainly the case that these groups have benefited materially from the EU. European integration has been first and foremost about creating a single market. But this market integration project has had the unintended outcome of giving some groups more opportunities to interact with people from other societies. These interactions have given them firsthand experience of their counterparts in other countries and made them feel positive affect for people who are like them.

The issues of identity, interest, and interaction are difficult to untangle, both theoretically and empirically. For example businesspeople who depend on trade for their livelihood are likely to spend time in other countries and get to know people from those societies. This interaction will reveal common interests and a common set of understandings. People will develop friendships and get to know other people with whom they will come to share a deeper identity. So, an Italian businessman who befriends a French businessman will find they share a common interest in having more opportunity to interact. They will come to see each other less as Italian and French and thus, foreign, and more as sharing common interests. These common interests will eventually bring them to see themselves more as Europeans and less as just having national identity. Of course, to the degree that these relationships are driven by material interest (i.e. the selling and buying of things), affect is more difficult to separate from interest.

These fictitious businesspeople begin by interacting with one another for business. They discover that people from other societies who occupy similar social positions are not so different from themselves. This makes them see that national identities are limiting and that a European identity gives them more freedom to associate with others who are *really* like them in other societies. They are all educated, rational people who prefer to find win-win situations, who prefer compromise to conflict, and who accept cultural differences as interesting and stimulating. It should not be surprising that the "agents" of European identity should be the educated middle- and upper-middle classes who espouse Enlightenment ideology.[2] After all, the Enlightenment reflected the cultural conception of those classes in the eighteenth century.

Evidence for "Who is a European"

I begin my search for Europeans by examining a number of datasets: three Eurobarometers that gather public opinion data, and a dataset I gathered on the founding of European-wide associations that was collected from the *International Handbook of Nongovernmental Organizations*. The appendix at the end of this chapter contains information on the data and measures reported in the tables that follow. I begin with the Eurobarometer data.

Table 6.1 reports on the degree to which people across Europe view themselves as Europeans. Only 3.9% of people who live in Europe view themselves as Europeans exclusively, while another 8.8% view themselves as Europeans and having some national identity. This means that only 12.7% of people in Europe tend to view themselves as Europeans. I note that this translates into 47 million people, a large number! Scholars who have looked at this data generally conclude that the European identity has not spread very far (Gabel 1998; Deflem and Pampel 1996).[3]

---

[2] Habermas (1992) views a European identity as part of the idea of completing the Enlightenment project. He argues that "reason" and "rationality" should guide people's interactions. Being a European is about trying to settle differences peaceably with respect for differences and others' opinions. A European state would be democratic and ideally would follow the creation of a European civil society where rational differences of opinion could be aired. Finally, he has recently argued that Europe should also stand for social justice and defense of the welfare state (2001). Such an identity, of course, was associated during the Enlightenment with the rising middle classes and in contemporary Europe with social democracy.

[3] In this volume, Favell presents interview data on people who have moved to other countries to live and work. His sample reflects people who are at the extreme tail of my distribution here.

Table 6.1 *"In the near future, will you think of yourself as a ...?"*

European only	3.9%
European and Nationality	8.8%
Nationality and European	43.3%
Nationality only	44.0%
Total:	
Mostly National	87.3%
Mostly European	12.7%
Sometimes European	56.0%

Source: Eurobarometer, EB 61, April 2004.

But this misses several interesting aspects of European identity. An additional 43.3% of people view themselves as having a national identity and sometimes a European identity (while 44% of people never view themselves as having anything but a national identity). The 43.3% of people who sometimes view themselves as Europeans can be viewed as "situational Europeans," that is, under the right conditions they will place a European identity over a national identity. So, if the right issue comes along, 56% of people will favor a European solution to a problem. If, however, all of the situational Europeans remain true to their national identity, 87.3% of people will be anti-European. This complex pattern of identity explains much about the ups and downs of the European political project. One can predict that most of the time, most of the population who live in Europe will see things from either a nationalist or a self interested perspective. But occasionally issues will arise that will bring together majorities of the population around a European perspective.

Table 6.2 reports the results of a logit analysis predicting whether or not a person has any European identity. The dependent variable in the analysis is whether or not the person ever thinks of him/herself as a European (i.e. the 56%) or as only having a national identity (i.e. the 44%). Here, the class bias of European identity is clearly revealed. People who are more educated, have higher incomes, and are owners, managers, professionals, or white collar workers are more likely to see themselves as European than people who are less educated, have lower incomes, and are blue collar. There are several suggestive

Table 6.2 *Statistically significant predictors of whether or not (+ = positive,
– = negative) a respondent ever views him/herself as a European, speaks
a second language, travels to another European country, and views the
EU as "good for their country" (see Appendix for more details)*

Independent variables	Some European identity	Speaks second language	Travels to other European country	Views the EU "good thing" for country
Gender (Male = 1)	+		+	
Age at leaving school	+	+	+	+
Income	+	+	+	+
Age	–	–	–	–
Left–Right politics (Left lower value)	+		–	–
Occupation[1]				
Owner	+	+	+	+
Professional	+	+	+	+
Manager	+	+	+	+
White collar	+	+	+	+
Not in labor force		+	–	+
Have some European identity				+

[1] Left-out category: Blue collar/Service.
Note: results include measures controlling for country.

demographic effects. Young people are more likely to see themselves as European than are old people, and men are more likely to see themselves as European than are women. This is consistent with our argument that young people and men have more opportunities to travel and interact with their counterparts in other countries, either for fun or for work. Finally, people who judge themselves as left wing politically are more likely than people who view themselves as right wing politically to be European. Since most right-wing parties in Europe favor the nation and national discourse, it makes sense that people in such parties would not have a European identity and would be against the EU more generally.

This analysis clearly supports a class-centered view of who the Europeans are. But it does not directly consider why those people might be Europeans. Here, I turn to other datasets to explore more carefully Deutsch's hypothesis that interaction produces common identity. One problem in the Eurobarometers is that the European identity questions have been asked infrequently and never in concert with questions about social interactions. So, I have to pursue a more indirect strategy in order to link the social class background with opportunities to interact across Europe.

I do this by choosing two indicators of social interaction: second language use, and data on European travel. The acquisition of a second language only makes sense if one intends to use it for business or travel. It is difficult to learn a second language, and if one does not use the language, it quickly disappears. People who intend to interact with others in different societies in a significant way are more likely to make the investment in a second language. I argue that the people who will make this investment will reflect those who have the opportunity to learn such languages and use them, that is, the young, the educated, and those with white-collar and professional occupations. An even more direct indicator of interacting with people from other societies is direct report of recent travel experiences. If people report having traveled to other countries recently, then it is a fair bet that they do so relatively frequently. If it is true that interaction produces collective identity, then the same people who have a European identity (again the young, the educated and white collar and professionals) will report traveling to other European societies more frequently.

Table 6.3 shows that 61.6% of people in Europe claim to speak a second language, as reported in a Eurobarometer conducted in 2000. This result should be interpreted with some caution. The actual level of skill in a second language was not directly measured by the survey. This was a self report and so one cannot be sure of its validity. Even if the degree to which Europeans actually speak second languages is overstated, the distribution of those languages and the relationship between speaking a second language and age is what one would predict: 57.5% of those who speak a second language report that language is English, 15.6% report the second language is French, and 11.3% report their second language is German. This variable is heavily skewed by age: 82.4% of people aged 15–24 claim to speak a second language, while only 34.1% of those 65 and above do so. There are also clear national differences in second language usage. The British have the lowest use of second languages, reflecting their clear advantage with English as the

Table 6.3 *Second language use in Europe overall and by country. "Do you speak a second language?"*

	No	Yes
Overall	38.4%	61.6%
By country:		
Belgium	37.6%	62.4%
Denmark	12.6%	87.4%
Germany	41.3%	58.7%
Greece	46.8%	53.2%
Italy	44.7%	55.3%
Spain	52.3%	47.7%
France	47.0%	53.0%
Ireland	46.6%	53.4%
Luxembourg	2.3%	97.7%
Netherlands	13.0%	87.0%
Portugal	53.5%	46.5%
Great Britain	64.3%	35.7%
Austria	52.7%	47.3%
Finland	28.8%	71.2%
Sweden	12.6%	87.4%

Source: Eurobarometer 54LAN, December 2000.

language of business. At the other extreme, 97.7% of Luxembourgois report speaking a second language. In general, people from smaller countries are more likely to speak second languages than people from larger countries.[4]

Table 6.2 also presents the results of a logit regression where the model predicts which social groups were more likely to speak a second language. Here, I observe once again the effects of social class. People who are educated, and who are owners, professionals, managers, white collar, and not in the labor force all report higher levels of second language use than the less-educated or blue-collar workers do. One of the strongest

---

[4] It is interesting to note that citizens of small countries generally have more European identity, speak second languages more, and travel more. Obviously, if you live in a small country, you need to know more than one language, and your opportunity to travel involves less time and money. But it also means that you are more aware of your neighbors, are more likely to interact with them frequently, and thus, more likely to see yourself as more like them.

Table 6.4 *Distribution of European travel in 1997.*
"Have you been in another European country in the
past 12 months?"

	No	Yes
Total	75.1%	24.9%
By country:		
Belgium	68.1%	31.9%
Denmark	65.2%	34.8%
Germany	58.8%	41.2%
Greece	88.7%	11.3%
Italy	88.4%	11.6%
Spain	88.6%	11.4%
France	77.6%	22.4%
Ireland	76.9%	23.1%
Luxembourg	43.9%	56.1%
Netherlands	57.7%	42.7%
Portugal	94.5%	5.5%
Great Britain	76.3%	23.7%
Austria	78.3%	21.7%
Finland	83.7%	16.7%
Sweden	68.3%	31.6%

Source: Eurobarometer 48.0 Fall 1997.

effects in the model is the effect of age. All Europeans are pushed to learn second languages in schools (with the exception of the British). This shows up clearly in the model. Language use is an indicator of social interaction of people across countries, and then there is a clear link between patterns of social interaction and social class position.

Table 6.4 presents data on whether or not the respondent in the survey has been in another European country in the past twelve months. These data come from a Eurobarometer conducted in 1997. Of those surveyed, 75.1% answered "no," while 24.9% answered "yes." These data show quite a bit of variation across country as well. Generally, people who live in the poorer countries in the South, like Greece, Spain, and Portugal, report traveling the least. People in the rich countries like Germany, Luxembourg, the Netherlands, and Sweden travel the most. Another interpretation of this data is that people in the North tend to travel more, suggesting that part of this travel is for recreation, not just for business. This makes my measure of interaction more problematic. It could be argued that tourists get on a plane, arrive at a beach where they are surrounded by their fellow citizens, and barely interact with the locals. While one must be cautious in overinterpreting the results of the analysis, the explanatory factors that work for the other variables hold up for this one as well.

Table 6.2 also presents results from a logit analysis where the dependent variable was whether or not a person had traveled outside of their country in the past twelve months. The effects in this analysis mirror the effects in the analysis of who regards him/herself as a European and who speaks a second language. The class differences are quite apparent, as educated people and people who are owners, managers, professionals, and white-collar workers travel more than less educated people and blue collar workers. This is the most direct evidence I have for the idea that interaction patterns follow social class lines. There are several other interesting effects in the models. Old people are less likely to travel than young people, and women less than men. This implies that both women and the elderly encounter people from other countries less frequently than do men or young people. People who are more right wing than left wing in their politics are also less likely to travel net of social class. This implies that people who tend to value the nation over Europe do not travel to foreign countries for work or pleasure.

These results provide strong, albeit indirect support for the idea that people who tend to think of themselves as Europeans are people who are more likely to interact with others across Europe. Managers, professionals, white collar, educated people, and males and the young are all more likely to report having been in another European country in the past twelve months, being able to speak a second language, and having a European identity. This conforms to my view that the EU has provided the opportunity for interaction for the most privileged members of society and that these members of all European countries are more likely to be European.

A European civil society?

One could argue that the evidence presented can easily be accounted for by "interest" driven arguments. That is, the EU has benefited these groups materially; it is no surprise that they favor Europe and think of themselves as Europeans. From this point of view, their speaking second languages and traveling abroad is not a cause of their identity, but an effect of their material interests. They make money by being able to travel and speak second languages and so it should be no surprise that they think of themselves as European.

This is a difficult argument to refute with the data. Indeed, it is possible to see that interest and identity are wrapped up together. But it is useful to put together one other dataset that measures the likelihood of interaction. One frequent claim is that if there are going to be Europeans, there needs to be a European "civil society" (Laffan *et al.* 2000). The definition of exactly what this would be is contestable (Calhoun 2003).

Here, I take a standard view and argue that one measure of a Europe-wide civil society is the existence of Europe-wide organizations or associations. My earlier results showed that people who tend to think of themselves as Europeans and who are more likely to travel or speak second languages are managers, professionals, the educated, and the young. I expect that the main Europe-wide associations founded by these people will be professional, scientific, trade, and interest group associations like hobby groups or special interest groups like environmental or peace groups. Professionals and middle- and upper-middle-class people create groups that reflect their occupational, political, and cultural interests. Professional, scientific, and trade groups reflect the interests of the educated and those involved in political and economic exchange to meet routinely. Social and cultural groups reflect the founding of a true European civil society, a society of nonprofits oriented toward charity and social activities that brings people together from around Europe. Their members will also be predominately the middle class, the upper middle class, and the educated and young in general.

If European political, social, and economic integration has increased over time, one would expect that the number of Europe-wide associations would increase, as these people would have the chance to routinize their interactions with each other by setting up nonprofit groups that would meet routinely to discuss matters of joint interest. This should particularly expand after 1985, when the EU began to complete the single market, thereby increasing the opportunities for interaction to occur.

The data I collected came from the *Yearbook of International Organizations* (2000). I created a database with every organization that was set up on a European basis. I eliminated organizations that were explicitly founded to lobby in Brussels. I was able to code 989

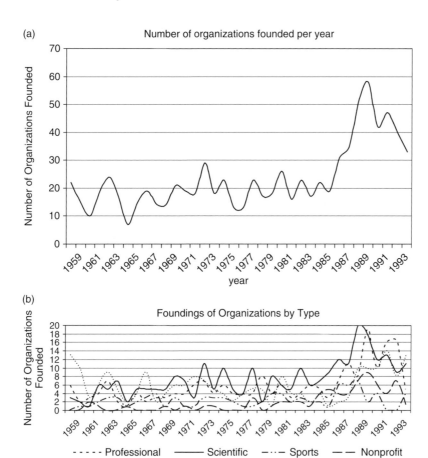

Figure 6.1: Europe-wide associations.
Source: Union of International Associations. 2000. *Yearbook of International Organizations*. Frankfurt: Sauer.

organizations. Figure 6.1a presents the founding of these organizations over time. Between 1959 and 1985, there were an average twenty such organizations founded each year. Starting in 1985 with the announcement of the Single Market, the number of organizations spiked to a peak of 58 founded in 1990, and dropped off thereafter. I note that this drop-off is partially due to the biases inherent in the data source. The *International Handbook of Nongovernmental Organizations* is slow to add organizations once they are founded, as they need to discover the existence of the organizations in order to add them to their database. This shows that the creation of such organizations was highly related to the increasing opportunity for people to meet and interact in the wake of the Single Market.

Figure 6.1b shows that the vast majority of organizations founded were professional and scientific organizations. A typical professional or scientific organization would be the European Association of Chiropractors or the European Association of Meteorologists. The third largest group was business or trade associations. Here, a typical association might be the European Association of Direct Marketing or the European Association of Chemical Producers. The most interesting part of the graph is the increase in sports/hobby organizations and nonprofit organizations after 1984. In the sports hobby category are included the European Association of Mushroom Gatherers and the European Association of Bicycling. In the nonprofit category are organizations such as the European Societies of Cancer and the European Save the Whales Association. These are the purest form of civil society organizations, in that they reflect how citizens decide to devote resources to Europe-wide organizations with no obvious material interest. While these organizations comprise a relatively small percentage of all organizations (about 15 percent of all cases), they show clearly that in the wake of the Single Market, some people took the opportunity to interact across national borders.

The vast majority of these organizations' main activities are to meet annually somewhere in Europe to discuss matters of mutual interest. These conferences and conventions are frequently held in warm and pleasant places. Like all professional meetings, the more instrumental purposes are supplemented by partying, networking, and vacationing. These conferences bring about increased interaction across national borders and furnish their participants with new friends, job contacts, and business opportunities. They are part and parcel of what creates Europe.

How should this matter for politics?

It is useful to summarize the results so far. Only about 12.7% of Europe's population basically sees itself as European. These people are disproportionately the most privileged members of society, that is, managers, professionals, and white-collar people, educated people, and the young. In this way, the European project has given the most opportunities to the people who are already the most privileged. But it is also the case that 56% of people who live in Europe have some European identity: 61.6% claim to speak a second language, and 24.9% have been out of their country in the past year. The educated and the middle and upper middle classes have taken the opportunities afforded by work and pleasure to create new patterns of association. They have founded Europe-wide organizations and associations. While some Europeans are clearly more affected by the EU than others because they have more opportunities to interact with people from other countries routinely, a substantial proportion of Europeans appear to have at least some interactions across borders in their lives. This interaction appears to have some impact on their identities as well.

One of the interesting questions is, what effect does this have on national politics? The assumption in much of the academic literature is that the EU has a democratic deficit. This is usually meant to imply that "average" people feel out of touch with decision making in Brussels. But this decision making is undertaken by the member state governments and their representatives in Brussels and the directly elected European Parliament. One obvious reason that "average" people do not experience a democratic deficit is that they still vote for their national politicians and even their representatives for the European Parliament. National political parties take a position on European integration, and voters are able to decide whether this issue is salient enough to them to vote for a political party on the basis of this position.

Haas argued that in the 1950s, European integration had no salience for voters across Europe (1958). He analyzed the political positions of various parties across Europe and observed little support or opposition for the European project. Haas thought that if the project were ever to go anywhere, this would need to change. Subsequent research has revealed that most people have almost no knowledge of the EU and its workings (for a review, see Gabel 1998). But, even here, large and important minorities of people across Europe find European issues salient to their voting. (For an interesting set of arguments that locate support for the EU in national politics, see Díez Medrano 2003).

It is useful to make an argument about why this might be. It follows from our analysis that middle- and upper-middle-class voters benefit directly from Europe, either materially or because they have formed identities whereby they relate to their peers across societies. These are certainly people who tend to vote, and it follows that political parties would want to take political positions on the EU that might attract such voters. While the EU is not going to be the only issue on which voters support parties, it might be one of the important issues (Featherstone 1999).

Table 6.2 explores this hypothesis by considering the determinants of whether the EU is viewed by respondents as good or bad for their country. In Europe, 56.2% of people in 2004 viewed the EU as a good thing for their country, while 24.9% viewed it as neither a good nor a bad thing for their country and only 19% viewed it as altogether a bad thing for their country. A logit analysis is used to separate the determinants of a more positive view of the EU. Once again, the class basis of support for the EU comes through. Higher educated, higher income people, as well as owners, professionals, managers, and white-collar workers are more likely to see the EU as a good thing for their country than are those who are lower educated, poor, or blue collar. Gabel (1998) has interpreted this from a rational choice perspective. Since the main beneficiaries of the EU's Single Market have been those who are better off, they continue to support the EU.

But there are a number of other effects in the model that can be given a more interactional and identity spin. Older people feel less positive toward the EU than younger people net of social class. Since younger people are more Europeanized in the sense that they are more likely to travel and speak second languages, it follows that they view the EU in a more positive way. There are two interesting effects of identity in the model. People who describe themselves as left wing are more likely to view the EU as a good thing for their country than are people who are more right wing. Right-wing politics in Europe tend to be more focussed on the "nation," and therefore people with those politics are going to be more skeptical of the EU and its effects on their country. Finally, if a person has some European identity, s/he is more likely to see Europe as a good thing for his/her country. Taken together, these results imply that there are indeed political constituencies within each European country who will favor the EU. Their support reflects both interest driven reasons (i.e. the economic opportunities afforded by the EU) and identity driven reasons (i.e. the opportunities to travel and interact, and the desire to protect the nation from "Europe").

This difference of perspective on the value of the EU has played out in interesting ways in European political parties over time. Since the 1950s, the center left/center right parties in the largest countries across Western Europe have converged in their support of the EU. I believe that this has not occurred as a result of these parties being driven by elites that have converged on this opinion. Instead, political parties on both the Left and the Right have experimented with taking both pro and con EU positions. They have discovered that by and large, even though there may be vocal and active minorities in each country who oppose European political and economic integration, there are not enough of these folks to actually get elected on an anti-EU platform. Moreover, given that middle- and upper-middle-class voters tend to be pro-EU, and given that these people tend to vote, center-left and center-right parties chase these votes, eventually realizing that the EU is not a good wedge issue to win elections.

The data used for this analysis come from Budge *et al.* (2001). They consist of an analysis of the platforms of political parties across Europe. I present data on the major political parties in England, France, and Germany over time. The variable I present is the negative mentions of the EU in the party platform, subtracted from the positive mentions of the EU in the platforms in a given election year. I choose to present this measure because it taps directly into the degree to which the EU is viewed in a mostly positive or a mostly negative way by each of the political parties.

The data for Germany are presented in Figure 6.2. All three major German political parties generally have more positive than negative things to say about the EU. This reflects the German political consensus that the EU is a "winning" issue. There is some interesting variation in this variable. In the 1987 election, the Social Democrats increased their negative comments on Europe, while the Christian Democrats increased their support. These negative comments were mainly about their

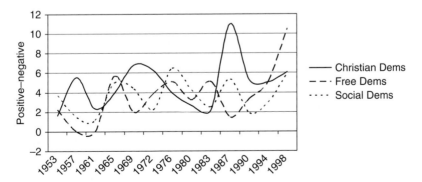

Figure 6.2: Net positive party attitudes toward the EU, Germany

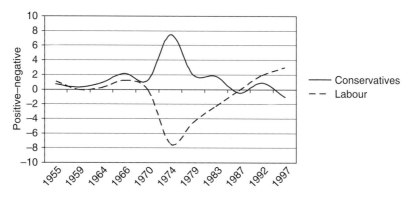

Figure 6.3: Net positive party attitudes toward the EU, Great Britain

opposition to the Single Market, which they tended to view as helping capitalists and hurting workers. This strategy did not work very well, and they shifted their position in the subsequent election to a more pro-European stance. The Christian Democrats took a more negative view of the EU in the 1990 political campaign. This reflected party members' negative reaction to the commitment made by its leaders to a monetary union. The Free Democratic Party was a moderate supporter of the EU throughout the period. In the wake of the Single Market and the run up to the euro, the party increased its positive mentions of the EU. By the late 1990s, the EU was a frequent topic in party platforms, and all three parties had converged to a positive position. In Germany, the way to get the votes of the middle and upper-middle classes was to be pro-Europe. That all parties eventually came to adopt this position demonstrates that there were few votes to be won by opposing the EU.

Figure 6.3 presents similar data for Great Britain. Here one can see that the Labour and Conservative parties both tried to use the EU as a political issue. In 1974, the Labour Party was negative about joining the EU, while the Conservatives were positive about joining the EU. During the 1980s, the political parties switched positions. Labour favored the EU and the Conservatives, led by Thatcher and Major, opposed it. In the 1990s, the Conservative Party moderated their view and the Labour Party became even more supportive of the EU. It is interesting that even though Europe appeared to be an important wedge issue in British politics, eventually both main political parties realized that they lost more voters by sub-scribing to an anti-EU point of view than they gained.

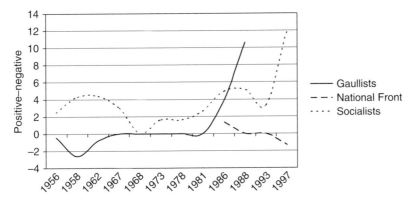

Figure 6.4: Net positive party attitudes toward the EU, France

Figure 6.4 presents the data for France. The Gaullist party during the 1950s and 1960s was both positive and negative about the EU (and the comments cancelled one another out). On the one hand, de Gaulle himself did not like the EU because of his concerns about sovereignty. On the other hand, French business did very well as a result of EU membership. The Socialist Party was vaguely Europeanist during this same period. This was partially to distinguish itself from the Gaullists, but also because of France's leadership in the EU. Beginning in the early 1980s, this positive support went up as France's leadership in the EU was a source of national pride and European economic integration was viewed as a possible solution to economic stagnation. After the fall of the Berlin Wall, both main political parties in France grew increasingly supportive of the EU. They viewed France's role in Europe as mainly a function of its leadership in the EU. Monetary union was popular in France, and the German–French alliance that drove the EU was viewed as a positive thing. The National Front (an extreme right-wing party) intentionally decided to take an anti-EU stand in the 1990s, with the idea that opposing the EU and supporting the "nation" would work to get them votes. This strategy has succeeded to some degree. The National Front played an important role in the defeat of the European Constitution in France; but they still have not been able to win a national election on an anti-EU platform.

In the three biggest EU polities, we see a remarkably similar pattern. Over time, the EU has become a more salient issue for political parties, and the center-left/center-right parties have converged in their support for the EU. During the 1970s and 1980s, the Labour and Conservative parties in Great Britain shifted their positions on the EU in order to attract middle-class voters. The defeat of the Conservative Party with their strongly anti-EU stance caused them to shift their position in the 1990s, and both the Labour and the Conservative Party now favor the EU. German political parties all have come to support the EU despite having briefly flirted with an anti-EU platform. In France, the National Front is the only political party to try to run on an anti-EU agenda since the 1980s. Since their votes have tended to be protest votes against both immigrants and foreign trade, it is not surprising that they have taken an anti-EU stand. No major center-left/center-right European political party in the largest countries is likely to run against the EU, precisely because it is unpopular to do so. Middle- and upper-middle-class voters benefit from the EU and identify with it sufficiently that no political party can win an election on an explicitly anti-EU program. Large majorities in every society think that the EU has generally been a good thing for their country. Vocal minorities have caused parties to experiment with anti-EU stands. But the basic sense that the EU is positive means that politicians continue to support some forms of European integration.

Conclusion

There is little evidence for an outpouring of sentiment among the citizens of Europe supporting a European nation. Even in Brussels, where people work for the EU, the socialization of citizens as Europeans has been less than one might expect (Hooghe 2005; Beyers 2005). In spite of the obvious limits of survey data, the results presented here help make sense of much of why this is the case. Only 12.7% of the people living in Western Europe think of themselves as Europeans. While overall, 56% of people in Europe sometimes think of themselves as European, 44% still have only a national identity. For the 43.3% who sometimes think of themselves as European, they still think of themselves as being members of a nation-state first. Moreover, in Great Britain, Finland, Sweden, and Austria, majorities of the population never think of themselves as Europeans. Put simply, there are not enough people with strong European identities to push forward a Europe-wide political integration project. While there is a majority in most countries who sometimes think of themselves as European, this is clearly a shallow and situational identity.

Building on the work of Karl Deutsch, I argue that for a national identity to emerge, a class alliance between elites and members of the middle and working classes has to become framed around a national "story." This story has to explain why everyone who lives within some geographic boundaries is part of a larger group, a group whose identity needs reinforcing by a state. The main mechanism by which this story gets told and spreads is through cultural communication. Groups from different classes have to meet in some organized setting, routinely interact, and come to view the other people as part of the same group.

It is the case that in Europe, the story of being "European" has only been told in a partial way. On the one hand, there has been increased communication and interaction among certain groups in Europe. People who are educated or are owners, managers, professionals, or white-collar workers have had opportunities to meet and interact with their counterparts in other countries because of the EU's market and political integration project. For these people, this interaction has pro-duced a positive European identity and support for the EU project, just as Deutsch would suggest. But for the vast majority of the population, these interactions are infrequent. For them, the national narrative still dominates. A substantial number of people in Europe sometimes think of themselves as Europeans (what might be called situational Europeans, that is, people who in some circumstances think of them-selves as Europeans). But these people obviously do not share as many interactions with other Europeans.

The economic and social construction that has accompanied the growth of the EU since its inception in 1957 has produced a complex, if explicable politics. The goal of the member-states' governments has consistently been to create a single market in Western Europe, one that would eliminate tariff and nontariff barriers and eventually open all industries to competitors from other countries. This goal has created a huge increase in cross-border economic activity, trade, investment, and the creation of Europe-wide corporations. On the social side, the people who have been most involved in this market-opening project have been managers and professionals who have the opportunity to travel and work with their counterparts in other countries. These groups have benefited financially but have also had the pleasure of discovering that people in other countries could be friends, and travel and work bring them to new and interesting places. Meeting people from other societies has been a good thing that has encouraged people to see themselves as both similar and different.

Perhaps the most interesting and subtle effect of all of this economic and social interaction is the creation of interest in European affairs in national political discourse. There is strong evidence that European affairs are covered in national papers and that national groups organize to protest to their governments about EU policies they don't like. There is also some evidence that on occasion, these discussions can be trans-European and result in policy coordination. But these discussions more frequently reflect the complex identities of people who live in Europe. Since the majority of those people have predominantly a national identity, it should not be surprising that many European political issues end up appealing to national as opposed to European-wide interests. This means that as issues confronting Europeans are discussed within national media, they are more likely to be filtered through national debates and self images than through European ones. So while there is certainly a wide awareness of European issues, the ability to produce European policies will always be difficult because of the institutional limits on the EU and the conflicting political demands that citizens place on their governments.[5]

It is useful to consider two scenarios for the future of European identity. One argues that we are at the limit of European identity and thus, the European national project will never happen. The other suggests forces that might push for an increase in European identity. First, let us consider the scenario for why European national identity will not emerge. For the majority of the European population, the opportunity to interact with people across borders has been greatly circumscribed, either by choice or by lack of opportunity. Blue-collar and service workers and the less educated have not had the opportunity to learn second languages or to interact for business or travel with their counterparts in other countries. As a result, they have lacked the impetus to see themselves as Europeans. Educated people and people with high-status occupations are more likely to become at least partly Europeans, but there are not enough of them to have a big effect on creating a mass "European identity."

---

[5] Díez Medrano reviews the literature on this topic in this volume and arrives at a similar conclusion.

For blue-collar and service workers, the EU has not delivered more jobs and jobs with better pay, but rather deindustrialization and globalization. There is the suspicion that the EU is an elite project that has mainly benefited the educated, and our evidence bears this out. The elderly still remember World War II and its aftermath. The elderly and the economically less privileged have less interest in knowing more about their neighbors and more in keeping a strong sense of national identity. Those politically on the right have created a politics to defend the nation. In some countries, they view the EU as intrusive on national sovereignty and by implication, on national identities. In others, they view immigrants as a threat to their livelihood and the nation. Perhaps the most divisive politics in Europe concerns the current rise in immigrants from Africa and the Middle East. Those who view this migration skeptically are distrustful of the EU and are satisfied with the national story.[6]

Now with enlargement to twenty-seven countries, a whole variety of people are entering the EU without a history of interacting with their counterparts across countries. The middle and upper-middle classes of what was formally Central and Eastern Europe do not necessarily feel affinity with the Western European project. There is already evidence that many of them feel ambivalent about their future in the EU, and their positions on Europe and having a European identity more closely approximate those who are skeptical than those who are optimistic. The existence of these new member-states will mean even fewer citizens who will see Europe as for them and about people like them.

It is possible to present a scenario implying that the process of European identity building is just starting and that over time, the forces producing more Europeans will rise. First, the European project has only really been going on since the mid-1960s. The biggest expansion of opportunities to interact with other people in Europe occurred beginning with the Single Market in the mid-1980s. It just might be too early to see a majority emerging to create a European nation. After all, national identities took hundreds of years to evolve, and Europeans have only been interacting in large numbers for 20–25 years. Second,

[6] Holmes's chapter in this volume discusses how the opponents of an enlightened, capitalist "Europe" think about what is going on. He argues that their version of what it means to be a "European" is more exclusionary of nonwhite and non-Christian groups.

demography is working in the EU's favor. Young people are more likely to know second languages, be educated, travel, and be more open to the EU. As older people pass away and are replaced by the young, there should be more people who think of themselves as Europeans. Third, as skill levels rise and education increases generally, people will be more interested in the cultural story of being with other Europeans. One of our more interesting results was the fact that educated people were the most likely to use a second language for travel and communication. As education levels rise, one would expect that the European identity would become more widespread. European issues are widely covered in the European press, and center-left and center-right parties generally continue to support the European project.

Finally, as European markets continue to integrate, people will have more opportunities to interact with people in other countries. This could happen through work. Interaction will occur more generally as media coverage, tourism, and the awareness of culture in other countries expands. So, for example, the creation of a European football league would spark even more Europe-wide interest in games being played across Europe. Games would be televised, people would have the opportunity to follow foreign teams, and they would travel even more to support their teams.

All of these processes have yet to play out for the citizens of Central and Eastern Europe. Over time, Central and Eastern Europeans will travel west for work and school. Businesspeople will gradually become more integrated with their Western European counterparts, particularly those who work for multinational enterprises. If my analysis is right, the middle and upper-middle classes in Eastern Europe will eventually come to interact with and relate to their colleagues in Western Europe. This interaction will make them become more favorable toward European integration.

All in all, my analysis suggests that, first, given that 87.3 percent of the European electorates mainly think of themselves as national in identity, the most likely outcome will be for the national story to continue to trump the European one. The challenges of the future will be decided by the part of the population that is situationally European. As issues play out, the middle-class voters who sometimes think of themselves as Europeans will empower their governments to cooperate either more or less with other European governments. Second, which way they go will be part of a political process that involves framing around identities. One can imagine a particular event that would bring people in Europe closer together. A Europe-wide terrorist event, for example, might push forward a Europe-wide response and the sense that European citizens were in it together. One could also imagine an event that would split Europe up. A severe economic crisis in one of the large member states might tempt citizens to vote for a party that offered to protect national jobs by leaving the monetary union and the EU. This is where real history and politics will matter for what is to come.

Appendix

The data analyzed in this chapter originate with the Eurobarometers. The Eurobarometers are financed by the European Commission and are carried out simultaneously in the European Union member countries. The surveys study the social and political opinions of persons living in the member countries. The material is collected by specialized organizations in each country. For example, in Finland, the material is collected by TNS Gallup Ltd (Gallup Finland). The collection is coordinated by INRA EUROPE (International Research Associates Europe). The surveys used here were provided through the Survey Research Center at the University of California and were accessed through the Interuniversity Consortium for Political and Social Research (ICPSR) at the University of Michigan. The identity questions were asked in Eurobarometer 61, which was conducted in February–March of 2004. The Eurobarometer used for the language data was 54.2, conducted in the fall of 2000. Eurobarometer 48.0 was conducted in the fall of 1997 and focussed on issues surrounding travel. All of the surveys used standard questions to obtain demographic data.

It is useful to review the questions and how the data were coded for the data analysis.

- Some European identity: 0 = national identity only; 1 = European identity only, European and national identity, national and European identity.
- "Do you speak a second language?" The dependent variable in the analysis is coded "0" if the respondent does not speak a second language and "1" if they do.
- Respondents were asked whether they had taken a trip in 1997. A variable was coded "0" if the respondent had not visited another European country in the past 12 months and "1" if they had.

- Views the EU as a good or a bad thing : 0 = bad thing, neither good nor bad thing; 1 = good thing.
- EU has a positive or a negative image: 0 = very negative, fairly negative, neutral; 1 = fairly positive, very positive.
- Gender: 0 = female; 1 = male.
- Age: Age in years.
- Age at school completion: Age in years during last year of school.
- Income scale: Income was reported from all sources. It was converted into local currency. It was then converted into five groups for each country based on the income distribution. "1" is the lowest income group, while "5" is the highest.
- Left–Right politics: The question asked was, "People talk about politics as being left and right. How would you place yourself on this scale?" Respondents were asked to place themselves on a five-point scale where "1" indicated the farthest "left" and "5" was the farthest right.

The occupational variables were coded based on the response to the following question: "What is your current occupation?" Respondents were given nineteen choices. I created a series of dummy variables whereby a person was coded "0" if they were in the category and "1" if they were not. The following groups were coded as "1" for each of the dummy variables.

- Owner: 1 = self employed, categories 5–9: farmer, fisherman, professional, owner of a shop, craftsman, other self employed, business proprietor, partner in a business.
- Manager: 1 = general management, middle management, supervisor, categories 11, 12, 16.
- Professional: 1 = employed professional, category 10.
- Other white collar: 1 = employed, working at desk, salesman, categories 14, 15.
- Blue collar and Service: Left-out category, categories 15, 17, 18.
- Not in the labor force: 1 = house caretaker, student, unemployed, retired, temporary ill, categories 1–4.
- Country dummy variables: 0 = if respondent not in the country; 1 = respondent in the country. The "left out" category for all of the analyses is Great Britain.

All of the data analyses were done using logit regression models in the computer program SPSS. Logit regression is the appropriate technique when the dependent variable in a data analysis is "limited" (discrete, not continuous). Researchers often want to analyze whether some event occurred or not, such as voting, participation in a public program, business success or failure, morbidity, or mortality. Binary logistic regression is a type of regression analysis where the dependent variable is a dummy variable (coded 0, 1). More details on logit regression and its interpretation are available from Demaris (1992). For nontechnical readers, a positive statistically significant coefficient implies that more of variable X implies that it is more likely that the respondent will be in category "1" rather than category "0." So a positive coefficient on gender below implies that men are more likely to think of themselves as Europeans. A negative coefficient implies that as X increases, the probability that the respondent will be in category "0" increases. So, for example, in the case of European identity, age is negatively related to having a European identity. This means that older people are less likely to see themselves as Europeans.

Table 6.A.1 *Means and standard deviations for logit analysis of determinants of European identity*

Variable	Mean	SD
Gender	.52	.50
Left–Right politics	2.32	1.06
Age at school completion	18.44	1.96
Age	44.83	10.57
Income scale	3.29	1.49
Owner	.08	.27
Manager	.10	.28
Professional	.13	.12
White collar	.11	.30
Service/Blue-collar	.21	.41
Not in the labor force	.37	.50
Some EU identity	.54	.49
EU good/bad thing	.56	.46
EU positive/negative image	.54	.48

Table 6.A.2 *Results of a logit regression analysis predicting whether or not a respondent ever viewed him/herself as a European*

Variables	B	S.E.(b)
Gender	.20**	.05
Age at school completion	.04**	.00
Income	.06**	.02
Age	−.004**	.002
Left–Right politics	−.06**	.01
Occupation:		
Owner	.25**	.11
Professional	.74**	.23
Manager	.51**	.10
White-collar	.35**	.09
Not in the labor force	−.01	.07
Belgium	.73**	.13
Denmark	.60**	.13
Germany	.71**	.11
Greece	.18	.13
Spain	1.09**	.13
France	1.32**	.13
Ireland	.60**	.13
Italy	1.59**	.13
Netherlands	.32**	.12
Luxembourg	.83**	.16
Portugal	.87**	.12
Finland	−.28*	.13
Sweden	.08	.12
Austria	.32**	.12
Constant	−1.19**	.16

* $p < .05$, ** $p < .01$

Table 6.A.3 *Results of a regression analysis predicting attitudes toward the EU (see Appendix for explanation of data coding)*

Variables	"Is EU a good/bad thing?" B	S.E.(b)
Gender	.06	.06
Age at school completion	.02**	.00
Income	.01*	.00
Age	−.019**	.001
Left–Right politics	−.01*	.003
Occupation:		
Owner	.07*	.02
Professional	.12	.08
Manager	.09**	.03
White-collar	.05*	.02
Not in the labor force	.05	.02
Belgium	.14**	.05
Denmark	.08	.05
Germany	.05	.04
Greece	.18**	.05
Spain	.17**	.04
France	−.09*	.05
Ireland	.34**	.05
Italy	.20**	.06
Netherlands	.06	.05
Luxembourg	.35**	.06
Portugal	.16**	.05
Finland	−.03	.05
Sweden	−.28**	.05
Austria	−.32**	.05
European identity	.35**	.02
Constant	2.18**	.06

* p < .05, ** p < .01

Table 6.A.4 *Means and standard deviations for variables used in data analysis*

Variable	Mean	SD
Gender	.51	.49
Age at school completion	17.44	4.96
Age	43.46	17.47
Owner	.09	.27
Manager	.11	.28
Professional	.10	.13
White-collar	.14	.30
Service/Blue-collar	.23	.41
Not in the labor force	.33	.50
Second language	.62	.48
Use language at work	.34	.50
Use language for social reasons	.76	.28

Source: Eurobarometer 54LAN, 2000.

Table 6.A.5 *Logistic regressions predicting second language use, use of language at work, and use of language for social purposes*

	Second language use	
Variables	B	S.E. (b)
Gender	.03	.04
Age at school completion	.04**	.00
Age	−.06**	.00
Occupation:		
Owner	.68*	.08
Professional	1.63**	.24
Manager	1.41**	.09
White-collar	.96**	.08
Not in the labor force	.60**	.06
Belgium	−.22**	.09
Denmark	1.99**	.11
Germany	.31**	.09
Greece	−.08**	.08
Spain	−.31**	.09

Table 6.A.5 (*cont.*)

Variables	Second language use	
	B	S.E. (b)
France	−.32**	.09
Ireland	.36	.19
Italy	.16	.09
Netherlands	.21**	.08
Luxembourg	4.96**	.57
Portugal	−.07.	.08
Finland	.70**	.09
Sweden	1.89**	.11
Austria	−1.04**	.08
Constant	1.39**	.09

* p < .05, ** p < .01
Source: Eurobarometer 54LAN, 2000.

Table 6.A.6 *Means and standard deviations for analysis of European travel data*

Variable	Mean	SD
Gender	.48	.50
Age at school completion	17.04	4.46
Age	43.54	17.92
Owner	.09	.27
Manager	.09	.28
Professional	.15	.13
White-collar	.13	.30
Service/Blue-collar	.20	.41
Not in the labor force	.34	.50
Left–Right politics	3.21	2.02
Income (harmonized)	31.71	40.72
Europe travel	.26	.44
EU good/bad thing	2.46	1.23

Source: Eurobarometer 47, 1997.

Table 6.A.7 *Logit regression for determinants of European travel*

Variables	European travel B	SE(B)
Gender	−.17**	.04
Age at school completion	.01**	.00
Income	.00	.00
Age	−.019**	.01
Left–Right politics	−.01**	.003
Occupation:		
Owner	.07*	.02
Professional	.26**	.08
Manager	.66**	.07
White-collar	.46**	.07
Not in the labor force	−.32**	.06
Belgium	.44**	.09
Denmark	.36**	.10
Germany	.87**	.09
Greece	−.97**	.12
Spain	−.89**	.13
France	−.17**	.11
Ireland	−.18**	.10
Italy	−.99**	.13
Netherlands	.75**	.12
Luxembourg	1.32**	.11
Portugal	−1.67**	.11
Finland	−.54**	.12
Sweden	.26 **	.11
Austria	−.17	.11
Constant	−1.73**	.12

* p < .05, ** p < .01
Source: Eurobarometer 47, 1997.

7 | Immigration, migration, and free movement in the making of Europe

ADRIAN FAVELL

Europe historically has been made, unmade, and remade through the movements of peoples. Despite the image today of Europeans as a rather sedentary and socially immobile population – particularly when compared to the highly mobile spatial and social patterns of North Americans – contemporary Europe has essentially emerged out of a crucible of local, regional, and international population movements over the centuries.

In this chapter, I consider the crucial impact of migration in Europe on European identity, by building a bridge between historical analyses of the phenomenon and emerging patterns that are shaping Europe as a distinctive new regional space of migration and mobility. My contribution points to how migration is making and remaking Europe, less at the level of identity in people's heads – in fact, if anything, most migrations are contributing to the growth of anti-European sentiment – but more in a territorial and (especially) structural economic sense. This is less easy to see if a purely cultural view is taken of the question of Europe. After sketching the role of population movements in the making and unmaking of Europe historically, I explore in depth the three kinds of migration/ mobility that are most salient to the continent today and its structural transformation: first, the ongoing, traditional "ethnic" immigration of non-Europeans into European nation-states; second, the small but symbolically important emergence of new intra-European "elite" migrations, engaged by European citizens enjoying the fruits of their EU free movement rights; and third, the politically ambiguous flows of East–West migrants – which fall somewhere between the other two forms – that have been connected to the EU enlargement processes formalized in 2004

This chapter started life as a lecture for the Sociology Department at the University of Copenhagen in late 2006, and is a new take on ideas first in Favell 2003a. I thank Nauja Kleist for the original invitation to speak, and the editors, my co-authors in the volume, and Thomas Risse for useful comments and criticisms in its development.

167

and 2007. The distinctiveness of Europe as a world region – hence in this sense, its economic and territorial identity – can best be grasped by briefly comparing it again to the US and North America as a similar but differently structured regional migration space, a theme I turn to in my conclusion.

Population movements in the making and unmaking of Europe

It is not uncommon to picture European nationals as somehow innately predisposed to not move. Europe is typically seen as a patchwork of "thick" inherited cultures – divided up by proudly preserved languages and social practices – that map out a continent of stubbornly rooted peoples with strong national and local identities, not much affected by the efforts of European institutions – or globalization – to get them to think differently. It is also seen as a continent largely hostile to new immigrants, struggling to integrate even the small numbers of ethnically and racially distinct minorities that do manage to get in.

The US, as is so often the case, is often referred to in order to underline this contrast. If the EU can be thought of for a moment as a kind of federal United States of Europe, the numbers are stark. While around 12% of Americans are foreign born (Batalova and Lowell 2006), less than one in fifty Europeans lives outside his/her state of national birth, and even intra-regional migration *within* European nation-states is lower than cross-state migration in the US, at 22% compared to 33% (European Foundation for the Improvement of Living and Working Conditions 2006). European society is thus seen as the product of historically rooted cultures; America unequivocally has been built on immigration and the melting pot of newcomers. Despite fluctuating political resistance to new immigration, the base numbers and percentages moving to the US are still bigger than anywhere in Europe, as is the sheer size of recent immigrant-origin populations over two or three generations – which in some states such as California now exceed 50%. And the attractiveness of the US for new generations of the internationally ambitious and talented is still unanswered by Europe as a global economic force: two-thirds of tertiary-educated migrants from developing countries choose America as their destination, with dramatically beneficial consequences for the American economy (Peri 2005). It appears, in short, that Americans are willing to move and accept movers; Europeans are not.

A short pause for thought on this assumption will quickly reveal its historical ineptitude (see also Recchi 2006). America, after all, was largely populated by Europeans who moved and moved again: over sea, and then over great stretches of land. Thought of less short-sightedly, Europe is and always has been a continent of migratory flux. Early modern Europe – the kind of Europe celebrated by nationalists everywhere in terms of culturally rooted folklore (Hobsbawm 1983; Anderson 1991) – in fact was already a patchwork of circular, seasonal, and career mobility well before industrialization. These revolutions then changed everything: sweeping peasants off the land, ripping apart rural communities, packing expansive cities full of new social classes, and creating economic channels of mobility that linked all of Europe, and eventually the world, in a new system of empire and capital (Moch 2003; Bade 2000; Hobsbawm 1987). On the ground, this meant continual flows of migration. By the late nineteenth century, unprecedented numbers were also moving across national borders as worker populations, and across seas as New World migrants and settlers (Hatton and Williamson 1998). Europeans went everywhere.

Why this is forgotten in the image of a sedentary Europe today is, of course, that the wars of the twentieth century stopped much of this migration. Nation-states finally reigned supreme as the dominant form of global social organization: cementing the institutionalized role of state-centered power as explosive population containers, using military service, citizenship, and welfare rights in the name of national identity, to build political distinctions between insiders and outsiders and fix people spatially (Torpey 2000; Mann 1993). This, then, became the familiar, legitimate political topography of the modern world, leaving numerous ethnic groups on the wrong side of territorial borders or in despised social locations, the stateless residual populations of a now thoroughly nationalized Europe. This left one disaster – the Jewish Holocaust – which scarred the continent forever, and an ugly aftermath of war that brutally shifted yet more populations east and west. Europeans were once again moved, in search of a stable political solution that might once and for all settle the ethnic and ideological frontiers of the so-called "shatter zone" in Central and East Europe (Mazower 1998; Brubaker 1996; Mann 2005). Europe gave up its empires, and the Iron Curtain created a new, nearly impermeable material and psychological barrier, freezing East–West mobility and literally severing the latitudinal land movements and interactions that had, in *longue durée* geographical terms, been the greatest civilizing resource of the continent (Diamond 1997).

In the West, generous welfare state structures in the postwar period – a kind of liberal democratic form of socialized nationalism prevalent throughout the continent up to 1970 (Mazower 1998) – cemented national populations in place like never before. The shrunken West European powers eventually re-emerged economically, but they did so by now servicing their migrant worker needs, first via a new wave of migrants from the peripheral South to North (from Italy, Spain, Portugal and Yugoslavia), then – as these movements too dried up – via a large, hitherto unprecedented immigration from former colonies and dependencies outside Europe (especially Turkey, North and Central Africa, the West Indies, South Asia, and Indonesia). This, of course, brought an even more explosive mix of race and cultural diversity into the fractious continent (Castles and Miller 2003).

A historical ground map to European population movements – breathless as this sketch is – is necessary for any discussion about the place of migration today in the making of a European identity. It is not an easy map to capture (see also King 2002). Conventional postcolonial and guest-worker immigration was supposed to have ended in the 1970s, leaving only limited channels of family reunification and asylum as entry points for migration. Immigrant populations were supposed to have settled and integrated as nationals and citizens, turning more or less culturally homogeneous national societies into reluctantly multicultural ones.

The 1980s, and especially 1990s, have changed all this again. A wave of "new migrations" has mixed up the continent once more (Koser and Lutz 1998). A globalizing economy has liberalized post-industrial societies, leading to a new dual service economy driven largely by a demand for cheap foreign labor (Sassen 2001; Piore 1979). Global transportation systems have facilitated movement to Europe from increasingly diversified and unpredictable sources (Held *et al.* 1999). European working classes, as in America, no longer wish to take on 3D (dirty, dangerous, and dull) tasks that might be left to more motivated and cheaper foreigners. Migration here, as elsewhere, has also dramatically feminized, as women from developing countries have become the carers and domestic workers of the highly developed. Asylum, which once functioned as a more symbolic gesture to enable small numbers of political refugees to escape to the West, has turned into an uncontrollable torrent as Europe has picked up the human pieces of numerous regional and global wars; asylum also has become effectively a channel of labor migration. Europe was supposed to become a fortress; by the early 2000s the reverse was happening (Favell and Hansen 2002).

Added to these new forms of immigration, novel *intra*-EU migrations have also become a feature of the European migrant tapestry. The European Union was built on the four freedoms, including the free movement of persons (the others being the free movement of goods, services and capital). Long-standing EU15 member states have enjoyed these rights for decades now. The numbers of West Europeans on the move have by no means been large, but they are highly symbolic. For every one who moves to work and settle freely in a neighboring member state of the EU, many more are moving temporarily as students, shoppers, commuters, and eventually retirees. Add to this the ever changing geographical definition of the Union with successive enlargements reuniting Europe, and the potential for a new kind of migration in Europe – "free movement" – looks set to again unmake and remake the settled patchwork of national societies that had, more or less successfully, used the EU to rescue the European nation-state in the postwar period (Milward 2005). The most visible intra-EU free movers now are, of course, after 2004 and 2007, the socially and spatially dynamic mobile populations of new Eastern and Central Europe, grabbing access to a European space that is now all theirs again. But, arguably, free movers will, due to the concentric logic of an externalizing, "neighborhood"-building EU, in future be coming from Ukraine, Turkey, and Morocco as well.

These combined phenomena leave a confusing setting for evaluating the impact of population movements on European identity. As I will show, untangling the impact of these various new migrations on the making and unmaking of Europe, it can be seen that Europe is struggling to maintain distinctions among three distinctive groups, but moving toward a new solution. Here, I will sketch the outlines of this likely future, before going on to explore this scenario in more depth in the rest of the chapter.

A first kind of migration – traditional, poor, "ethnic," extra-European immigrants from Africa and Asia – insofar as they can be distinguished as such – is being processed, with a great deal of social and political conflict, in line with the established methods for dealing with postwar, post-colonial, and guest-worker migrants. These immigrants continue to be framed as the legitimate concern of national societies, not the EU; recent years have seen the return of nationalist integration policies across all of Europe, alongside a growing instrumental role they play in fueling the symbolic closure of anti-EU and anti-globalization politics. However, in Europe as elsewhere, this often ugly politics of immigration does not square with the economics of migration. Nostalgia for contained, culturally secure, citizenship and nation-based societies sits badly with a globalized dual labor market within service-sector-driven economies run by multinationals, which demand an almost endless reserve army of flexible foreign labor.

The experiences of a second group of migrants, at the other end of the social scale – West European movers I call "Eurostars" – tell a different story about Europe today. Unsurprisingly, they reflect a Europe at its most enthusiastically cosmopolitan and post-national. Yet, even with all formal barriers to migration down, they encounter limitations and resistance to their movement that suggest the resilience of national ethnicities in even the most structurally global and multinational of locations – London and Amsterdam being my examples.

A third group of migrants – the new East European movers – are the most ambiguous of all. Are they cadet "Eurostars," as the theory of European integration predicts they will one day become? Or are they still more like traditional "ethnic" immigrants, and likely to be treated this way? I argue that both are true. They are making a new European space of movement and fulfilling a new idea of European citizenship; but they are also being shuffled into economic roles in the West European economies assigned in the postwar period to traditional non-European immigrants. Herein lies the punch line. A kind of European fortress may yet be built on the back of this ambiguous spread and opening of Europe to the East. A tempting racial logic is at stake for Europeans today. Opening to populations from the East may enable the more effective closing of Europe to the South, filling the structural need for which Western Europe had historically to turn to colonial and developing country immigrants from more distant societies and cultures. Racial and cultural distinctions might be used to achieve what concrete, electronic surveillance, and barbed wire cannot.

The three migrations in Europe

I will now explore in greater detail each of the three migrations identified above: traditional non-European "ethnic" immigrants; West

European "Eurostars"; and the new East–West post-Enlargement movers. It is essential to analytically distinguish them before showing how the new migration scenario is blurring many of these supposedly clear distinctions.

Traditional non-European "ethnic" (im)migrants

New forms of migration and mobility have changed the context of population movements in Europe, but the dominant story about immigration today in Europe is still, mostly, the ongoing classic post-colonial and guest-worker scenario. Unquestionably, European economies still generate a strong demand for migrant workers, alongside an alluring image that generates a supply – alluring enough to offset the often highly costly and uncertain calculations that lie behind migrants' decisions to move from Africa or Asia. Where the story has changed is in the increasingly diverse source origins of ongoing immigration: now from a range of countries with little or no colonial connexion to the destination countries. Previous generations of post-colonial immigrants could at least count on a symbolic connexion to the metropolitan destinations, together often with having been socialized to some extent in the language and culture of the country. Nowadays sources and destinations are equally scattered, a factor that increases the tensions that emerge politically around the migration in the receiving society. For example, on this score, the reception context of British West Indian migrants in the 1960s differs dramatically from the Sri Lankis or Kurds arriving in Denmark today. National integration systems thus find it that much harder to deal with the new migrations.

In addition, channels of migration today are much more "bottom-up" than in the days of relatively planned post-colonial and guest-worker recruitment migration. Some of the most remarkable migration systems that have emerged have been very specific in their internal self-organization: Senegalese street vendors in Italy (Riccio 2001), Cape Verdean domestic workers in Italy and Spain (Andall 1998), Chinese migrants in Britain and France (Benton and Pieke 1998), Middle Easterners in Scandinavia (Diken 1998), and so on. In the main, though, the largest groups of migrants – from Turkey and Morocco – are rather predictable and continuous migration systems built on long histories and easy connexions with a range of countries (for some sources: Lesthaege 2000; Kastoryano 1993; Bousetta 2000; Phalet *et al.* 2000).

As everyone knows, these various immigrations have visibly put black, brown, and yellow faces in white Europe, including in some of the least likely places. Issues of multiculturalism or inter-ethnic conflict that were most familiar to former colonial powers like Britain and France are now raised in every country in Western Europe, and increasingly in East and Central Europe too. As a majority of these new immigrants hail from predominantly Muslim countries, the Islamic dimension of this immigration – whether by practicing religious affiliation or merely the parent culture – has become the defining issue of twenty-first-century European "identity" most associated with immigration today (see also Byrnes and Katzenstein 2006).

This is of course an issue imprisoned in broader geopolitical struggles linked to the "war against terror," and at the mercy of reductive, inflammatory visions of the so-called "clash of civilizations" (Huntington 1996). It is now difficult to see past the rhetoric to assess qualitatively how different these new migrations and the multicultural problems are from those of the "old" immigration of the 1950s and 1960s. In fact, the trajectory of these visible, so-called "ethnic" immigrants in European society is a quite familiar one. At a macro-level, they have been a key structural feature of all postwar European societies. What impacted first the large post-colonial and guest-worker countries has had similar effects in asylum-receiving countries in northern Europe, and later in new destinations in southern Europe. Each nation-state has faced similar "multicultural questions," albeit with different timings and political saliency (Favell 2001; Joppke and Morawska 2003). Europe as a whole has become a continent of immigration, and (with more difficulty) a continent of Islam; but the political and social processes raised by these questions have everywhere been dealt with as predominantly national ones, now raging at the core of domestic national politics everywhere, from Britain to Denmark, and the Netherlands to Spain.

Immigration, then, is certainly a European question; but the politics of immigration are still dominantly national in locus. Cooperation at the European level has had its effects, particularly on border control and entry policies; but the EU has little effect on the policies or processes of immigrant settlement. The basic problems for these non-European immigrants – "Third Country Nationals" as they are known in EU jargon – is one of attaining formal national citizenship and recognized national membership: they are not European citizens, even when they have permanent residency. Naturalization into their adopted host state provides the one sure route to becoming a European, but successful naturalization is inevitably a nationalizing process (Hansen 1998). The effect on European identity of these new immigrations is, in this sense, negative: it helps to preserve the nation-centered status quo. Whatever transnational, even pan-European social forms migrants might develop – Islam, for example, has taken specific "Euro" forms in the visions of young leaders like Tariq Ramadan – the socialization pressures faced by Muslim immigrants are overwhelmingly national. Nearly every European nation-state has formulated in recent years a policy on "integration" of immigrants that reflects mainly nation-building concerns about imparting national culture and values to newcomers, and very little of the kinds of post-national responses to immigration that would be the consequence of a through Europeanization of the issues involved (Favell 2003b). The most encouraging message all such immigrants get from their host societies is: "integrate – or else ..."

Immigration is thus dominantly a national issue everywhere because of the integration question. Even progressive, inclusionary movements are always framed in terms of inclusion into *national* identities: finding your place in "multi-ethnic" Britain, or "republican" France, or the "tolerant, pluralist" Netherlands, and so on. As recent debates in all these countries reveal, immigration issues and the vulnerable populations who embody them are consistently projected by both pro- and anti-immigration politicians and media into grand national debates about citizenship, national culture, language acquisition, and absorption in national welfare and labor market systems. Ongoing "ethnic" immigration in fact has become one of the primary ways in which nation-building continues its classic operations in Europe today, despite other Europeanizing and globalization processes. If by the making of Europe or a European "identity" is meant something over and above the nation-state – something post-national, cosmopolitan, a European "society" and so on – then "Europe" is simply not very relevant to most traditional immigration policy questions.

Moreover, the anti-immigrant reactions seen across Europe in the toughening of politics on immigration and integration are also a crucial pillar in the anti-EU backlash. They are again a distinct part of the un-making of European identity (in a post-national sense), although, as Doug Holmes (this volume) points out, these politics themselves have Europeanized nationalists and nativists in support of their own, different vision of Europe – a Europe of nation-states. Populations remain, on the whole, hostile to migrations of all kinds. Progressive immigration policies – on citizenship rights and so on – have generally only been advanced politically in Europe by depoliticizing the issues into legal and technical arenas, and typically during periods of low saliency of immigration politics (Guiraudon 1998). In terms of Neil Fligstein's analysis (this volume) about how and why people might feel "European," immigration in fact is one of the issues leading nationals of member states to feel much *less* European – including the immigrants themselves, who have no option, if they wish to be included in their host society, but to comply with the integrating/nationalizing pressures attached to citizenship and membership acquisition. The effects of immigration, in fact, suggest an opposite dynamic to the Deutsch hypothesis: more mobility and more interaction leading to a less integrated Europe.

A different view about the aggregate effects of new immigration might be taken if we were to view the question in structural, economic terms, rather than the cultural ones reflected in political debates and discussions on identity. Far from the maelstrom of rhetorical national politics, policy makers in the EU certainly have been talking about coordinating or formulating immigration policies at the EU level; indeed, the only EU policy field where there is rapid integration today is in security-based externalization efforts on immigration and border control. This is more a question of nations efficiently devolving control mechanisms to more effective agency than anything supranational as such; but it has certainly Europeanized police forces and other state agencies in ways they would have not expected. There seems to be a huge effort in redirecting the internal European integration project to external border construction and policy – particularly to the south. In this sense, immigration does appear to be helping in the (negative) construction of Europe – as the "fortress" hoped for by alarmed national populations.

Economics, though, may yet defeat this particular vision of Europe. The numbers of extra-EU immigrants are still rising, despite the efforts to control and limit them. This migration does still seem to be fulfilling a structural demand for migrants, driven by the demographic demand of declining childbirth and aging populations, and the economic restructuring of European national welfare state economies into a global service economy. No European nation-state can escape the changing structure of labor markets, and their rescaling at a wider European level, as they become organized everywhere around highly polarized, service-industry driven global cities. Every European economy is witnessing a division of labor and widening of inequalities between the primary sectors of middle- and upper-class employment, and lower grade working-class jobs that native nationals are less and less willing to fill: notably cleaners, domestic workers, restaurant and shop workers, taxi drivers, construction and agricultural workers, and so on. There is national level resistance to this process, as well as variation across the "varieties of European capitalism" (Esping-Andersen 1999) – Britain is much more polarized and hence open to migrants than, say, Denmark – but these structural economic effects *are* impacting all.

These processes are thus integrating Europe under a new economic rationale. On their convergent economic trajectories, European economies are coming to look more and more like North America in their structural demand for migration to fill the secondary labor market demand. This will mean high levels of tacit migration, social and economic marginalization for immigrants, and policies at the border that "talk the talk" of control but are porous and liberalizing in their effects – what is referred to in the American context as "smoke and mirrors"-style border control policies (Massey *et al.* 2002). Viewed this way, immigration *is* still building a new Europe, in a structural sense – although host populations don't much like politically the apparently neoliberal Europe that is being built by these processes (see also Díez Medrano in this volume).

Eurostars and Eurocities

What happens when you remove race, class, ethnicity, inequality, borders, barriers, and cultural disadvantage from immigration? Answer: you get "free movers." Nationals of European member-states are also European citizens, among whose basic rights are those that ensure their unfettered ability to move, shop, work, live, and settle wherever they want abroad in Europe, whenever and however. Globally speaking, the European Union is a unique space in this sense: there is nothing like this kind of politically constructed post-national space anywhere else on the planet. Free moving European citizens don't need visas; they don't need to worry about citizenship or integration; they often don't even need residency to live and work where they choose – they can come and go in a free European space. European free movement laws – which date back to the original Treaty of Rome in 1957 – undid the nationalizing logic of nation-states as population containers just as the postwar settlement and the completion of European welfare states was cementing this national system firmly in place.

In theory, then, European free movement could be an avenue for building a very different kind of Europe. Yet, numbers of such migrants have historically been small. Still, today, less than one in fifty Europeans lives outside their country of origin, and numbers have not grown appreciably with any of the major steps toward European integration. The interest in this small population in comparison to traditional immigrants is precisely as an unexpected limit case: they reveal exactly what other types of immigrants have to face to achieve anything like level playing field conditions with national citizens (the following discussion is based on Favell 2008a).

The "Eurostars," as I call them, are at the heart of the EU Commission's efforts to build Europe through dynamic mobility policies; the talk nowadays is not of moving coal miners and factory workers from the South to the North – as it was when Freedom of Movement of Persons was established as one of the basic provisions of the Treaty of Rome in 1957. The talk at the heart of the much touted 2000 Lisbon agenda, rather, is the movement of professionals, the skilled and the educated: the circulation of "talent" in a "knowledge economy," with its beneficial side effect the building of European identity – through the kinds of cross-border interactions discussed by Fligstein in this volume. This movement is likely to be a predominantly urban hub phenomenon – hence the emergence of "Eurocities," a network of cosmopolitan places driving the new European economy: familiar big cities such as London, Amsterdam, Brussels, Milan, Munich, Berlin, Barcelona, Vienna, and so on, that enjoy semi-detached identities from the national societies in which they are situated.

Unquestionably, London has benefited the most from these trends since the 1990s. Offshore from the continent, a global hub and gateway for all of Europe, London is *the* European destination of free movement *par excellence*, an urban economy that has in the last ten to fifteen years creamed off the brightest and best of a whole generation of French, German, Italian, and Spanish movers (and others), frustrated with stagnant economies or parochial career hierarchies back home. What began as a large but rather invisible migration of West Europeans has laid a path now for a new generation of young, talented, and educated Poles, Hungarians, Romanians, and others heading in the same direction – not least because other countries (such as France and Germany, most notably) have unwisely kept doors shut for these very same grade-A migrants from new accession countries. European mobility of this kind is also promoted as the model for future post-Enlargement migrations. At the very least, mobile East European EU citizens taking their new European chances as "free movers" – no longer "immigrants" – are likely to largely exceed the paltry numbers of West Europeans who have moved with these same rights during the previous three to four decades.

For sure, those movers found pioneering the life of Eurostars are the most likely to both feel and make a post-national/cosmopolitan European identity. As the PIONEUR survey documents in some detail (Recchi and Favell, in press), they embody in flesh and blood – albeit in small numbers – what the philosophers and cosmopolitan social theorists of Europe have long been dreaming of.[1] This much is no surprise. In Fligstein's terms, these people undoubtedly are the prototypical Europeans – although, as PIONEUR shows, they find little difficulty in combining their new European identity with identities rooted in both their nation of origin and nation of residence (Rother and Nebe, in press).

But are they really making or changing Europe in a macro-structural sense? The irony is, of course, still patent: break down all barriers, create all kinds of incentive structures, paint a Europe without frontiers and only opportunities, and still you only get low, statistically insignificant levels of movement. Typically, the assumption here is that this is because Europeans don't like to move; that they are inherently rooted to where they were born by culture and language. But this culturalist view of Europe is unsustainable given its longer and dramatic migration history and the fact that English has provided a common second

---

[1] The EU Framework V funded PIONEUR project (2003–6) "Pioneers of European Integration 'from below': Mobility and the Emergence of European Identity among National and Foreign Citizens in the EU," directed by Ettore Recchi of the University of Florence, completed the first ever systematic survey of the migrant population of West European citizens within the EU, interviewing randomly 5,000 foreign residents from the five (EU15) largest states in the five largest states (i.e., Germans in Britain, France, Italy and Spain; British in Germany, France, Italy and Spain; French in the four other countries and so on). It posed questions about the socioeconomic and geographical profile of these migrants, their reasons for migration, their social and spatial mobility, their feelings of European identity, their media consumption, and their political participation. See our web site: www.obets.ua.es/pioneur.

language that can be used interchangeably by Europeans in most professional circles or multinational corporations located in major cities. But whatever the reason for immobility, European cross-border movement is a perilously slow and marginal way of making Europe. So much for philosophy and economic theory. This exceptional "most likely case" scenario is, however, revealing of the stark limitations of any post-national Europeanized space under even the best possible theoretical conditions.

So being European for these free movers is certainly a banal fact in terms of identity survey questions. Yes, there are forms of new Europeanized life, highly Europeanized spaces in cities, and slowly growing numbers of "new Europeans" in these terms out there. But more importantly, even with the low numbers, when the lives, experiences and trajectories of these would-be cosmopolitans are studied ethnographically, the movers can be seen to face surprising local and national barriers blocking their aspirations in even the most ostensibly cosmopolitan of locations.

After London, another vastly popular hub of European mobility is Amsterdam. The Netherlands is often rated the number one open global economy in the world, and Amsterdam is seen as the liberal capital of Europe, widely seen as the most open and tolerant urban culture on the continent. It is a very popular destination with Irish, British, German, and Southern European migrants. Yet even here, EU movers often find themselves excluded on an informal level in their chosen places of residence by locally specific, highly ethnicized processes of exclusion. These center in Amsterdam, as in other Eurocities, on the competitive struggle for highly sought after prizes of settlement – high-quality urban lifestyles – in the most desirable locations of global cities. The Dutch are open, tolerant, cosmopolitan – for sure – but they simply do not make it easy for foreigners to settle on an everyday level, ensuring that even the closest European neighbors have minimal access to the internal secrets of a national "culture" reserved to native speakers. This "culture" structures the confusing rules and regulations that police organizational life, access to the best housing, and attainment of the elusive quality of life that native Amsterdammers spend years strategizing to attain. Despite its appeal and the very high numbers of foreigners who move there, very few stay, turnover is high, and the Netherlands has one of the smallest foreign resident populations in the continent. It takes elite capital, and the adoption of a disconnected "expat" life in the city, to surmount these barriers – a stratification which ensures that European mobility cannot be massified downwards to the middle classes, or effect a bigger structural change on the Europe of nation-states. It will remain an exclusive property of elites, if any, and European spatial mobility opportunities will not lead to dramatic new social mobility or the emergence of a more widespread cosmopolitan sensibility (as the theorists dream) (see also Recchi, in press, for a quantitative analysis of PIONEUR findings in these terms).

It is a fair retort to suggest that expecting Europeans to build Europe by moving and resettling long term abroad is setting the bar too high in some respects. Yet, these same Europeans consistently (in Eurobarometer surveys) rate their rights of free movement as the most important benefit of EU membership – ahead of the economy and security – and around a third claim to be ready to move abroad if the opportunity and demand arose (European Year of Worker's Mobility 2006).[2] Perhaps other forms of more transient/temporary mobility in Europe will be more significant: businessmen, students, retirees, shoppers, cross-border traders, commuters, and so on. Again, the broader terms of Fligstein's search for the Europeans establishes the evidence, such as it can be shown through the limited available attitudinal sources of the Eurobarometer surveys. Maybe the experience of any cross-border mobility, even the most short-term, may have big Europeanizing effects. However, if mobility consists primarily of holidaying with co-nationals on a beach in the Costa del Sol, or going on the rampage as a hooligan at a European football championship, European identity will not be the result. Thus far the evidence is ambiguous, even for the most likely beneficiaries such as Erasmus students or retirement migrants. Most of the evidence on these other forms of mobility suggests that experience of these benefits of EU is not particularly destructive or transformative of national cultures or identities (as PIONEUR also underlines; see also King *et al.* 2000; King and Ruiz-Gelices 2003), and that when Europeans go home, they go home to their primary national identities. Eurostars, on the other hand,

---

[2] Of those surveyed, 37% think they would be willing to move to another country that offered better conditions, 53% think the "freedom to travel and work in the EU" is the most important single benefit of membership – ahead of the euro (44%) and peace (36%) – and 57% have travelled internationally within the EU in the last two years. Yet, less than 4% have ever lived and worked abroad.

are explicitly trying to live a post-national life; most of them find that it is a rather difficult proposition in the EU today.

East–West movers

Setting up the contrast between these two types of migrants in Europe – "ethnic" immigrants and "elite" professional movers – unfortunately emphasizes what has become a clichéd view of the polarized mobility opportunities alleged to index the winners and losers of globalization and regional integration processes (Bauman 1998). The image, in fact, is far from empirically accurate (on this, see Smith and Favell 2006). "Ethnic" immigrants often contain a fair number of middle-class and highly qualified movers, who frequently use their relatively privileged homegrown social and economic capital to engineer what becomes a social move downward into higher paying, but lower level work in the West. It is a universal fact of migration that it is *not* the poorest and least capable of migrating that move, but those with some degree of human capital or networks-based social capital (Hammar *et al.* 1997). Among the intra-European migrants, meanwhile, there is much evidence that free movement rights in Europe have been most effectively mobilized by a new generation of "social spiralists" – upwardly mobile, ambitious, provincial, working- and lower-middle-class migrants, often from the South, often women, using international migration in Europe as an escape from career and lifestyle frustrations at home (Favell 2008a: 64).

The caricature of "ethnic" immigrants and "elite" movers is even less applicable to the new form of migration that has in the last few years grown to become the most important visible proof of a changing Europe: post-Enlargement migration. This migration is dated post 2004 and 2007, although in truth the migration was already well established, both informally and semi-formally, before these dates, and encompasses countries not even now among the twenty-seven official members of the EU. EU A8 movers, new accession country citizens, and by extension migrants from all candidate, possibly candidate, associate, and neighboring countries may fall under this logic – because of the territorial, "concentric" effects of integrating markets on a regional scale across these borders through the European neighborhood policies (Rogers 2000; Favell 2008b). The question, though, is whether post-Enlargement migrants are following the classic "ethnic" trajectory, or whether they are, rather, "free movers" destined to become the full and free European citizens of the future? Which scenario best applies?

Demographic and economic theory is highly hopeful here. The newly freed "free movers" are seen as the avatars of an all-triumphant theory of European integration, which predicts a win-win-win outcome for Europe from these new movements (ECAS 2005, 2006): the migrants win through satisfying their ambitions and mobility goals; the receiving society wins from creaming off their talent and enthusiasm; and the sending society will benefit from the positive development dynamics initiated by the movement of talented individuals who circulate money and networks within the new Europe, and who will bring back their talents at some point to the newly integrated Eastern economy – where all the best opportunities will be located in future. In short, movement theoretically promotes European integration, efficient economic dynamics, and a circulation of talent and capital flowing back into development. True to this theory, more spatial/social mobility is seen among East European movers. This generation of new Europeans *are* ambitious, dynamic movers ready to get what's theirs from the West, while benefiting from ease of mobility back and forth from West to East. Well over half a million citizens from the A8 accession countries of 2004, for example, took the chance to move into Britain's boom economy since 2004. In this, at least, they are unequivocally making Europe – regardless of how they or others might express their feelings in Eurobarometers or identity terms. This movement marks arguably the biggest social change in Europe in half a century: the definitive end of the Cold War, and a European social experiment that will leave neither West nor East unchanged.

But, at the same time, a negative political scenario continues to react to these migrants as "immigrants" rather than "free movers." Identity can be mobilized negatively on this issue if migrants are seen by domestic populations as threats rather than benevolent economic complements to domestic economies. On this point, the evidence is equivocal. A pragmatic reaction has on the whole greeted many of these migrants. Over Romanians in Milan and Bilbao, Poles in Berlin and London, Russians and Yugoslavs in Paris or Amsterdam, overt politics has certainly not reacted anything like as violently as it has against the (somewhat) more visible North African or African populations in the same places. For sure, Polish plumbers and the "invasion" of Roma have grabbed headlines in France and Britain; France remains mostly closed to new accession members, and Britain shut its doors to Romanians and Bulgarians. But, overall, the reaction has been slow and measured, more in tune with the growing realization that these new faces are part of a rather permanent looking East–West economic system that might have even deeper consequences than the limited settlement of new "ethnic" immigrants.

This reaction can apply even when these migrants are white, Christian, skilled and in high demand – and it can happen equally to the Romanian farm worker in Italy, the Polish shop owner in Germany, or the highly skilled Hungarian office worker in England (see the ethnographies collected in Favell and Elrick 2008). The ambiguity of their presence is sharpened by the fact that it is not so clear that the old traditional nation-building integration response is so applicable here. Older immigrant populations might resent that East Europeans can come and go, taking the same jobs, but facing none of the integratory pressures that are put on traditional immigrants to demonstrate that they "belong" in their West European host countries. There is still room for these migrants to be enveloped in the traditional nation-building processes of exclusion/inclusion, but for the main part they are establishing patterns of circular, temporary, and non-residential mobility in the new European space (Morawska 2002; Wallace and Stola 2001). Locals react with horror when they see the wives and children of Polish workers cluttering up state school and medical facilities. They understand quite well that the solution is to make sure that low cost airlines are plentiful, mobility easy, and economic conditions back home promising enough to ensure it is a temporary residence. West European nations, if they stay open and porous enough, might just get this migration/development equation right with Poland, although more permanent brain- and brawn-drain is an ongoing threat for the new Balkan member states.

An evaluation of the future of this new European migration system, then, needs to stress both dimensions of the Europe it is building. Yes, the integrating Europe of mobility promised by demographers and economists is happening. But the system they are moving into is more often than not a system based on a dual labor market – in which East Europeans will take the secondary, temporary, flexible roles based on their exploitability in terms of cost and human capital premium. Europe thus comes to resemble the US–Mexico model: where East–West movers do the 3D jobs or hit glass ceilings, and where underlying "ethnic" distinctions between East and West are unlikely to disappear. In a sense, this mode of inclusion continues the iniquitous longer-standing historical relationship between East and West analyzed in this volume by Holly Case. Eastern Europeans will get to move, and they will learn the hard way that the West only wants them to do jobs that Westerners no longer want. The danger, in short, is they will become a new Victorian service class for a West European aristocracy of university educated working mums and "creative class" professionals, who need someone to help them lead their dream lives.

The concentric, externalizing logic of regional integration is meanwhile pushing the EU to begin negotiations out across the Eastern borders, micro-managing border scenarios with new neighbors to encourage trade and mobility while controlling unwanted security and policing implications. The idea, again, is that free movement of all kinds can be governed; and that when it is governed well it is a win-win for both sides. This feature of European integration puts it far ahead of other steps toward regional economic integration around the world. Via bilateral external accords and neighborhood polices, the regional integration project in Europe stretches far east to the Urals, extends south to the Atlas mountains, and laps up against the borders of the Dead Sea. It can be expected that population movements of all kinds will increase within this concentric European space, and that those moving within this space will claim new rights as de facto European free movers rather than non-European immigrants.

Conclusion: Migration and comparative regional integration processes

Migration of all kinds is making Europe in new ways, but the new migration system engendered by successive EU enlargements and other externalizing efforts will prove the most momentous. In these terms, it is true that the founding fathers would perhaps not believe the European regional integration process that they put in train. As the logic of enlarging has triumphed over deepening, a functional new regional European space is being built, squaring the demography/economy/securitization question – although the borders of that space certainly do not end at the borders of EU27. When political integration of the EU hit the rocks, all the growth energy of the EU was turned into the activities of governing the porous borders of a new regional space, hence opening mobility and the four freedoms (in at least a partial way) to an EU45 or EU55 through the extension of the European market beyond all previous ideas of Europe.

The key question of course will be: Where lie the borders of this "space" and "system"? Who is in/out? What, in other words, will be the relationship of the newly fluid East European "free movers" – both new and potential members – to those post-colonial, "non"-European "immigrants" who have filled the secondary economic roles for Europe in the past?

One way of answering this question is to go back to the US–Europe comparison and lay out the emergent European regional space against the North American one. Viewed this way, it becomes instructive to compare the expanding, explicitly political logic of European regional integration with the politically ungoverned and socially disastrous scenario that the US now faces with Central America. Where Europe is increasingly turning to the East for its migrant labor sources, the US relies massively on Latino migration from the South to fill the same roles. And as the recent politics of immigration in the US testify, the Mexico–US immigration scenario (and by extension the relationship with all of Central America) is now tragically hamstrung between the irreconcilable paradoxes of the national container "migration state" (Hollifield 2004), unable to take effective political steps toward a post-national regional integration in the European mold, while structurally dependent on cross-border mobility (Massey *et al.* 2002). America desperately needs a rational economic solution; but its politics will not allow it.

The US remains an economy and society driven by immigration. The American economy more than ever is based on its porous borders. The Californian agricultural economy would collapse without it; Texas is much the same. What do Los Angelenos do when there is a hole in their roof, a problem with the garden sprinkler, or a fence that needs patrolling at night? They phone up Carlos, a recently naturalized Mexican-American, who has in fact been living in the city for twenty-five years. He then phones up some "guys" he knows, and you stop asking questions. Or if you need some help getting the house clean or the baby monitored, your neighbor's home help, Susana, always has a "sister" or "cousin" willing to come by, for cash in hand. The middle and upper class can get back to work making money franchising cable comedy shows, or get busy with their yoga class after dropping the kids off at school. This is how the city works, how everyone makes money and creates time for themselves. Nowadays it's exactly how New York, Chicago, Atlanta and Houston work too, and it's getting to be that way in Dalton, Georgia, Las Vegas, Nevada, or even (someday soon) Des Moines, Iowa. European middle classes in London, Paris, or Rome are learning the same economic logic; and the home helps they are turning to, and becoming increasingly dependent on, are increasingly East European in origin.

Politically, though, the two continents are divergent. Nativism is on the rise in the US, usually based on spurious cultural and linguistic arguments that are woefully outdated in their views of the population dynamics of major urban centers i.e., Huntington 2004. Congress has recently failed in several attempts to pass legislation to regularize undocumented migration and to square the economic demand for workers with the push for more political control. Only border control and internal security has tightened. But as a recent satirical movie made clear, "A day without a Mexican" is the day the miracle American economy grinds to a halt. The scenario was actualized in the massive one-day Mexican protests in Los Angeles and elsewhere in the spring of 2006. America has tried to look east to fill its voracious immigrant demand – one can argue that the US is so soft on immigration from Korea, Japan, China, and Vietnam precisely for this reason – but it still needs Carlos and his crew. White supremacists in the US have had their day, thanks to demographics. Even the Bush presidency understood that a Republican with no Asian or Latino voters is now a Republican out of office. Nativists will always want to build fences to the sky, and they may still feel empowered and legitimated to take their rifles out as minutemen to patrol the Arizona desert. But as is shown by the trucks pouring northwards across that border, while American capital and tourism pours south, the US economy does not and will not ever end at El Paso or Tijuana – arguably a lot more of the Central and South American continent than US citizens would like to admit is indisputably North America (see also Pastor 2001). But, as ever, this reality is driven by economic facts way in advance of any political understanding. It awaits a political leadership able to grasp it.

Europe faces similar issues with immigration, but politically and economically it is choosing a different path. In the twentieth century, Europe's greatest weakness in relation to the US was that its borders were ambiguous and its internal politics and economics fractious – to the tune of millions dead. Discounting its practically empty neighbor Canada, the US took a lead as the major container nation-state in the world because it had seas on either side and vast deserts to the south. It was a nation-state like no other, and it pursued a policy of essentially open doors to immigration – and a flattening of barriers to all internal migration – that fueled its growth and power to a scale that dwarfed all its rivals. Europe, too, eventually opened its societies to immigration and intra-regional migration, and now it seeks to manage a migration scenario that is close to being as dynamic and unruly as the one that dominates North American debates. London, *the* boomtown of European mobility, has in fact shadowed the mythical immigrant city of New York in terms of immigrant-led population growth in the period 2000–2005. But there is one major difference between the continents. The US has to look south for its sources of cheap labor. Europe, on the other hand, can look east; and this is what it has been increasingly doing.

But where does this leave Europe's own South? Put another way, this is the ethnic question of European identity again: the crucial issue of whether or not Moroccans and Turks – by far the largest immigrant populations in Europe, and the closest "ethnic" neighbors – are also mobile Europeans by the logic of regional integration. The politics currently do not look good: Europe may choose to heed nativism and treat its Moroccans and Turks in the same dismal fashion in which the US treats its Central American "alien" workforce. Yet, by a purely economic/concentric logic of regional integration, their mobility should come to resemble less and less the traditional nationalizing/integrating immigrant trajectory, and more that of new and potential East European members. Other contiguous populations to the south and east might also make this claim – although the space of the European neighborhood, as any space, has to end somewhere. Physical borders matter; to some extent you can build walls and patrol seas. The US is trying this again on its southern border, although as tens of thousands of have discovered at great human cost, it does not stop migration. But other mechanisms can make migration a lot more unpleasant. What if Europe could remove its reliance on ethnic workers in the lower, secondary slots in the economy; if demand itself could be removed by a racial and ethnocentric logic? For the time being, this seems the underlying logic determinate in defining who can be a "free mover" and who cannot. The strong suspicion is that the eastward expansion of Europe is being built with a racial logic, seeking to open borders to the East while closing them to the South.

This is politically functional, economically attractive, and a dynamic solution in the short term.

European enlargement and externalizing agreements have made it possible for Europe to look east. These same policies are being used to more effectively border and police borders in the South – reinforcing borders and, through neighborhood policies, enticing southern states in Africa and the Middle East financially and politically in order to implement more effective means of remote control. The payoff for a Europe, which is uneasy primarily about a neighboring Islamic South rather than a less familiar Balkan East, is clear. Most Poles, Romanians and Ukrainians are white and Christian; most Turks, Moroccans, Senegalese, or Somalians are not. But there is a sting in the tail of this logic: it will not solve the longer term demographic question. East Europeans have similarly low birthrates to their West European neighbors. The tension here between a porous East and a bordered South is thus likely to be a central defining feature of the ongoing regional integration being built through Enlargement. As always with the study of population movements, this dramatic macro-process can be very effectively viewed and humanly grasped through the micro-level experiences of the various migrants enacting these processes in Europe at the ground level.

PART III

European identity in context

8 Identification with Europe and politicization of the EU since the 1980s

HARTMUT KAELBLE

Since the 1980s, the European Union (EU) has undergone a process of profound politicization and a deliberate, though less striking process of de-politicization. These developments have left their mark on the identification of Europeans with Europe and the EU. This identification has some specific qualities: it is predominantly liberal; it attempts to encompass Europe's substantial internal diversities; it is based on common social and cultural rather than political experiences; and it is disappointingly weak in the view of some, surprisingly substantial in the view of others. These qualities, I argue, have much to do with the distinctive politicization the EU has experienced since the early 1980s. I start with a short outline of the history of the politicization and de-politicization of European affairs since the 1980s. In the second section I analyze changes in the identification with Europe under five separate headings. The final section develops my answer to the question of how politicization and identification with Europe have become deeply intertwined.[1]

---

[1] Research by historians on the politicization of the EU in the 1980s is lacking, and research on European identity is also scarce. The vast majority of books and articles on European identity are written by social scientists, lawyers, philosophers, or specialists on literature. A few have been written by historians such as Wlodzimierz Borodziej and Heinz Duchhardt (Borodziej *et al.* 2005), Federico Chabod (1995), Etienne François (2006), Robert Frank (2004), Ute Frevert (2003), René Girault (1993, 1994), Hartmut Kaelble (2001a, 2001b, 2002a, 2002b), Maria G. Melchionni (2001), Luisa Passerini (1998, 1999), Kiran Patel (2004), Wolfgang Schmale (2003), Alexander Schmidt-Gernig (1999), and Bo Stråth (2001, 2002). If they write on this topic at all, historians usually work on the history of the European idea rather than on identification with Europe. Major reasons are the strong traditional link of European historiography with national history, the lack of appropriate sources for the history of European identity beyond and below the elites, and sometimes the fear of being involved once again in the construction of an identity that might be misused by politicians – the fear of a new jingoism introduced purposefully or involuntarily by historians.

Politicization and de-politicization since the 1980s

Since the 1980s, the EU has experienced a period of politicization, as profound decisions affecting the character and future course of the EU became matters of public debate. Previously, there had existed a diffuse and largely uncontroversial general support for complicated expert decisions, for example on the creation of a common market, a common agricultural policy, and various European funds. After the mid-1980s, debates on Europe became more contentious, with increasingly clear contrasts between supporters and opponents of the European project. Besides Europe's economic integration, important new fields became part of a broadly based and widely debated process of Europeanization including labor markets, consumer and environmental protection, human rights, foreign workers, student exchange programs, university exams, drivers' licenses, identity cards, and border controls. In addition, various national referenda on new European treaties stirred at times intense political debates.

A crucial part of the politicization of identities was intellectuals' rediscovery of Europe as a topic for political analysis. In the mid-1980s, scholars such as Edgar Morin, Richard Löwenthal, Antony Giddens, Umberto Eco, Jürgen Habermas, and later Bronislaw Geremek and many others started to write and talk about the EU. This ended a long period of disinterest and disdain with which intellectuals, for the most part, had treated the area of the EU since the 1950s – as a small, purely economic, technocratic, culturally unattractive, and conservative project.

It is important to put this rediscovery of Europe in a larger historical context. Over the last two centuries, one can distinguish three periods of debate about Europe. After intensifying greatly during the Enlightenment, the debate declined during the rise of European nation-states and the building of European empires. It was reignited only at the end of the nineteenth century, provoked first by the rise of the US as the largest and most modern economy and society, and later by the deep economic and moral crisis Europe experienced during and after the two world wars. The discourse about Europe receded during the Cold War, as intellectual and political attention shifted to the "West," which included North America, divided Europe, and excluded Eastern Europe. Only in the 1980s did a new debate on Europe re-emerge. With the fall of the Soviet empire, the dissolution of the third world bloc, and the increase in the EU's power, intellectuals began to identify Europe as a major topic for political discussion rather than an esoteric occasion for the manifestos of small idealistic circles (Frank 1998; Girault 1994; Kaelble 2001a, 2002a; Osterhammel 1998; Pomian 1990).

These cycles of intellectual engagement differed in the eastern part of Europe during the nineteenth century and after 1945 (see Case in this volume). In the nineteenth century, the debate on European topics concentrated largely on common culture, values, economy, society, religion and the Church. Since Europe lacked a political center, the discourse skirted around common political issues. In contrast, starting in the early and mid-1980s, public debate began to recognize the EU as a centre of politics and to discuss common European political issues decided by European institutions.

In addition, since the mid-1980s a European public sphere has begun to distinguish itself (see Medrano in this volume). Based on a connected network of national rather than Europe-wide media, it is reflected in the simultaneous appearance of the same news in the media of different nation-states, presented from a European rather than a purely national perspective; in the growth of an expert public sphere particularly in political science, law, and economics; and in the rise of new European symbols, all based on a substantial increase in the knowledge of foreign languages (Eder and Spohn 2005; Risse 2002; Kaelble 2002b, 2007a; Kaelble *et al.* 2002; Machill *et al.* 2006; Medrano 2003 and in this volume; Meyer 2007). However, whether a European public sphere has emerged fully remains a point of considerable controversy among specialists.

Three major upheavals contributed to the politicization of the EU. First, since the mid-1980s the power of the EU has grown substantially, partly in response to Eurosclerosis in the early 1980s, partly due to the breakdown of the Soviet empire and the challenge that German unification posed for all European states. A series of agreements and treaties between 1986 and 2007 (the Single European Act, the treaties of Maastricht, Amsterdam and Nice, and finally the treaty of Lisbon) redesigned the EU. Expanding its competence well beyond the sphere of economics, the EU began to make decisions in external and internal security, social policy, migration and consumer policy, and cultural policy. As a consequence, it began to intervene in many ways in the daily lives of citizens, becoming the inevitable target of political criticism. Significantly, the expansion of its power occurred in a period of growing economic difficulties, increasing energy prices, rising unemployment, and spreading skepticism about the economic future of Europe. Hence, the EU could no longer profit indirectly from the exceptional economic boom of the postwar years (the "trente glorieuses"); instead, Europe's image suffered under the impact of these economic challenges, thus providing grounds for even further criticism.

The geographic expansion of the EU was a second factor contributing to its politicization. To be sure, important enlargements had occurred earlier. However, these remained within the borders of Western Europe, as set by the Cold War, and were not tied to dramatic institutional change. In contrast, the accessions prepared and decided since the early 1990s – by Europe's neutral states, by the Central European countries, and finally by Romania and Bulgaria, as well as ongoing negotiations regarding Turkish membership – had a different character. They raised fundamental questions concerning Europe's boundaries, and criteria for democratic governance had to be specified. Finally, in a time of economic difficulties and political volatility, the membership of poor Central and Eastern European countries with a strong need for subsidies and liberalization of migration policies were widely seen as posing serious economic and political challenges for national and European decision makers. The debate about the boundaries and the basic values of the EU further increased politicization.

A third factor was the American and East Asian waves of globalization that have reached Europe since the 1980s. In trade, capital investment, corporate ownership and management, migration, transport, communication, knowledge transfers, and culture and media, Europe became more closely linked to global markets. And while its lack of political and military power denied it superpower status, Europe's importance in world affairs increased visibly on questions of trade, capital flows, migration, human rights, and environmental issues. Europe was also on the receiving end of global changes. Immigration from the eastern and southern Mediterranean, sub-Saharan Africa, the Caribbean, India, and East Asia was beginning to lead to the establishment of new, permanent ethnic and religious minorities in Europe. Furthermore, awareness was spreading that the era of Western global superiority might be coming to an end, and that the rise of China and India signaled the arrival of new actors on the global scene who might well surpass Europe in the not-too-distant future. Although Europe often operates as a global actor, Europeans frequently saw it as a victim of globalization. On crucial issues of economic and social policy,

Europeans typically expected EU policy to be more effective than national policy. This, too, contributed to the politicization of the EU.

Politicization, to be sure, was accompanied at times by a policy of de-politicization, in line with national political experiences. At the level of the EU, specific institutions of de-politicized decision making existed or emerged in this period: the European Court in Luxembourg, which became a central enactor in European integration; the European Central Bank, which was established with the introduction of the euro currency; the European Court of Auditors; and various European agencies regulating different arenas of policy. The European Court of Justice and European Central Bank became totally autonomous from and unconstrained by the European Council and European Commission. In its design, the ECB followed very closely the model provided by the German Bundesbank – a case of voluntary de-politicization after the disastrous experience of totalitarian politicization during the Third Reich and uncontrolled inflation after military defeat.

The introduction of direct elections to the European Parliament in 1979 failed to enhance the political standing of that body and thus acted as a further de-politicizing factor in European politics. In contrast to national elections, elections to the European Parliament have not provided a genuine choice among competing programs and political teams that might sway the direction of the European Commission; instead, they have typically become a further electoral test of the political performance of national governments. As it turned out, European elections were not about Europe but were rather by-elections over national controversies. As a consequence, participation fell continuously in all EU member states except Denmark and Spain (Kaelble 2008).

Developments in European civil society also reinforced de-politicization. More than at the national level, European actors tend to organize unobtrusively, preferring telephone calls, petitions, personal encounters, expert statements, and discussions of white and green papers to public mobilization and strategies of politicization. In a word, to the extent that it has begun to emerge embryonically, European civil society is bypassing the public sphere and eschewing strategies of politicization.

Yet these factors working toward de-politicization were too weak to stop the politicization of the EU. The broadening and deepening of its political agenda over the last two decades has moved the EU quite a distance, from an administrative body to a political institution subject to genuine political debate.

Identification with the EU

The politicization of European affairs had a substantial effect on how Europeans have identified with Europe. Strength, unity, and clash are categories that do not capture European, national, or Western identifications. Identification did not become stronger; no single European identity emerged; and European identity did not begin to clash with that of other civilizations. Five possible changes in identification, spanning internal and external developments, command our attention.

A liberal identification with Europe

The era of Europe's politicization did not result in a weakening of liberal identification with Europe. Rather, a politicized debate over the character of Europe and the EU gave liberal identification with Europe a stronger political profile. Yet, we should readily acknowledge that a single European identity has never existed in Europe's past and did not emerge in the 1980s. Identification with Europe has always been a subject of dissent and debate, a choice among different options, a contest between or coexistence of different concepts, a history of varieties and multiplicities of identifications rather than the existence of one unchallenged, hegemonic idea of Europe.

A brief, cross-national glance at the history of identification with Europe reveals the existence of five different types of identification since the late eighteenth century.

First, identification with a superior Europe, more advanced than all other societies of the world and in all fields of human endeavor: economy, political institutions, warfare, technology, science, urban planning, education as well as the arts, lifestyle, and social organization. Europe was seen as the harbinger of progress for the world, sometimes linked to concepts of culture, at other times to concepts of race. This was the predominant identification of the nineteenth and early twentieth centuries. Some European critics, to be sure, regarded Europe's superiority as a disadvantage, a burden, even a menace for the non-European world. Tending to idealize the non-commercialized China, India, or Africa, they were in a clear minority. In recent decades the view of European superiority is the rarely articulated in public and exists for the most part only as a concealed or suppressed worldview.

A second identification is with European inferiority – cultural, economic, political, or moral – in the face of a threat posed by the outside world. It expresses the fear of decline and of Europe's colonization by others. Paradoxically, this identification with an inferior Europe has often elicited more passion than the identification with a superior Europe. It had already developed before World War I, became predominant in the interwar period, and only gradually weakened in the 1950s and 1960s. Although it declined in the 1980s, the sense of European inferiority did not fully disappear. The more recent widespread perception of the rise of Asia and the Islamic world has elicited once again this kind of identification.

A third identification focusses on Europe as part of the modernized world and as an actor in a mission of global modernization. Although non-European societies such as the US have played the leading role, Europe is an important, indeed indispensable, part of modernity. This identification was particularly common between the 1950s and 1970s and has become less compelling since the 1980s. A fourth identification with Europe sees it as one civilization among several others, endowed with both positive and negative traits, engaged in friendly competition with other non-European societies and civilizations, learning from others and exporting its own ideas and practices to other parts of the world, appreciative of immigration from other parts of the world as an enriching experience. This identification already existed in the nineteenth century. It became important only after the fall of the European overseas empires and after the early decades of the Cold War. Fifth and finally, there exists an inward-looking identification with Europe that focusses on Europe's internal diversity, as summarized in the formula "European unity in diversity."

In light of such a multitude of identifications with Europe during the last two centuries, it is far-fetched to assume that history has now run its full course, ending with the emergence of a single identification. The result of the history of the last several decades is the same as for the last several centuries: the persistence of various identifications that are primarily, though not exclusively, liberal, tolerant, and also cosmopolitan. With many gradations, three basic orientations toward Europe prevail: Europe as one civilization among others; Europe as marked by great internal variety; and Europe as an inferior victim exposed to the threats posed by a globalizing world.

Especially for liberals, during the recent era of Europe's and the EU's politicization, history has played an increasingly important role. From the liberal perspective, identification with Europe as it now exists stands as a refutation of a Europe occupied, exploited, and oppressed by a murderous Nazi regime in a disastrous war accompanied by unfathomable war crimes, and a Europe ravished by genocide and a Holocaust perpetrated by Nazi Germany. Liberals support the EU as a very different model, infinitely preferable to the Europe ruled by Nazi Germany (Giesen 1999; Eder and Giesen 2001). In addition, liberal views are informed by new post-colonial sensibilities and a renewed interest in the history of European colonial empires, in Europe's "mission civilisatrice" and Europe's carrying the "white man's burden," and in the history of the universalistic claim of European values that rings hollow when measured against the mostly deplorable conduct of European imperialists. Here too, liberal views are reinforced greatly by the European past as the political "other" that contemporary Europe has rejected.

At the same time, history also became an important source for a positive identification with Europe. Schuman, de Gasperi, Adenauer, and also Churchill were celebrated as Europe's mythical founding fathers after World War II. May 9 was introduced as the day of Europe, celebrating Robert Schuman's declaration in 1950, following Jean Monnet's design. Plans were launched for the eventual creation of European museums in Brussels and in Aix-la-Chapelle. The *comité de liaison*, a group of historians backed by the European Commission, was established in 1982. A network of historians of European identity was founded in 1989 by the late René Girault, thereafter directed by Robert Frank (Girault 1993, 1994; Frank 2004; cf. Loth *et al.*, in press). European history schoolbooks have been published (François 2007), as have numerous handbooks. After a decline of interest in European history in the 1960s and 1970s and a long period in which the subject was not attractive to historians, it has now returned as a widely appreciated topic in the 1990s, part of the liberal identifications with Europe.

Even though liberal identifications have predominated since the 1980s, one should not forget the other forces in this history of identification with Europe. A closer look reveals that important pioneers of the European unity movement did not wish to see a liberal, democratic Europe. For example, Coudenhove-Kalergie, usually considered one of the great visionaries of European unity, believed that unity could also be achieved in partnership with a dictator such as Mussolini, whom he greatly respected (Conze 2004). Usually regarded as an innovative period of European unity plans and movements, during the interwar period three important non-liberal trends of European identification were influential: the understanding of Europe developed first by Italian fascism and later by the German Nazi regime; the conservative Catholic and Protestant concept of the Occident, skeptical of mass democracy; and finally the concept of a superior European civilization that was frequently suffused by racial and racist concepts and, typically, firmly in opposition to the principles of liberal democracy (Conze 2005; Frevert 2003; Kaelble 2001a; Kletzin 2000; Laughland 1997; Li 2007; Loth 1995; Pagden 2002; du Réau 1996; Rößner 2007; Schmale 2003; Wilson *et al.* 1995; Case, this volume).

Hence, the long history of debate by Europeans does not lead in a straight line to the modern, liberal identification with Europe. That history serves as a useful reminder that new anti-democratic identifications with Europe may well emerge once again. Douglas Holmes (this volume) is thus correct to explore the renewed identification of right-wing extremists with Europe.

Identification with Europe's internal diversity

Identification with Europe's internal diversity is a second change directly linked to the politicization of the EU. Simply put, as the EU became a readily identifiable center of power, it also began to be viewed as a threat to European diversity of culture. Conservation of Europe's diversity in the arts, sciences, intellectual and political culture became an alternative source of identification with Europe. For this conception of identity, Europe's *unity in diversity* offers an attractive paradox. Here, identification is constituted at its core by the appreciation of differences among countries, regions, political orientations, and individuals. The interest in and tolerance of the different "other," and a culture of individualism of persons and collectivities, is seen as one of Europe's greatest achievements, worthy of full identification. Difference is seen as a humanitarian achievement and also as a major stimulant for economic and cultural innovation, as well as for effective democratic institutions.

This celebration of Europe's strength and its harbinger of modernity tends toward Euro-centrism. It typically presumes, quite erroneously, that in its internal differentiation Europe is unrivaled among the world's major civilizations. Since the 1980s, this identification has been quite common in the debates about Europe (Brague 1992; Castiglione and Bellamy 2003; Checkel 2007b; Delanty 1995; Frevert 2003; Habermas

2003; Kaelble 2001a, 2002a; Katzenstein 2006; Kohli 2000; Landfried 2005; MacDonald 2000; Mendras 1997; Müller 2007; Osterhammel 1998; Passerini 1998, 1999; Risse 2004; Stråth 2001; Shore 2000; Swedberg 1994). Edgar Morin called this the "dialogique," the fundamental inner logic of Europe based on the dialogue between diverging tendencies (Morin 1987, p. 128; see also Eisenstadt 2003). Stein Rokkan (1983; see also Flora 1999) built elaborate taxonomies around the construct of diversity. Many other social science approaches in more specific fields have followed Rokkan's lead, usefully summarized by Göran Therborn (1995). Some scholars go as far as to argue that each nation develops its own characteristic identification with Europe, based on its specific national experiences including perceptions of national security, national past and future, and basic national values. The identification with Europe's internal diversity and the European predilection for difference thus has become well established. As opinion polls show, European identities readily combine identification with country, region, or locale with an identification with Europe (Bruter 2005; Duchesne and Frognier 1995; Herrmann *et al.* 2004; Kohli 2000; Malmborg and Stråth 2002; Risse 2004). Identification with Europe's internal diversity is implicitly based on the reasonable assumption that Europeans normally prefer multiple identities.

The predilection for difference is even more important as it touches on the role of intellectuals. With the increase in EU power, especially since the late 1980s, a new, critical, engaged European intellectual has emerged who remains independent of Brussels. One important way of illustrating such intellectual autonomy is the sustained critique of the EU's homogenization of culture and lifestyles and the plea for the conservation or revitalization of differences in Europe. The concept is particularly attractive for social scientists with their well-established research methods, including the building of typologies, international comparison, and the study of flows, transfers and encounters. Identification with European diversity is thus a reaction to the rising and homogenizing power of the EU.

Does the identification with internal divergences indicate a more flexible European self-understanding, more easily integrating differences between East and West as well as North and South? Two observations suggest that this is not the case. First, even though internal differences were enormous, turning the observation of difference into identification with difference has not been a long-standing tradition in

European history. Instead, this kind of identification can primarily be found only since the 1980s. To be sure, appreciation of Europe's internal diversity has existed for a long time; but direct identification with internal differences emerged only when the EU became recognized as a powerful actor of homogenization; when European mental maps had to include once again, as before the Cold War, Eastern and South-Eastern Europe with their very different historical experiences; and when even the EU started to invest in liberal precepts extolling the virtues of productive competition among different European states.

Second, Europe's internal differences did not increase in the 1980s. In a longer historical perspective of the last two centuries, economic and political variation among European countries and regions increased until the middle of the twentieth century. This was followed, after the 1950s, by a period of distinct convergences, first within the western, then within the eastern part of Europe, and finally, after 1989, across the entire continent (Kaelble 2007b). Obviously, there is no direct parallel between changes in divergence and the identification with difference. On the contrary, there exists a paradoxical connexion between identification with European diversity and periods of convergence when internal divergences do not threaten unity. The identification with diversity in Europe depends on a very specific and possibly transient constellation of factors in recent history (see also Case in this volume). It may not last.[2]

Identification with European lifestyles and values

During the period of politicization of the EU, identification with European lifestyles and values increased, a lived and often unreflected identification with a way of life rather than a self-consciously adopted political program. This identification is rooted in consumption and consumer tastes, work and leisure, family life, and cities and landscapes,

---

[2] This argument should be explored further through a comparison of Europe with other civilizations that are marked by internal divergences and debates on internal difference – such as the United States, India, Africa, the Arab world, Latin America, and East and Southeast Asia. To be sure, there have been varying interpretations of such differences by central power holders, by spokespersons of the periphery, and by more recent research. In its political, social, cultural, and economic diversity, Europe is distinctive, not unique (Eisenstadt 2003, 2006; Katzenstein and Shiraishi 2006).

but also in values such as well-developed social security systems, secularization, human rights and tolerance, a strong role for intellectuals, civility, strict limitation on private and public violence (and hence opposition to the death penalty), equality between men and women, and universal education (Joas and Wiegandt 2005; Kaelble 2007b). This kind of identification prompted the late French historian René Girault to draw a distinction among the concepts of *Europe vécue* – the unconscious and implicit identification with common norms and lifestyles and established solidarities; *Europe pensée*, the debates on Europe; and *Europe voulue*, the creation of European institutions (Girault 1994).[3] Behind such categories looms the larger question of whether the identification with Europe was stimulated primarily by a convergence in Europe's social structures, lifestyles, and values, along with the intensifying transfers and interconnections between European societies; or by public debates in the media; or by the governance of the EU (see also Bach 2000; Münch 2001; Risse 2004).

An implicit identification with common European lifestyles and values does not necessarily signify a decline in the identification with national ones. To the contrary, the two might go together. Furthermore, identification with European values does not necessarily mean a rejection of non-European values.[4]

Lacking adequate empirical research on the identification with European diversity, we can only point to the most important trends that reinforce and undermine identification with European norms and lifestyles. First, since the 1950s and 1960s, European lifestyles have become increasingly internationalized. More consumer goods began to be imported from other European countries, more than from the US or East Asia. Hence, identification with hybrid European consumption tastes and patterns became easier. In addition, cross-border travel, study, marriage, work, and retirement have enormously enhanced direct,

---

[3] Along these lines, Luisa Passerini has explored with great imagination the European cultivation of love between women and men as an implicit European identity (1999).

[4] While it does not address the precise question posed, one of the few relevant empirical studies (Delhey 2004; see also Bach 2000) has established that Europeans' confidence in other European countries has increased somewhat during the last decades, especially for Northern European states with their remarkable record of economic prosperity and efficient public administration. Confidence in one's own country tends to correlate positively with confidence in other European countries.

personal experiences with the lifestyles of other European countries. Although such international exposure is not limited to Europe, it tends to take place mostly between European countries. Moreover, the identification with *Europe vécue* was reinforced by strong trends toward European social convergence in important fields such as work, health, migration, education, urban life, social welfare programs, and media, as well as by weakening divergence among states, transnational regions, and between East and West (Kaelble 2007b). Finally, the representation of other European countries has changed. The impact of the experience and memory of war and war propaganda has gradually eroded, allowing confidence in other European countries.

In contrast, two trends work in the opposite direction, undermining identification with European lifestyles and values: competition on the labor market, resulting in anxiety about job loss to immigrants from other European countries; and the dearth of institutions of European solidarity providing help among Europeans in times of personal crisis or disaster. In the absence of much needed empirical research, trends working in favor of identification with Europe appear to be stronger than those undercutting it.

A cautious and restrained identification with Europe?

Many scholars and public intellectuals argue that, compared to national identities, the identification with Europe is weak in its statistical, political, and symbolic impact. I shall first present the evidence in more detail, and, in the following section, cover the opposite, and to me more obvious argument.

In terms of statistics, only slightly more than half of Europeans identify with Europe and regard themselves as Europeans. In some European countries such as Britain, Sweden, Austria, and Hungary, only a minority does so. Furthermore, over the last three decades, opinion polls on the relative strength of national and European identities record no clear rise in the identification with Europe (Bruter 2005; Kohli 2000; Díez Medrano 2003).

In addition, political solidarity as a crucial indicator of identification remains underdeveloped across Europe. The charter of fundamental rights signed in the Treaty of Nice (2000) and later incorporated into the proposed European constitution addresses only citizen and human rights, without explicit reference to the duties and obligations of citizens

such as paying taxes and contributing to public social insurance programs –
not to speak of social or military service (Kohli 2000; Offe 2001).

Moreover, European symbols have remained far less potent than
national ones. To be sure, there have been efforts to create common
European symbols, particularly during two major periods since the end
of World War II. During the late 1940s and early 1950s, when a strong
European movement was active in the initial period of European integration, many European symbols were proposed: various designs of a
European flag (not only the flag eventually adopted by the Council of
Europe, but also an alternative design with a green E on a white back-
ground); postage stamps; historical places commemorating Europe, such
as Strasbourg; human rights charters; historical figures such as
Charlemagne, reinforced by the Charlemagne prize of Aix-la-Chapelle;
institutions for advanced education, such as the College of Europe in
Bruges; and rituals such as the lifting of border barriers by young
Europeans or the signing of international treaties by elder statesmen.
The 1980s and 1990s – that is, the era of politicization of the EU – also
witnessed numerous inventions of European symbols, often created by the
EU: a European anthem, a Europe day, a European flag, two European
charters of rights (1989, 2000), the Erasmus program, the buildings of the
European Parliament in Strasbourg and Brussels, and finally the euro
currency (Hedetoft 1998; Jones 2007; Kaelble 2003; Passerini 2003).

But only the European flag (blue with twelve golden stars), the Erasmus
program, and the EU currency (the euro) have fully succeeded. Relative to
national symbols, most other European ones have remained weak or
ambiguous. The European anthem and Europe Day[5] remain largely unob-
served and unknown. References to outstanding European historical
figures are infrequent. French and Germans successfully reinterpreted
Charlemagne as a European symbol after 1945; but he is not a figure of
common identity for British, Polish, Swedish, or Portuguese citizens. French
historian Jacques Le Goff disavows Charlemagne as a major European
symbol. For him, the origin of Europe lies in the European network of
intellectuals that emerged in the thirteenth and fourteenth centuries rather
than in Charlemagne's conquest of the Carolingian empire (Le Goff 2003).[6]

---

[5] In fact, there are two Europe Days, one created by the European Council (May 5),
one by the EU (May 9).
[6] Whether Robert Schuman or Winston Churchill played the crucial role
among the founding fathers remains disputed.

Further, a common European history, another symbol of European unity, remains to be written. European schoolbooks are the exception, not the rule (François 2007). Lacking are the typical ingredients of national history – a common war of independence, a common period of defeat and suffering, a common period of subsequent reaffirmation of the body politic, a history of common frontiers, and a common historical memory. To be sure, common European places and objects of memory (*lieux de mémoire*) can be traced, but they are much less evident than national ones (François 2006). Europe lacks a symbolic capital such as Paris or London. Brussels is an administrative center, but no capital with which to identify, for lack of what one would expect from a capital: a purposeful architectural ensemble of buildings for the European Parliament, the European Commission, and the European Council; a European museum, a European opera and theater, a European academy of sciences, a major European university, a European library, European monuments, and European street names.

One major factor accounting for variation in the identification with Europe has to do with the "other," which can be close or alien, amicable or inimical, helpful or menacing, linked to or separate from Europe. Each identification is probably rooted in opposition to one or several others. The loss of the United States as a conspicuously emphatic "other" after the fall of the Wall, and the loss of the Soviet Union/Russia as an alien and menacing "other" are major reasons for the recent weakness of the identification with Europe. During the Cold War, identification with Europe was undermined for a different reason, as Europe was encompassed by a broader Western or international communist identity.

Another explanation for the weakness of identification with Europe is its complex relationship with national identity. Some see a strong national identification as the main reason for a weak identification with Europe. Hence, the weak British identification with Europe has been attributed to the strong British national identity, based partly on the unique British role and success in defeating Nazi Germany. Discredited nations, such as Germany after World War II and Spain after Franco, are instead developing a strong identification with Europe. In a view that is now contested in the social sciences, this argument suggests that the relationship between the two forms of identification is mutually exclusive (Eisenstadt and Giesen 1995; Risse 2004).

A final explanation for weak identification with Europe is a relatively weakly developed European public sphere in which a European identity could be created, renegotiated, and reaffirmed. European media, intellectuals, films and bestseller lists, a European education system, political debates, competing politicians and political camps, and election campaigns with rival candidates are largely lacking. To be sure, while some indicators point to the rise of a European public sphere, it is both different from and reliant upon different national public spheres (Eder and Spohn 2005; Risse 2002; Kaelble 2002b; Díez Medrano 2003; Meyer 2007).

In sum, Europe is not a cultural nation (*Kulturnation*), which emerges before the establishment of a political nation (*Staatsnation*), as was true of historical developments in Italy, Germany, and Poland in the nineteenth and early twentieth centuries. Europe is not a demos in search of a state. Hence many social scientists and lawyers believe that the creation of European institutions without a European demos is not likely or even possible.

A distinctive identification with Europe

This discussion yields an obvious question: Is identification with Europe weak simply because it differs from what we know about national identities? European identifications, I argue here, are distinctive in the sense that all transnational identifications differ from national ones.

First, identification with Europe does not aim at being a primordial identification, as national identity does in purposefully seeking to displace regional and local identities. It is, instead, part of an ensemble of multiple identities. Hence, under normal circumstances, European and national identities should be complementary rather than competing.

Moreover, during the second half of the twentieth century, identification with Europe has included a very special relationship to violence and war. Learning from the two world wars, identification with Europe usually meant avoiding conflict and violence against ethnic or religious groups in Europe, rather than glorifying a war of independence as in many European nations and former colonies. European identity, today, is not grounded in violence, war, and death.

Furthermore, identification with Europe was clearly influenced by the attempt to overcome Europe's colonial past and colonial hierarchies both outside and inside Europe. Hence, EU membership on relatively equal terms between large and small member states, rather than a hierarchy of power, is constitutive of Europe's identity and crucial for the identification with Europe. The more small states joined the EU, the less the identification with Europe could be centered solely on large countries. In addition, identification with Europe typically does not stand for identification with a model for the rest of the world, as national identity often does.

Finally, the relationship between trust and identification with institutions at the European level is also distinctive. At least in recent years, trust in and expectations of specific policies of the EU have been stronger than overall identification with the EU. These specific policies are above all foreign policy, defense policy, environmental policy, and the fight against organized crime and terrorism; they have been much weaker on questions of education, health, housing, and pensions. According to Eurobarometer polls, and with unavoidable variations among states, in these policy fields Europeans trust the EU more than they do their national governments in these fields (DGPC Division of the EU: Eurobarometer 2004, pp. 59–94; see also Eisenstadt 2006, pp. 223–49). The share of Europeans who expect positive actions from the EU is higher than those who identify with it. Even in countries with particularly weak identifications with Europe, such as Sweden or Austria, a majority of the citizens favor a European foreign and defense policy. Though more refined historical research is needed, one can conclude with some confidence that, viewed against the historical experiences of the nineteenth and twentieth centuries, the rise in Europeans' trust in the EU as an international political body is a new and noteworthy development. Identification with the EU might be weak. Trust in the EU is not.

In addition, an important upheaval took place in the relationship between EU citizens and political decision makers during the 1980s. European citizens' identification with the EU started to matter politically as the EU initiated policies to create or reinforce loyalty to the EU. This policy consisted of the creation of European symbols mentioned above; developing an EU social policy and thus establishing the image of a social Europe; strengthening the human rights jurisdiction with the European Court in Luxembourg; developing policies in favor of enhancing European mobility by abolishing passport controls and the emergence of European-wide networks as in the Erasmus and European research programs; and strengthening cross-border exchanges and communications by enforcing cost reductions for international remittances and telephone calls, and by abolishing the costs of doing business with multiple currencies in a common market through the creation of a common currency (Eder and Giesen 2001; Hedetoft 1998; Kaelble 2002a; Kohli 2000). The EU policy had an unintended consequence: To the extent that the French referendum of 2005 was more than a plebiscite on the performance of an inept French president, the failure of the first European constitution illustrated that the average European favored a Europe different from that of the elites. The "Non" vote showed that Europeans took Europe and European affairs seriously, and that they identified with the EU. The average French citizen did not opt out of the European project, but while voting "Non" had a different project in mind. That vote was identification by voice rather than exit (Medrano, this volume).

The history of identification with Europe follows a model in which public institutions precede identification, rather than the other way around as in the evolution from *Kulturnation* to *Staatsnation* – from demos to state. This model occurs frequently in the European history of "state-nations" – in France, Britain, Spain, Portugal, Switzerland, the Netherlands, Sweden, and Denmark. Analogously, the identification with Europe was emerging in the framework of an international institution, the EU – which was first created by an international elite and only several decades later became the object of trust, confidence, and incipient identification by European citizens.

Conclusion

I have argued here that the politicization of the EU was not just a typical process as experienced by many other countries throughout modern history. Quite to the contrary, this politicization had peculiar characteristics that need to be considered. It was induced by intellectuals, journalists, experts, and national politicians rather than by European political parties or interest groups. Media, rather than the European Parliament or the European Council, provided the platform. Despite this, the EU's media policy has remained surprisingly restrained and cautious, with no attempt being made to control the existing media or to create new media supervised by the EU. The EU's major response to this politicization has been a persistent effort to create bonds of loyalty among European citizens and the EU through a plethora of symbolic, social, economic, and constitutional policies.

Moreover, the EU chose a policy of controlled politicization, inviting experts to hearings, conferences, and reports much more frequently than national administrations did, and experimenting with a process of preparation of major decisions by green and white books. The EU also adopted a policy of de-politicization, through the creation of institutions such as the European Central Bank, the European Court in Luxembourg, and the European Court of Auditors. Elections for the European Parliament and the activities of European civil society also remained outside the politicization process.

Finally, the process of politicization happened in specific circumstances: the breakdown of the Soviet empire; an expansion of the power of the EU, to a substantial degree caused by German unification; globalization and the gradual dissolution of the Third World; and a weakening of the political assumption of the superiority of the Western model of capitalist development. Politicization was not triggered, as in many national cases in the past, by an authoritarian regime, dictatorship, colonial rule, or a menacing foreign power.

Politicization has had a strong impact on identification with the EU since the 1980s. It explains why public debate about identification with Europe and the EU has became more vivid and at the same time more diverse and controversial. With the re-establishment of democracy after World War II, identification with a democratic Europe was bolstered by the contrast of a Europe run by Nazi Germany. More recently, politicization supported the predominance of liberal identifications with the EU at a moment of triumph for Western democracy, while communism fell. In recent years, that liberal vision has been encountering opposition from a New Right, with its own views on Europe.

Under these specific circumstances, identification with Europe has often been grounded in a profound appreciation of Europe's distinctive internal diversity. Politicization triggered by internal dictatorship or external threat would have led to different, more homogenous representations of Europe. The widespread preference for internal diversity was caused by politicized disputes over the homogenizing effects of EU policies, and, paradoxically, by the recent convergence of European societies, occurring at times quite independently of the policies pursued by the European Commission.

Politicization also led to more intensive reflection and public debate on common European values and lifestyles touching on issues of societal security; opposition to violence, both private (ownership of weapons) and state (death penalty and war); the role of religious values in the context of Europe's multiple secularisms; protection of the environment; strict separation of work and non-work; family intimacy; equality of men and women; and a specific European consumption style, shaped by specific European design and use of consumption for the creation of social distinctions. As a consequence, identification with the EU remained restrained and cautious in part because Europe was spared a major external threat or attack.

Politicization of the EU also helped to reinforce identification with Europe. It clarified for European citizens that the power of the EU was substantially enlarged. Hence, identification with the EU became based on substantial trust and high expectations for the decisions of this more powerful institution in specific policy arenas such as foreign affairs, international and internal security, unemployment, and the environment. At the same time, politicization was reflected in growing tensions between elite and mass public concepts of Europe, illustrated by national referenda on the European constitution. Politicization led to an identification with the EU that was grounded at least in part in controversy at the very time that weak identification increased, non-reflexively. Since the early 1980s, politicization and identification have been constant themes in European history. The past is once again becoming prologue.

9 Conclusion – European identity in context

PETER J. KATZENSTEIN AND
JEFFREY T. CHECKEL

Europe's identities, this book argues, exist in the plural. There is no one European identity, just as there is no one Europe. These identities can be conceived as both social process and political project. Understood as process, identities flow through multiple networks and create new patterns of identification. Viewed as project, the construction of identities is the task of elites and entrepreneurs, operating in Brussels or various national settings.

Process and project involve publics and elites; they are shaped by and shape states; they are open-ended and have no preordained outcomes; and they serve both worthy and nefarious political objectives. Bureaucrats crafting a Europe centered on Brussels, xenophobic nationalists, cosmopolitan Europeanists, anti-globalization Euro-skeptics, and a European public that for decades has been permissive of the evolution of a European polity – they are all politically involved in the construction of an evolving European identity.

Following the 2004 and 2007 enlargements, a politically cohesive Western Europe centered on the European Union (EU) is receding, while a politically looser and more encompassing Europe is rising. Europe is no longer what it was during the Cold War, an integral part of an anti-communist alliance. In the wake of 9/11, for many in Western Europe, Europe now represents an alternative to American unilateralism and militarism. For Central and Eastern European states seeking to build their own democratic and capitalist futures, Europe has become both a place of return and an inescapable destination. Globalization and the Single Market, a common foreign and security policy, and the threat of a virulent Islam are central to Europe's future – refracted through prisms provided by multiple intersections of different senses of belonging.

Where that sense of belonging is reacting to threats or challenges posed by others – Islamic fundamentalism, US unilateralism, East Asian competition – it often reveals a Europe that is perceived as a community of shared values. Threats and fears are powerful identity mechanisms. Threats make us choose sides. And threats are egalitarian. The politics of threat and fear are one kind of European identity politics.

Where that sense of belonging is challenged to create something on its own – in the EU's constitutional process or in choosing between the continent's secular and religious heritages – Europe often reveals itself to be a community of strangers. As a political project, European identity is an important concern for political, economic and academic elites and parts of the middle class, who are drawn to a European construct as complementing the primacy of national identity. Yet, at the level of mass society, "European" often means little else than the geographic expansion of a specific national identity – a supranational nationalism – onto European beaches and into European soccer arenas.

This variation reflects the reality of contemporary Europe, where debates over the EU and its constitutionalization increasingly intersect with other arenas of identity construction such as professional networks, transnational religion, everyday individual practices, social movement politics, and party competition.

In this closing chapter, we begin by summarizing our main findings on the construction of identity in today's Europe. A second section places these findings in a broader global context. We then return for a more detailed look at European identities, arguing that while they are distinctive, the dynamics creating them are in no sense unique or *sui generis*.

Identities in the new Europe

In its empirical chapters, this book has looked to domains of identity construction found in discourses, institutions, daily practice, and the cultural substrates of societies that interact with European politics, broadly understood as developments affecting both state and society. We thus shift the analysis of identity partially away from the EU and its institutions.

While the old EU with its fifteen member states clearly incorporated a great deal of variety, the enlargements of 2004/2007 are nonetheless creating a Union that differs greatly from its smaller predecessors. It is true that Western Europe will now act as an even stronger agent of modernization for Eastern Europe. But it is a fundamental mistake to see the EU's new Eastern members as little more than vessels capturing the political visions, programs, and policies of its old Western members. The new members have their own visions, programs, and policies grounded in a history that points to persistent differences in experiences and memories (Case, this volume). For years to come, the contested politics of European identity will have the potential to spill into many different policy domains.

East and West, new and old will have to forge new political bonds, requiring considerable adjustment of the old West and, very likely, dramatic change in Brussels. Students of the EU and of European identity must come to grips with the reality that Enlargement has fundamentally altered their core units of analysis. Before the late 1990s that unit was *secular* identities, illustrated by the work of normative theorists like Jürgen Habermas (Castiglione, this volume) or empirical findings on the role EU institutions play in creating new (secular) senses of belonging in Europe (Herrmann *et al.* 2004; Bruter 2005; Hooghe 2005; Beyers 2005; Zürn and Checkel 2005).

Yet, in the form of Polish Catholicism, the 2004 Enlargement reintroduced religion into Europe. Put bluntly, although Poland itself is divided on the issue of religion, the Polish Church and its powerful political allies are seeking to re-Christianize a godless Europe lost in the grip of secularism. Since 1945, West European Christian Democracy has been supportive of the European integration movement. But its vision was never as bold as that of Polish Catholicism. Furthermore, orthodox Christianity is now an official part of the EU as well. As a result, *confessional* identities are interacting with secular ones in ways that are utterly novel (Byrnes and Katzenstein 2006). This dynamic was illustrated clearly by the row that broke out in 2003–2005 over whether the (secular) EU constitution should contain a reference to Europe's Christian heritage. And it is rehearsed daily by political conflicts over the manifold and complicated relations between Europe and Islam.

What have we learned?[1] The history of nation-states or state-nations does not provide useful material for analyzing the emergence of a collective European identity. European identity politics are not like those in a cultural nation, where processes of cultural assimilation precede political unification (Kaelble, this volume). The number of unambiguously committed Europeans (10–15% of the total population) is simply too small for the emergence of a strong cultural

---

[1] We thank Neil Fligstein for discussion on these points.

European sense of belonging. The number of committed nationalists (40–50% of the total) is also too small for a hegemonic reassertion of nationalist sentiments. The remaining part of the population (35–40% of the total) holds to primarily national identifications that also permit an element of European identification.

But neither do European identity politics resemble that of a state-nation, where the process of political unification precedes cultural assimilation. Over a period of centuries, state-building European elites did their best to minimize or suppress ethnic, linguistic, religious, and regional differences. Collective national identities that complemented and eventually supplanted these alternative identities centered around common institutions such as schools, the army, or the Church, and were forged across alliances that connected economically privileged groups with economically disadvantaged ones.

This book suggests that European identities are supported by factors too weak or inchoate to replicate processes of nation-state identity formation. Instead of one strong European identity, we encounter a multiplicity of European identities. As Europe's market integration has accelerated, multiple factors are fragmenting the very possibility of a collective European identity. The chapters analyze the proponents and opponents of Europe, capturing both their identity projects and the variety of identity processes of which they are a part.

The proponents are many and varied, including West Europeans (Case, Castiglione, and Kaelble), EU and national elites (Díez Medrano, Favell, Fligstein), middle- and upper-middle-class business elites (Fligstein), and young Eurostar migrants (Favell). These agents favor a rational, technocratic Europe, marked by tolerance of the Enlightenment and rational discourse (Castiglione, Díez Medrano, Kaelble). Opponents are from lower strata, those with less education, the losers in the integration process (Holmes, Fligstein, Favell), and those favoring various national identity projects that are threatened by migration streams from east to west and south to north (Case, Holmes, Favell, Kaelble). Instead of technocracy, the opponents favor a more authentic national or post-national identity. Authenticity means a return – to national values and national culture – and less disruption by international competition and transnational movements (Holmes). Their vision is a Europe in which the national community is primary and non-nationals or religious others are marginalized. And opponents feel excluded from what they regard as a dominant, liberal, and exclusionary vision (Case, Kaelble).

Advances in European integration during the last two decades have created the winners of integration, who are available for a certain kind of European identity. At the same time, the building of Europe by stealth through de-politicization – relying on the courts and the European Central Bank, the creation of a united currency zone, the establishment of the Schengen area, and the process of Enlargement – has increased opposition everywhere. The chapters by Holmes, Díez Medrano, and Favell suggest that de-politicization has been followed by a re-politicization, especially of identity and of a quite different kind.

When we view identity in Europe as process, there is again no unified storyline. On the one hand, as Neil Fligstein documents in his chapter, the EU's internal market has created growing transnational networks of like-minded elites who are comfortable viewing themselves as European. While their absolute numbers are small, this is indisputably a key arena and social process of identity construction. Driven initially by a simple market logic, repeated contact has led a number of these individuals to report a sense of community that, analytically, goes beyond a simple calculus of economic self interest and, geographically, spans national borders.

On the other hand, that same market-opening logic has stimulated other social processes that seemingly undercut those outlined by Fligstein. Especially after the 2004 and 2007 enlargements, the influx into West Europe of migrants from the East, who are both "European" (they are, after all, EU nationals) *and* foreign, has unleashed a new and increasingly politicized set of identity dynamics. Are these individuals – be they Poles in France, Czechs in London or Romanians in Italy – migrants or Europeans? Is their movement strengthening or undermining more encompassing senses of community in Europe (Favell, this volume)? Even in the case of intra-West European migration – Favell's "Eurostars" – we see processes of identity construction that do less for the creation of prototypical European citizens than for the reinforcement of national senses of belonging.

The findings we sketch here have clear implications for how to study identity in Europe. It is no longer sufficient to explore EU institutions and their effects on identity in isolation from broader social and political processes; nor is it sufficient to examine nationalist movements as if they exist separate from European institutions. Rather, the challenge is to connect these disparate political phenomena through research that crosses disciplinary boundaries. As Holmes, Fligstein, Favell, and others in this volume demonstrate, the payoff of such boundary crossing is high, giving us a more complete picture of the politics of European identity construction.

The return of Eastern Europe to the European identity mix, as Case argues in her chapter, has additional implications for research practice. Datasets need to be extended to the East (Díez Medrano, this volume). More important, our capacity for political analysis needs to improve through a more intimate knowledge of East European politics. And the historical experiences and memories of political actors in the East must be given their proper due. As Shmuel Eisenstadt (2002) reminds us, in a world of multiple modernities, modernization and political change are dialectical, not unilinear. Religious fundamentalism is a modern form of politics that is contesting different forms of secularism; and anti-European backlash is a modern form of oppositional politics that resists Europeanization. Given these facts, it is highly unlikely that the EU will operate as some great modernization machine, streamlining its new East European members to fit a West European mold.

Identities in comparative perspective

Europe is one among several civilizational polities, including the United States, China, Japan, India, and Islam (Katzenstein 2007). The civilizational label became increasingly frequent in the mid-eighteenth century, as talk of Latin Christendom declined. Civilizations operate at the broadest level of cultural identity. Not fixed in time or space, civilizational ideas and identities are multiple. Because civilizations are culturally integrated, they can assume a reified form when encountering other civilizations. And because they are differentiated, civilizational ideas and identities transplant selectively. The practices of civilizational polities and the peoples they rule lead to processes such as Americanization, Sinicization, Japanization, and Europeanization. It is these polities and their characteristic processes and practices that allow us to place European identities in a broader comparative setting.[2]

Civilizational identities are often shaped by and reflected in institutionalized memories – 150 years of national humiliation for China, the

---

[2] Because the EU is *sui generis* in its institutional structure, focussing only on political institutions at the regional level makes it much more difficult to create a comparative context (Katzenstein 2005).

civil war and the global fight for rights for the United States, World Wars I and II and the Holocaust for Europe, for example. But acts of remembrance are myriad and occur in innumerable frames. Even though polities and states, through education and other means, seek to regulate memory, there is no unity in memory. Official acts of remembrance thus are only one part of the politics of collective memory. "There is no chorus of memory," writes Yale historian Jay Winter (2007, p. 3); "instead there is a party line, and then a host of other stories not easily combined." Civilizational memories are a cacophony.

Greece as the foundation of European civilization is a perfect example. Widely regarded by Greeks and Europeans alike as Europe's foundational civilization, its history tells a very different story. Greek civilization was not foundational in the sense of having existed apart from the influence of Africa, Egypt, and the eastern Mediterranean, to which it was linked intimately. Athena was most likely neither black (Bernal 1987) nor white (Slack 2006), but brown. Greece as the civilizational foundation of a Europe set apart from Islam is also difficult to comprehend – in light of the country's incorporation into the Ottoman empire for half a millennium.

Analogously, the notion of a China or Japan as largely closed off from the rest of the world remains one of the staples of Chinese and Japanese self-understanding, despite massive evidence to the contrary (Hansen 2000; Hamashita 2008). And in the case of America, conflicting notions of secularism and religion, non-intervention and imperial expansion create multiple political traditions that remain deeply contested (Smith 1993; Mead 2002).

In the face of civilizational hybridities, memories and myths clash within civilizations in a kaleidoscope of different political colorations and in the cacophony of multiple voices. There is in fact nothing unusual in the European story when it is compared to that of Asia and the Americas.

Asia

Like Europe, Asia's collective identities are distinctive. These identities are multiple, contested, and complementary, rather than a substitute for typically stronger national, subnational, and local identities. And they operate in an area with a very different setup of regional institutions from that of Europe (Katzenstein 2005, pp. 60–75). While Europe looks back at half a century of institutionalizing the growth of a European polity, the most characteristic institution in East and Southeast Asia at the regional level has been the market, specifically production alliances between different firms increasingly centered around China, heavily concentrated in electronics, and fully linked to global markets.

In comparison to Europe, the civilizational content of identities in Asia is less significant than the fact that political leaders invoke universal, regional, and local referents, sidestepping specific cultural features in the interest of instrumental political purposes (Katzenstein 2005, pp. 76–81). The political temptation of invoking unified and essentialized conceptions of the Occident, or West, is in Asia as appealing as the urge of European politicians to invoke the East, or Orient, as a differentiating myth. Such cognitive and symbolic political moves are designed to impose clear boundaries where none exist, on one Eurasian landmass, a handful of civilizations, and scores of nations and states. Singapore is a case in point of how the construction of civilizational identities in Asia, as in America and in Europe, is highly variable and deeply contested (Katzenstein 2005, pp. 78–9).

Singaporean identity was crafted deliberately as an act of state creation, championing Asian civilizational values. Such an abstract and embracing ideological construct has the enormous political advantage of sidestepping all of the racial and cultural specificities that divide Singapore's Chinese, Malay, and Indian populations. In the 1970s, Singapore funded identity entrepreneurs employed in government-run think tanks to develop a legitimacy-enhancing state ideology. Eventually, in the 1980s and 1990s, that state ideology radiated outward into Asia and from there to Washington, DC. The abstractness of the category of Asian values leaves open which values are to be furthered, and thus the extent to which Asian and Western values disagree or clash. The incontrovertible truth is that Singapore offered other Asian polities a dramatic, early illustration that modernization without Westernization was indeed a viable path for Asian societies.

This dramatic modernization notwithstanding, the Asian past throws a long and dark shadow over its future. For the last two decades, and with increasing intensity in recent years, Japan's unwillingness to atone for past transgressions toward its neighbors has become a seemingly insurmountable obstacle for the evolution of a politically relevant sense of Asian civilizational identity. Old wounds simply have not been permitted to heal (Katzenstein 2005, pp. 86–8). For numerous reasons,

Japan has been unable to atone for the horrors of the Pacific War in a way that is acceptable to its neighbors: continuity in political leadership before and after 1945; a centralized education system run by a conservative bureaucracy in the Ministry of Education; the gradual ascendance of the views of that bureaucracy over those of the left-wing Japan Teachers' Union; the rise of a new nationalist movement that Prime Ministers Koizumi and Abe courted in the early years of the new millennium; and, more recently, resentment and envy over China's growing importance in East Asian and world affairs and anger and nervousness about North Korea's nuclear policy (Katzenstein 2008).

The Americas

Identity formation in the Americas is shaped by a history that is very different from those of Europe and Asia (Katzenstein 2005, pp. 226–31). While the political salience of the United States for Europe and Asia assumed enormous importance only after World War II, this has been a long enduring feature for Latin America. Indeed, it dates back to the Latin American independence movements in the early nineteenth century and the Monroe Doctrine of 1823. The essential purpose of the inter-American system was anti-European. The goal was to keep the leading European powers at bay – Spain and Britain in the nineteenth century; imperial Germany, Nazi Germany, and the Soviet Union during the twentieth century. It was thus only natural that the other states in the Americas looked to Europe, and especially to the Iberian peninsula, as a natural balancer to pervasive American influence.

The proliferation of regional institutions in the Americas is primarily focussed on market integration. This is not to say that Latin American institutions have the political character of Europe's emerging polity. Rather, in contrast to Europe, they are often working at cross-purposes. Because of the dual role played by the United States – as both a regional and a global power – Latin American states seek to build and undermine regional institutions at one and the same time. In contrast to the evolving European polity, during the second half of the twentieth century, the Inter-American system remained a bargaining relationship between conflicting and often vitally important state interests.

The shadow that the US throws over the Americas is exceptionally long because, in contrast to Europe and Asia, it plays the parts of both the regionally dominant state and a world power. This makes the politics of civilizational identities in the Americas complex and contested. In contrast to Asia, the Americas feature many multilateral institutions. And in sharp contrast to Europe, the US is deeply involved in the regional architecture of the Americas. Multilateral institutions are not merely ways of solving collective action problems. They are also central sites for rivalry and competition between Latin and Central American states and the US. Patron–client relations and coercive diplomacy are hallmarks of intra-American political relations for which one finds Asian analogues, but for which European analogues exist after 1945 only in exceptional circumstances.

The emergence of the Americas as a distinctive Western hemisphere – warmly welcomed as such inside, and grudgingly recognized outside of the region – occurred in the first three decades of the nineteenth century. Only by the 1880s, however, did Pan-Americanism gain some momentum. Within the latter, anti-Americanism became one form of collective identity uniting Latin America (Sweig 2006). In Asia and Europe, in comparison to Latin America, regional variations in anti-American sentiments are stronger – for example, between East and West Europe, and between East, Southeast and South Asia. But as is true of Europe and Asia, anti-American sentiments in the Americas are cyclical. The visits of Presidents Nixon in 1958 and Bush in 2006 were high points of anti-Americanism. In the intervening decades, these sentiments, though not absent, were much less intensely felt throughout the region.

Compared to the southern hemisphere of the Americas, the civilizational identities of North America are even less developed. Canada's and Mexico's history and relations with the US differ greatly, and Canadian and Mexican anti-Americanisms are considerably weaker than in Latin America. James Bennett (2004) argues that North America is deeply divided between the American-Canadian Anglosphere and Mexico. This view is mistaken, as it overlooks the internal split of Canada and the vitality and growth of the Hispanic strand in the repertoire of United States identities. It is, however, correct in pointing to the existence of no more than a thin veneer of a civilizational identity that, while perhaps comparable to Asia's, is arguably lagging behind Europe's.

Anti-Americanism in North America is more muted than in the South (Bow *et al.* 2007). This is aptly illustrated by the case of Canada, where Anglophone and Francophone varieties of anti-Americanism differ considerably. Each has had its distinctive roots and historical trajectory.

The Anglophone Canadian, in the words of historian Frank Underhill, is "the first anti-American ... the ideal anti-American as he exists in the mind of God" (quoted in Hillmer 2006, p. 63). If there is a common theme in this ideal anti-Americanism, it rests in what Freud called the narcissism of small differences to foster group cohesion and a positive self-image. Not being American is one of the few readily available markers of Canadian identity. When mixed with a dose of resentment and fear, as has occasionally been the case, Anglophone anti-Americanism can be of considerable political importance, as it was at the outset of the twentieth century, the early 1960s, and the late 1980s. More typical, however, is the muting of anti-Americanism by extensive and direct personal contacts with America and Americans.

In contrast, Francophone anti-Americanism has nearly always been a non-issue for the simple reason that the politically relevant and resented "other" has been Anglophone Canada. America by way of contrast has normally been admired and, with the exception of its militarist tendencies, the United States is often viewed as a potential ally in the enduring struggle that pits Francophone against Anglophone Canada.

European identities

The historical evolution of Europe and its contested identities is marked neither by total rupture nor by unending sameness. Instead, that evolution is a blending of old and new elements, along a road that has many novel twists and turns even though its general direction is quite familiar. During the last four decades, how old and new Europe combine has been a source of deep interest – and not only to the editors and authors of *Dædalus* (1964, 1979a, 1979b, 1997). And what is true of scholars is true of politicians. They, too, are engaged in the never-ending redefinition of what it means to be a European, and what Europe stands for. If there is something noteworthy about these identity dynamics today, it is their politicization at the intersection of globalization – in the form, for example, of migrants or foreign cultural values – and Europeanization – in the form of an expanded European Union searching for legitimacy. They are no longer a purely national affair, if in fact they ever were (Case, Kaelble, this volume).

Europeans have been preoccupied with the many dramatic changes that have transformed their regional politics in the aftermath of the Cold War. They are too ready to assume that there is something very special and unique about a Europe that stands simultaneously for both a contested idea and a unifying metaphor (Delanty 1995). Yet, as the preceding section demonstrates, there is nothing unusual in thinking of a region – Europe, in this case – as a self-conscious idea, encountering others, and as an unthought metaphor for self-interpretation. In meeting other civilizational discourses and actors, Europe can look like an active partner, even a fortress. And in encountering its own conflicts and contradictions, Europe can look like a maze. This is not particularly remarkable, and certainly not unique.

This book's core claims thus do not traffic in European exceptionalism or uniqueness. Depending on the political context, Asia and the Americas also resemble fortresses and mazes. As is true of Asia and the Americas, Europe has its own distinctive set of often conflicting and sometimes converging identities that help shape European politics. Remarkably, Europe has evolved from a would-be to an actual polity (Lindberg and Scheingold 1970a; Olsen 2007). This polity links states that are pooling some of their sovereignty, and it fosters novel ties across national borders between different segments of Europe's different civil societies.

With Europe lacking internal characteristics that can generate a strong sense of collective self, one source of its identity lies in its relations with other international actors (Neumann and Welsh 1991; Neumann 1996, 1999; Meyer 2004, pp. 120–65). In the past, Europe's "other" has traditionally been located to the east and taken on either religious or civilizational forms. Historically, both Turkey and Russia have imposed on Latin Christendom a degree of coherence that would otherwise have been lacking (Nexon 2006). Represented by the Holy Roman Empire of the German Nation, most Europeans may not have known who they were and with which Europe to identify. But they did know who they were not and with whom not to identify – the Ottoman and Muscovite empires to the east. However loosely coupled civilizational empires may be internally, they do manage to identify themselves at their fuzzy borders where they encounter the "other" (Case, this volume). Europe's relations with Turkey and Russia (Morozov 2007) remain today deeply contested. During the Cold War, anti-communism had similar, perhaps more powerful effects, since the Iron Curtain between East and West was so unambiguous.

Many Europeans continue to have a difficult time acknowledging what is now increasingly recognized – multiculturalism is not a passing phase, but a new chapter in Europe's evolution. Multiculturalism in an era of radicalized Islam has, since 9/11, given a new political urgency to this question and to conflicts over European identities – in Britain, France, Spain, the Netherlands and Germany, and throughout Europe more generally. Apart from the political fissures in the Turkish and Muslim communities, numerous conflicts pit political forces preferring Europe's distinctive Christian or secular legacies, on the one hand, against coalitions that regard the move to a new form of multicultural-ism as both inevitable and, in the light of Europe's deep and long-standing entanglement with the Islamic world, desirable.

European identities also crystallize in relation to America. European anti-Americanism has a long pedigree, especially in France. America has always been both a dream and a nightmare, especially for Europe's cultural and political elites, as Hannah Arendt (1994) observed half a century ago. After the 9/11 attacks, *Le Monde* famously exclaimed that "we are all Americans now." However, since the summer of 2002 and the American choice to wage war against Iraq without UN support, anti-Americanism has once again become a political force affecting all European states, those opposing and those supporting the Bush adminis-tration. Anti-war and anti-American demonstrations staged on February 15, 2003 drew some of the largest crowds ever recorded in European capitals. This is not the first time there has been a strong anti-American shift in European sentiments. The late 1960s movement against the war in Vietnam, and the early 1980s peace movement, are useful reminders that anti-Americanism is a cyclical rather than a secular political phenomenon (Katzenstein and Keohane 2007; Markovits 2007).

Europeans are coming to terms with a sense of self that exhibits a broader range of identities and values than Europe was willing or able to accommodate in the past. The definition of a European self in relation to the other, be it to its east or to its west, is comparable to demarcating the European self of today from the Europe of the past. In the views of an overwhelming majority of Europeans, today's Europe is much pre-ferable to the dark continent of war, repression, and genocide of a couple of generations ago (Mazower 1998, pp. 138–81). Submerging the memory of Auschwitz in a liberal, modernizing European project that readily accepts the soft dimensions of power and post-national identities is an opportunity that many Europeans have come to embrace, often with considerable eagerness. Viewing Auschwitz in a broader, non-European perspective, as the European manifestation of genocidal warfare that European imperialists practiced with great eagerness on a global scale, is not as readily acknowledged. The universal significance of Europe's global mission, however, is associated not only with the European Enlightenment but also with the dark sides of European imperialism. This, too, is a Europe from which many Europeans seek to distance themselves.

European ambivalence – between pro- and anti-Americanism, between pro- and anti-Islamic sentiments, between old national and new supranational allegiances, and between the fearsome European past of the 1930s and 1940s and the peaceful and prosperous Europe of today – is captured well by Castiglione and Bellamy when they write, with specific reference to the EU, "most people believe it to be useful without feeling deeply attached to it" (Castiglione and Bellamy 2003, p. 21).

European identities today thus remain plastic and open to multiple interpretations. They are neither defined primordially from within, nor simply imposed politically from without. They emerge instead from the confluence and blending of a variety of projects and processes. With some justification, John Meyer (2000, p. 3) concludes that "the exact definition of Europe and its people is uncertain, variable, and for most participants unknown."

Identity matters

Nothing in this book or concluding chapter should be read as a claim that identity does not matter. It matters crucially, both to the future of the European project centered on the EU, and to a set of identity processes and European politics more generally. After all, if identity has played a key role at many points in Europe's luminous and dark pasts (Nexon 2006), why should that role diminish now?

Rather, our concern has been to argue that developments in contemporary Europe require a different kind of scholarship on identity. Both disciplinary and epistemological boundary lines should be questioned – and crossed. European identity construction is occurring at the multiple intersections of elite projects and social processes; at both supranational and national-regional levels; within EU institutions but also outside them, in daily practice and lived experience; driven by the economic logic of an aging continent that needs migrants but simultaneously fears them.

If our hunch and analytic direction in this book are correct, then the coming years will see students of European identity elaborating contingent, multi-causal frameworks that connect the national and the supranational, that integrate variables or mechanisms across the social sciences, and that view epistemological differences as an opportunity for learning rather than barriers to be reified (Katzenstein and Sil 2005; Johnson 2006; Lebow and Lichbach 2007). Empirically grounded, middle-range theory (Glaser and Strauss 1967) appears more apposite to the task at hand than overly ambitious and universalizing models of politics.

At the same time, our arguments about identity should not be read as saying that anything goes or that everything matters.[3] Statements of this sort say everything – and thus nothing. On the contrary, the anthropological explorations of Holmes; the sociological investigations of Favell, Fligstein, and Díez Medrano; the historical analyses of Case and Kaelble; and the normative problematization of Castiglione are models of analytic rigor. However, it is a rigor more concerned with explicating identity dynamics than with fitting them into preconceived theoretical frameworks.

Capturing such dynamics results in an argument about identity that resembles a rich tapestry more than a tight framework. There may be a time and place for parsimonious, deductive reasoning on identity (Laitin 1998); but post-Cold War, enlarged, quasi-constitutionalized Europe is neither that time nor that place (Hopf 2002). Students, scholars and policy makers are better served by nuanced, cross-disciplinary inquiries and arguments that more closely approximate the multiple worlds Europeans experience on a daily basis.

---

[3] We thank Adrian Favell for pushing us to elaborate our thinking on these points.

Bibliography

Adamic, Louis. 1941. *Two-Way Passage*. 1st ed. New York: Harper & Brothers.
Adevărul Cluj. 1995. (July 21): 1, 4.
Adler, Emanuel. 2002. "Constructivism and International Relations," in Walter Carlsnaes, Thomas Risse, and Beth Simmons (eds.), *Handbook of International Relations*. London: Sage Publications.
   and Michael Barnett, eds. 1998. *Security Communities*. New York: Cambridge University Press.
Amato, Joseph. 1975. *Mounier and Maritain: A French Catholic Understanding of the Modern World*. Birmingham, AL: University of Alabama Press.
Andall, Jacqueline. 1998. "Catholic and State Constructions of Domestic Workers: The Case of Cape Verdean Women in Rome in the 1970s," in Koser and Lutz (eds.), *The New Migration in Europe*, pp. 124–42.
Anderson, Benedict. 1983. *Imagined Communities*. London: Verso.
   1991. *Imagined Communities*. London: Verso.
Anderson, Christopher. 2006. "Workshop Memo." Prepared for a Workshop on "European Identities: Between Cosmopolitanism and Localism." Ithaca, NY: Cornell University (20–21 October).
Appiah, Kwame Anthony. 2005. *The Ethics of Identity*. Princeton, NJ: Princeton University Press.
Arendt, Hannah. 1994. "Dream and Nightmare," in Hannah Arendt (ed.), *Essays in Understanding 1930–1954*. New York: Harcourt, Brace, pp. 409–17.
Aron, Raymond. 1974. "Is Multinational Citizenship Possible?" *Social Research* 41(4): 638–56.
Aughey, Arthur. 2007. *The Politics of Englishness*. Manchester and New York: Manchester University Press.
Bach, Maurizio, ed. 2000. *Die Europäisierung nationaler Gesellschaften*. Sonderheft 40, Kölner Zeitschrift für Soziologie.
Bade, Klaus. 2000. *Europa in Bewegung: Migration vom späten 18. Jahrhundert bis zur Gegenwart*. Munich: C. H. Beck Verlag.
Bakunin, Mikhail Aleksandrovich. 1971. *Bakunin on Anarchy; Selected Works by the Activist-Founder of World Anarchism*. 1st ed. New York: Vintage Books.

Balibar, Etienne. 2004. *We, the People of Europe? Reflections on Transnational Citizenship*. Princeton, NJ and Oxford: Princeton University Press.

Banks, Marcus and André Gingrich. 2006. "Introduction: Neo-nationalism in Europe and Beyond," in André Gingrich and Marcus Banks (eds.), *Neo-nationalism in Europe and Beyond: Perspectives from Social Anthropology*. Oxford: Berghahn Books, pp. 1–26.

Barber, Benjamin. 1984. *Strong Democracy, Participatory Politics for a New Age*. Berkeley: University of California Press.

Barth, Fredrik. 1969. *Ethnic Groups and Boundaries*. Long Grove, IL: Waveland Press.

Batalova, Jeanne and B. Lindsay Lowell. 2006. "'The Best and the Brightest': Immigrant Professionals in the US," in Smith and Favell (eds.), *The Human Face of Global Mobility*, pp. 81–102.

Bauman, Zygmunt. 1998. *Globalization: The Human Consequences*. Cambridge: Polity Press.

Baun, Michael. 1996. *The New European Union*. New York: Harper.

Beiler, Markus, Corinna Fischer, and Marcel Machill. 2006. "The Debate about the European Public Sphere: A Meta-Analysis of Media Content Analyses." *European Journal of Communication* 21(1): 57–88.

Bellamy, Richard and Dario Castiglione. 1998. "Between Cosmopolis and Community: Three Models of Rights and Democracy within the European Union," in Daniele Archibugi, David Held, and Martin Köhler (eds.), *Re-Imagining Political Community: Studies in Cosmopolitan Democracy*. Cambridge: Polity Press, pp. 152–78.

2003. "Legitimising the Euro-'polity' and its 'Regime': The Normative Turn in European Studies." *European Journal of Political Theory* 2(1): 1–34.

2004. "Lacroix's European Constitutional Patriotism: A Response." *Political Studies* 52(1): 187–93.

2008. "Beyond Community and Rights: European Citizenship and the Virtues of Participation," in Per Mouritsen and Knud-Erik Jørgensen (eds.), *Constituting Communities*. Basingstoke: Palgrave, pp. 162–86.

Benhabib, Seyla. 1992. *Situating the Self*. Cambridge: Polity Press.

2004. *The Rights of Others: Aliens, Residents, and Citizens*. Cambridge: Cambridge University Press.

Bennett, James C. 2004. *The Anglosphere Challenge: Why the English-speaking Nations Will Lead the Way in the Twenty-First Century*. Lanham, MD: Rowman & Littlefield.

Benton, Gregor and Frank Pieke, eds. 1998. *The Chinese in Europe*. London: Macmillan.

Berezin, Mabel. 2006a. "Appropriating the 'No': The French National Front, the Vote on the Constitution, and the 'New' April 21." *PS: Political Science and Politics* 39 (April): 269–72.

2006b. "Great Expectations: Reflections on Identity and the European Monetary Union," in Robert Fishman and Anthony Messina (eds.), *The Year of the Euro: The Cultural, Social and Political Import of Europe's Single Currency.* South Bend, IN: University of Notre Dame Press.

2007. "Revisiting the French Front National: The Ontology of a Political Mood." Special Issue: Racist and Far Right Groups. *Journal of Contemporary Ethnography* 36(2): 129–46.

In press. *Illiberal Politics in Neoliberal Times: Security, Democracy, and Populism in the New Europe.* Cambridge: Cambridge University Press.

and Juan Díez Medrano. Forthcoming. "Distance Matters: Place, Political Legitimacy, and Popular Support for European Integration." *Comparative European Politics.*

and Martin Schain, eds. 2003. *Europe without Borders: Remapping Territory, Citizenship, and Identity in a Transnational Age.* Baltimore, MD: The Johns Hopkins University Press.

Berindei, Dan. 1991. *Românii Şi Europa : Istorie, Societate, Cultură.* Bucharest: Ed. Museion.

Berlin, Isaiah. 1976. *Vico and Herder: Two Studies in the History of Ideas.* London: Hogarth Press.

1979. *Against the Current: Essays in the History of Ideas.* London: Hogarth Press.

1990. "Joseph de Maistre and the Origins of Fascism I–III." *New York Review of Books*, September 27, October 11, October 25.

1997. *The Crooked Timber of Humanity*, ed. Henry Hardy, Princeton, NJ: Princeton University Press.

Bernal, Martin. 1987. *Black Athena: The Afro-Asiatic Roots of Classical Civilization.* New Brunswick, NJ: Rutgers University Press.

Betz, Hans-Georg. 2002. "Contre la mondialisation: xénophobie, politiques identitaires et populisme d'exclusion en europe occidentale." *Politique et Sociétés* 21(2): 9–28.

Beyers, Jan. 2005. "Multiple Embeddedness and Socialization in Europe: The Case of Council Officials." *International Organization* 59(4): 899–936.

Blair, Tony. 2006. "Our Nation's Future: Multiculturalism and Integration." Speech delivered to the Runnymede Trust, Downing Street, December 8, 2006. www.number10.gov.uk/output/Page 10563.asp.

"Books." *New Europe* (Nov. 1941): 336.

Borneman, John and Nick Fowler. 1997. "Europeanization." *Annual Reviews of Anthropology* 26: 487–514.

Borodziej, Wlodzimierz, Heinz Duchhardt, Małgorzata Morawiec, and Ignác Romsics, eds. 2005. *Option Europa. Deutsche, polnische und ungarische Europapläne des 19. und (frühen) 20. Jahrhunderts.* 3 vols. Göttingen: Vandenhoeck & Ruprecht.

Börzel, Tanja. 2002. *States and Regions in the European Union: Institutional Adaptation in Germany and Spain.* Cambridge: Cambridge University Press.

Bousetta, Hassan. 2000. "Political Dynamics in the City. Citizenship, Ethnic Mobilisation and Socio-Political Participation: Four Case Studies," in Sophie Body-Gendrot and Marco Martiniello (eds.), *Minorities in European Cities: The Dynamics of Social Integration and Social Exclusion at the Neighbourhood Level.* London: Macmillan.

Bow, Brian, Peter J. Katzenstein, and Arturo Santa-Cruz. 2007. "Anti-Americanism in North America: Canada and Mexico." Paper presented at the International Studies Association Annual Convention, Chicago (February 28–March 3).

Bowen, John R. 2007. *Why the French Don't Like Headscarves: Islam, the State, and Public Space.* Princeton, NJ: Princeton University Press.

Boyer, Dominic. 2005. *Spirit and System: Media, Intellectuals, and the Dialectic in Modern German Culture.* Chicago: University of Chicago Press.

Brague, Rémi. 1992. *Europe, la voie romaine.* Paris: Criterion.

Brenner, Robert. 1989. "Economic Backwardness in Eastern Europe in Light of Developments in the West," in Daniel Chirot (ed.), *The Origins of Backwardness in Eastern Europe: Economics & Politics from the Middle Ages until the Early Twentieth Century.* Berkeley and Los Angeles: University of California Press, pp. 15–52.

Breuilly, John. 1993. *Nationalism and the State.* Chicago: University of Chicago Press.

Brewer, Michael B. 1993. "Social Identity, Distinctiveness, and In-Group Homogeneity." *Social Cognition* 11: 150–64.

1999. "Multiple Identities and Identity Transition." *International Journal of Intercultural Relations* 23: 187–97.

and William Gardner. 1996. "Who Is We?: Levels of Collective Identity and Self Representation." *Journal of Personality and Social Psychology* 71: 83–93.

Brubaker, Rogers. 1992. *Citizenship and Nationhood in France and Germany.* Cambridge: Cambridge University Press.

1996. *Nationalism Reframed: Nationhood and the National Question in the New Europe.* Cambridge: Cambridge University Press.

and Frederick Cooper. 2000. "Beyond Identity." *Theory and Society* 29: 1–47.

Bruter, Michael. 2005. *Citizens of Europe? The Emergence of a Mass European Identity*. London: Palgrave Macmillan.

Budge, Ian, Hans-Dieter Klingemann, Andrea Volkens, Judith Bara, and Eric Tanenbaum. 2001. *Mapping Policy Preferences*. Oxford: Oxford University Press.

Bureau of Public Secrets. "May 1968 Graffiti," www.bopsecrets.org/CF/graffiti.htm. Accessed March 14, 2007.

Burke, Edmund. 1993 [1790]. *Reflections on Revolution in France*. Oxford: Oxford University Press.

Byrnes, Timothy A. 2001. *Transnational Catholicism in Postcommunist Europe*. Lanham, MD: Rowman & Littlefield.

2006. "Workshop Memo." Prepared for a Workshop on "European Identities: Between Cosmopolitanism and Localism." Ithaca, NY: Cornell University (20–21 October).

and Peter J. Katzenstein, eds. 2006. *Religion in an Expanding Europe*. Cambridge: Cambridge University Press.

Calhoun, Craig. 2003. "The Democratic Integration of Europe: Interests, Identity, and the Public Sphere," in Berezin and Schain (eds.), *Europe without Borders*, pp. 243–76.

California University Committee on International Relations. 1939. *Foreign Policies of the Great Powers*. Berkeley: University of California Press.

Caporaso, James. 1971. "Fisher's Test of Deutsch's Sociocausal Paradigm of Political Integration: A Research Note." *International Organization* 25: 120–31.

and Min-hyung Kim. 2007. "The Dual Nature of European Identity: Subjective Awareness and Coherence." Unpublished Mimeo. Seattle: Department of Political Science, University of Washington (December 7).

Maria Green Cowles, and Thomas Risse, eds. 2001. *Transforming Europe: Europeanization and Domestic Change*. Ithaca, NY: Cornell University Press.

Case, Holly. Forthcoming. *Between States: The Transylvanian Question and the European Idea during WWII*. Stanford, CA: Stanford University Press.

Castiglione, Dario. 2004. "Reflections on Europe's Constitutional Future." *Constellations* 11(3): 393–411.

and Richard Bellamy. 2003. "Legitimizing the Euro-'polity' and its 'Regime': The Normative Turn in EU studies." *European Journal of Political Theory* 2: 7–34.

and Justus Schönlau. 2006. "Constitutional Politics," in Knud-Erik Jørgensen, Mark Pollack and Ben Rosamund (eds.), *Handbook of European Union Politics*. London: Sage, pp. 283–300.

Justus Schönlau, Chris Longman, Emanuela Lombardo, Nieves Pérez-Solórzano Borragán, and Miriam Aziz. 2007. *Constitutional Politics in the EU: The Convention Moment and its Aftermath*. Basingstoke: Palgrave.

Castles, Stephen and Mark Miller. 2003. *The Age of Migration: International Population Movements in the Modern World*. 3rd ed. London: Palgrave Macmillan.

Cederman, Lars-Erik, ed. 2001. *Constructing Europe's Identity: The External Dimension*. Boulder, CO: Lynne Rienner.

Cerutti, Furio. 2006. "Constitution and Political Identity in Europe," in Ulrike Liebert, Josef Falke, and Andreas Maurer (eds.), *Postnational Constitutionalisation in the New Europe*. Baden-Baden: Nomos.

Chabod, Federico. 1995. *Idea di Europa e politica dell'equilibrio*. Bologna: Mulino.

Checkel, Jeffrey T. 2005. "International Institutions and Socialization in Europe: Introduction and Framework." *International Organization 59*: 801–26.

2007a. "Constructivism and EU Politics," in Knud-Erik Jørgensen, Mark Pollack, and Ben Rosamond (eds.), *Handbook of European Union Politics*. London: Sage Publications.

ed. 2007b. *International Institutions and Socialization in Europe*. New York: Cambridge University Press.

Churchill, Winston. 1995. "The Sinews of Peace," in Mark A. Kishlansky (ed.), *Sources of World History*. New York: HarperCollins, pp. 298–302. www. historyguide.org/europe/churchill.html. Accessed March 16, 2007.

Cicero. 1999. *On the Laws, in On the Commonwealth and On the Laws*, ed. James E. G. Zetzel, Cambridge: Cambridge University Press.

"Civilian Resistance in Czechoslovakia," section on "Graffiti," www.fragments web.org/TXT2/czechotx.html. Accessed March 14, 2007.

Cobb, Roger W. and Charles Elder. 1970. *International Community: A Regional and Global Study*. New York: Holt, Rinehart and Winston.

Colley, Linda. 1992. *Britons: Forging the Nation 1707–1837*. New Haven, CT: Yale University Press.

Conze, Vanessa. 2004. *Richard Coudenhove-Kalergi. Umstrittnere Visonär Europas*. Zürich: Muster-Schmidt.

2005. *Das Europa der Deutschen. Ideen von Europa in Deutschland zwischen Reichstradition und Westorientierung (1920–1970)*. Munich: Oldenbourg.

Coudenhove-Kalergi, Richard Nicolaus. 1926. *Pan-Europe*. New York: A. A. Knopf.

Council of Europe, Parliamentary Assembly. 1997. *Voices of Europe: A Selection of Speeches Delivered before the Parliamentary Assembly of the Council of Europe, 1949–96*. Strasbourg: Council of Europe Publications.

Cowan, Jane. 2003a. "Who's Afraid of Violent Language? Honour, Sovereignty and Claims-making in the League of Nations." Special Issue on "Violence and Language," *Anthropological Theory* 33: 271–91.

2003b. "The Uncertain Political Limits of Cultural Claims: Minority Rights Politics in Southeast Europe," in Richard A. Wilson and Jon P. Mitchell (eds.), *Human Rights in Global Perspective: Anthropological Studies of Rights, Claims and Entitlements*. London and New York: Routledge, pp. 140–62.

2006a. "Culture and Rights after Culture and Rights." *American Anthropologist* 108(1): 9–24.

2007a. "The Success of Failure? Minority Supervision at the League of Nations," in Marie-Bénédicte Dembour and Tobias Kelly (eds.), *Paths to International Justice*. Cambridge: Cambridge University Press.

2007b. "The Supervised State." *Identities: Global Studies in Culture and Power* 14(5).

Crozier, Michel. 1973. *Stalled Society*. New York: Viking.

Curran, James. 1991. "Mass Media and Democracy," in James Curran and Michael Gurevitch (eds.), *Mass Media and Society*. London: Edward Arnold.

Dædalus. 1964. "A New Europe? A Timely Appraisal." 95(1).

1979a. "Looking for Europe." 108(1).

1979b. "Old Faiths and New Doubts: The European Predicament." 108(2).

1997. "A New Europe for the Old?" 126(3).

de Gaulle, Charles and French Embassy, Press and Information Division. 1965. *Major Addresses, Statements and Press Conferences of General Charles De Gaulle*. New York: French Embassy.

de Puy, Henry W., ed. 1852. *Kossuth and his Generals: With a Brief History of Hungary; Select Speeches of Kossuth, etc.* Buffalo, NY: Phinney & Co.

de Wilde, Pieter. 2007. "Politicisation of European Integration: Bringing the Process into Focus." Paper presented at the ARENA Research Seminar. Oslo: Arena Centre for European Studies, University of Oslo (October 2).

Declaration of the Rights of Man, Approved by the National Assembly of France, August 26, 1789. www.yale.edu/lawweb/avalon/rightsof.htm. Accessed September 7, 2007.

Deflem, Michael and Frederick Pampel. 1996. "The Myth of Post National Identity: Popular Support for European Unification." *Social Forces* 75: 119–43.

Delanty, Gerard. 1995. *Inventing Europe: Idea, Identity, Reality*. New York: St. Martin's Press.

Delhey, Jan. 2004. "Nationales und transnationales Vertrauen in der Europäischen Union." *Leviathan* 32: 15–45.

Demaris, Alfred. 1992. *Logit modeling: Practical Applications*. Newbury Park: Sage Publications.

Dereje, Cornelia. F., Cathleen Kantner, and Hans-Jörg Trenz. 2003. "The Quality Press and European Integration. European Public Communication between Consonances and Dissonances." Paper presented at the International Conference "Europeanisation of Public Spheres? Political Mobilisation, Public Communication, and the European Union," Wissenschaftszentrum Berlin für Sozialforschung (WZB), June 20–22, 2003.

Deutsch, Karl W. 1953. *Nationalism and Social Communication.* Cambridge: Technology Press, and New York: Wiley.

1969. *Nationalism and its Alternatives.* New York: Knopf.

Lewis J. Edinger, Roy C. Macridis, and Richard L. Merritt. 1957. *Political Community and the North Atlantic Area.* Princeton, NJ: Princeton University Press.

1967. *France, Germany, and the Western Alliance: A Study of Elite Attitudes on European Integration and World Politics.* New York: Scribner.

Diamond, Jared. 1997. *Guns and Germs and Steel: The Fates of Human Societies.* New York: W.W. Norton & Co.

Díaz Nosty, Bernardo. 1997. *Comunicación Social. Tendencias/1997.* Madrid: Fundesco.

Díez Medrano, Juan. 2001. "Die Qualitätspresse und die europäische Integration," *Forschungsjournal Neue Soziale Bewegungen* 15: 30–41.

2003. *Framing Europe. Attitudes to European Integration in Germany, Spain, and the United Kingdom.* Princeton, NJ: Princeton University Press.

and Paula Gutierrez. 2001. "Nested Identities: National and European Identity in Spain." *Ethnic and Racial Studies* 24(5): 753–78.

Diken, Bülent. 1998. *Strangers, Ambivalence and Social Theory.* Aldershot: Ashgate.

Dinan, Desmond. 2002. *Ever Closer Union.* London: Palgrave Macmillan.

Directorate General Press and Communication Division of the European Union. 2004. Eurobarometer: Public Opinion in the European Union, No. 61. Brussels: The European Union.

Downs, Anthony. 1957. *An Economic Theory of Democracy.* New York: Harper and Row.

du Réau, Elisabeth. 1996. *Europe au XXe siècle. Des mythes aux réalités.* Brussels: Editions Complexe.

Duchesne, Sophie and Andre-Paul Frognier. 1995. "Is there a European Identity?" in Oskar Niedermeyer and Richard Sinnott (eds.), *Public Opinion and International Governance.* New York: Oxford University Press.

Eder, Klaus. 1999. "Integration durch Kultur? Das Paradox der Suche nach einer europäischen Identität," in Reinhold Viehoff and Rien T. Segers (eds.), *Kultur, Identität, Europa.* Frankfurt-am-Main: Suhrkamp, pp. 147–80.

and Bernhard Giesen. 2001. *European Citizenship. Between National Legacies and Postnational Projects.* Oxford: Oxford University Press.

and Cathleen Kantner. 2000. "Transnationale Resonanzstrukturen in Europa. Eine Kritik der Rede vom Öffentlichkeitsdefizit," in M. Bach (ed.), *Die Europäisierung nationaler Gesellschaften.* Sonderheft 40, Kölner Zeitschrift für Soziologie und Sozialpsychologie. Wiesbaden: Westdeutscher Verlag, pp. 306–31.

and Willfried Spohn (eds.). 2005. *Collective Memory and European Identity. The Effects of Integration and Enlargement.* Aldershot: Ashgate.

Eichenberg, Richard and Russell Dalton. 1993. "Europeans and the European Community: The Dynamics of Public Support for European Integration." *International Organization* 47: 507–34.

Eisenstadt, Shmuel N. 2002. "Multiple Modernities." *Dædalus* 129(1): 1–29.

2003. *Comparative Civilizations and Multiple Modernities,* 2 vols. Leiden: Brill.

2006. *Theorie und Moderne. Soziologische Essays.* Wiesbaden: Verlag für Sozialwissenschaften.

and Bernhard Giesen. 1995. "The Construction of Collective Identities." *European Journal of Sociology* 36: 72–102.

Ellenzék. 1941. (Dec. 6): 1–2.

Engels, Frederick. 1973. "Democratic Pan-Slavism," in Karl Marx and David Fernbach, *Political Writings.* London: Allen Lane/New Left Review.

Erickson, Jennifer. 2007. "Market Imperative Meets Normative Power: Human Rights and European Arms-Transfer Policy." Paper presented at the Sixth Pan-European International Relations Conference, Turin (September).

Eriksen, Erik Oddvar. 2006. "The EU – A Cosmopolitan Polity?" *Journal of European Public Policy* 13(2): 252–69.

Esping-Andersen, Gösta. 1999. *The Social Foundations of Post-Industrial Society.* Oxford: Oxford University Press.

Esterházy, Péter. 2005. "How Big is the European Dwarf?" in Daniel Levy, Max Pensky, and John Torpey (eds.), *Old Europe, New Europe, Core Europe: Transatlantic Relations after the Iraq War.* London and New York: Verso.

European Citizenship Action Service. 2005. *Who's Afraid of EU Enlargement?* Brussels: ECAS.

2006. *Who's Still Afraid of EU Enlargement?* Brussels: ECAS.

European Foundation for the Improvement of Living and Working Conditions. 2006. *Mobility in Europe: Analysis of the 2005*

Eurobarometer Survey on Geographical and Labour Market Mobility. Dublin.

European Year of Workers' Mobility. 2006. *Europeans and Mobility: First Results of an EU-wide Survey.* Brussels: European Commission.

Favell, Adrian. 2001. "Integration Policy and Integration Research in Western Europe: A Review and Critique," in Alex Aleinikoff and Doug Klusmeyer (eds.), *Citizenship Today: Global Perspectives and Practices.* Washington, DC: Brookings Institute, pp. 349–99.

  2003a. "Games without Frontiers? Questioning the Transnational Social Power of Migrants in Europe." *Archives Européennes de Sociologie* 44(3): 106–36.

  2003b. "Integration Nations: The Nation-State and Research on Immigrants in Western Europe." *Comparative Social Research* 22 (Nov.): 13–42.

  2005. "Review Article: Europe's Identity Problem." *West European Politics* 28(5): 1109–16.

  2008a. *Eurostars and Eurocities: Free Movement and Mobility in an Integrating Europe.* Oxford: Blackwell.

  2008b. "The New Face of East–West Migration in Europe." *Journal of Ethnic Migration Studies* 34(5): 701–16.

  and Randall Hansen. 2002. "Markets against Politics: Migration, EU Enlargement and the Idea of Europe." *Journal of Ethnic and Migration Studies* 28(4): 581–601.

  and Tim Elrick, eds. 2008. "The New Face of East–West Migration in Europe." Special edition of *Journal of Ethnic and Migration Studies* 34(5).

Featherstone, Kevin. 1999. *Socialist Parties and European Integration.* New York: St. Martin's Press.

Ferguson, James. 1990. *The Anti-Politics Machine: "Development," Depoliticization, and Bureaucratic Power in Lesotho.* Cambridge: Cambridge University Press.

Firat, Bilge. 2007. "Negotiating Europe/Avrupa: Turkish Europeanization and the Cultures of Lobbying in Brussels." Doctoral Research Prospectus. Department of Anthropology, State University of New York at Binghamton.

Fisher, William E. 1969. "An Analysis of the Deutsch Sociocausal Paradigm of Political Integration." *International Organization* 23: 254–90.

Fligstein, Neil. 2008a. *Euroclash: The EU, European Identity, and the Future of Europe.* Oxford: Oxford University Press.

  2008b. *Limits of Europeanization.* Oxford: Oxford University Press.

  Wayne Sandholtz, and Alec Stone Sweet, eds. 2001. *The Institutionalization of Europe.* Oxford: Oxford University Press.

Flora, Peter, ed. 1999. *State Formation; Nation-Building and Mass Politics in Europe. The Theory of Stein Rokkan.* Oxford: Oxford University Press.

Fogarty, Michael P. 1957. *Christian Democracy in Western Europe 1820–1953*. Notre Dame, IN: University of Notre Dame Press.

Fossum, John Erik and Agustin Menendez. 2005. "The Constitution's Gift? A Deliberative Democratic Analysis of Constitution-making in the European Union." Working Paper 13/2005. Oslo: Arena Centre for European Studies, University of Oslo (March 14).

François, Etienne. 2006. "Europäische lieux de mémoire," in Gunilla Budde, Sebastian Conrad, and Oliver Janz (eds.), *Transnationale Geschichte*. Göttingen: Vanden hoeck & Ruprecht, pp. 290–303.

   2007. "Le manuel franco-allemand d'histoire: une entreprise ineditée." *Vingtième Siècle. Revue d'histoire* no. 94 (April).

Frank, Robert. 1998. "Les contretemps de l'aventure européenne." *Vingtième Siècle*, no. 60 (Oct.–Dec.).

   ed. 2004. *Les identités européennes au XXe siècle*. Paris: Publications de la Sorbonne.

   In press. In Loth *et al.* (eds.), *Experiencing Europe*.

Fraser, Nancy. 1997. *Justice Interruptus: Critical Reflections on the "Post-Socialist" Condition*. New York: Routledge.

Frevert, Ute. 2003. *Eurovisionen. Ansichten guter Europäer im 19. und 20. Jahrhundert*, Frankfurt: Fischer (to be published in English).

Gabel, Matthew J. 1998. *Interests and Integration*. Ann Arbor: University of Michigan Press.

Gaillard-Starzmann, Gerald. 2006. "Regarding the Front National," in André Gingrich and Marcus Banks (eds.), *Neo-nationalism in Europe and Beyond: Perspectives from Social Anthropology*. Oxford: Berghahn Books, pp. 177–96.

Gal, Susan 2007. "Circulation in the 'New' Economy: Clasps and Copies." Paper presented at the 106th Meeting of the American Anthropological Association, Washington, DC, November 29–December 2, 2007.

Gellner, Ernest. 1983. *Nations and Nationalism*. Ithaca, NY: Cornell University Press.

Genov, G.P. *et al.* 1941a. *Vsebŭlgarski sŭyuz "Otets Paisiĭ": urediavane idei, tseli, zadachi, zhivot, deĭnost, postizhenia*. Sofia: n.p.

   1941b. *Rukhna poslednata postroĭka na vesaĭlskata sistema*. Sofia: Vsebŭlgarski sŭyuz "Otets Paisiĭ."

Gerhards, Jürgen. 1993. "Westeuropäische Integration und die Schwierigkeiten der Entstehung einer europäischen Öffentlichkeit." *Zeitschrift für Soziologie* 22: 96–110.

   2000. "Europäisierung von Ökonomie und Politik und die Trägheit der Entstehung einer europäischen Öffentlichkeit," in Maurizio Bach (ed.), *Sonderheft 40 der Kölner Zeitschrift für Soziologie und Sozialpsychologie:*

Die Europäisierung nationaler Gesellschaften. Opladen: Westdeutscher Verlag, pp. 277–305.

Giesen, Bernhard. 1999. "Europa als Konstruktion der Intellektuellen," in Reinhold Viehoff and Rien T. Segers (eds.), *Kultur, Identität, Europa. Über die Schwierigkeiten und Möglichkeiten einer Konstruktion.* Frankfurt: Suhrkamp, pp. 130–46.

——— 2003. "Generation und Trauma," in J. Reulecke (ed.), *Generationalität und Lebensgeschichte im 20 Jahrhundert.* Munich: Oldenbourg, pp. 59–71.

Girault, René, ed. 1993. *Les Europe des européens.* Paris: Publications de la Sorbonne.

——— ed. 1994. *Identité et conscience européenne au XXe siècle.* Paris: Hachette.

Glaser, Barney G. and Anselm L. Strauss. 1967. *The Discovery of Grounded Theory: Strategies for Qualitative Research.* New York: Aldine de Gruyter.

Goulard, Sylvie. 2002. "Frankreich und Europa: die Kluft zwischen Politik und Gesellschaft," in M. Meimeth and J. Schild (eds.), *Die Zukunft von Nationalstaaten in der europäischen Integration: Deutsche und französischen Perspektiven.* Opladen: Leske & Budrich, pp. 85–96.

Granville, Johanna. 2004. *The First Domino: International Decision Making during the Hungarian Crisis of 1956.* College Station: Texas A&M University Press.

Grass, Günter and Krishna Winston. 2002. *Crabwalk* [Im Krebsgang]. 1st ed. Orlando, FL: Harcourt.

Grasseni, Cristina. 2003. *Lo Sguardo della Mano: Patricche della località e antropologia della visone in una comunità montana lombarda.* Bergamo: Sestante. English Translation forthcoming as *Developing Skill, Developing Vision. Practices of Locality in an Alpine Community.* Oxford: Berghahn Books.

——— 2006. "Conservation, Development and Self-Commodification: Doing Ethnography in the Italian Alps." Paper presented at the 105th Annual Meeting of the American Anthropological Association, San Jose, CA, November 15–19, 2006.

——— 2007. "Conservation, Development and Self-Commodification: Doing Ethnography in the Italian Alps." *Journal of Modern Italian Studies* 12(4): 440–9.

Graziano, Paolo and Maarten Vink, eds. 2006. *Europeanization: New Research Agendas.* London: Palgrave Macmillan.

"The Great Debate Begins." *The Economist* (February 12, 2005).

Grimm, Dieter. 1995a. "Braucht Europa eine Verfassung?" Munich: Carl Friedrich von Siemens Stiftung.

——— 1995b. "Does Europe need a Constitution?" *European Law Journal* 1(3): 282–302.

Gross, Felix. 1941. "Europe's Ideological Crisis." *New Europe* (July).

Guiraudon, Virginie. 1998. "Citizenship Rights for Non-Citizens: France, Germany and the Netherlands," in Christian Joppke, *Challenge to the Nation State*. Oxford: Oxford University Press, pp. 272–319.

Haas, Ernst B. 1958. *The Uniting of Europe: Political, Social, and Economic Forces, 1950–1957*. Stanford, CA: Stanford University Press.

    1961. "International Integration: The European and the Universal Process." *International Organization* 15: 366–92.

    1964. "Technocracy, Pluralism and the New Europe," in Stephen R. Graubard (ed.), *A New Europe?* Boston: Houghton Mifflin, pp. 62–88.

    1968. *The Uniting of Europe: Political, Social, and Economic Forces, 1950–1957*. Stanford, CA: Stanford University Press.

    1975. *The Obsolescence of Regional Integration Theory*. University of California, Berkeley, Institute of International Studies, Research Series No. 25.

    2000. *Nationalism, Liberalism, and Progress: The Rise and Decline of Nationalism*. Ithaca, NY: Cornell University Press.

Habermas, Jürgen. 1987. *The Theory of Communicative Action*, vol. 1 *Reason and the Rationalization of Society*, vol. 2 *Lifeworld and System: A Critique of Functionalist Reason*, trans. Thomas McCarthy. Boston: Beacon.

    1991 [1962]. *The Structural Transformation of the Public Sphere. An Inquiry into a Category of Bourgeois Society*. Boston: MIT Press.

    1992. "Citizenship and Identity: Some Reflections of the Future of Europe." *Praxis International* 12: 1–19.

    1996. *Between Facts and Norms*. Cambridge: Polity Press.

    1997. *Solidarietà tra Stranieri. Interventi su "Fatti e Norme,"* ed. L. Ceppa. Naples: Guerini e Associati.

    1998. *The Inclusion of the Other*. Cambridge: Polity Press.

    2001. "Why Europe Needs a Constitution." *New Left Review* 11: 11–32.

    2003. "Europäische Identität und universalistisches Handeln." *Blätter für deutsche und internationale Politik* 7: 801–6.

    2006a. *The Divided West*. Cambridge: Polity Press.

    2006b. *El pequeño occidente escindido: Pequeños escritos políticos*. Madrid: Trotta.

    and Jacques Derrida. 2005. "Feb. 15, or, What Binds Europeans Together: Plea for a Common Foreign Policy, Beginning in Core Europe," in Daniel Levy, Max Pensky, and John Torpey (eds.), *Old Europe, New Europe, Core Europe: Transatlantic Relations After the Iraq War*. London and New York: Verso.

Hall, Peter and Rosemary Taylor. 1996. "Political Science and the Three New Institutionalisms." *Political Studies* 44 (Dec.).

Hamashita, Takeshi. 2008. *China and East Asia in the World Economy*, ed. Linda Grove and Mark Selden. London: Routledge.

Hammar, Tomas, Grete Brochmann, Kristof Tamas, and Thomas Faist, eds. 1997. *International Migration, Immobility and Development*. Oxford: Berg.

Hannerz, Ulf. 2006. "Afterthoughts," in André Gingrich and Marcus Banks (eds.), *Neo-nationalism in Europe and Beyond: Perspectives from Social Anthropology*. Oxford: Berghahn Books, pp. 271–82.

Hansen, Randall. 1998. "A European Citizenship or a Europe of Citizens? Third Country Nationals in the EU." *Journal of Ethnic and Migration Studies* 24(4): 751–68.

Hansen, Valerie. 2000. *The Open Empire: A History of China since 1600*. New York: W.W. Norton.

Hatton, Timothy J. and Jeffrey G. Williamson. 1998. *The Age of Mass Migration*. Oxford: Oxford University Press.

Havel, Václav and Jan Vladislav. 1986. *Václav Havel, Or, Living in Truth: Twenty-Two Essays Published on the Occasion of the Award of the Erasmus Prize to Václav Havel*. Amsterdam, London: Meulenhoff, in association with Faber.

Hedetoft, Ulf, ed. 1998. *Political Symbols, Symbolic Politics. European Identities in Transformation*. Aldershot: Ashgate.

Hegel, Georg Wilhelm Friedrich. 1952. *Philosophy of Right*, ed. T.M. Knox. London: Oxford University Press.

Held, David, Anthony McGrew, David Goldblatt, and Jonathon Perraton. 1999. *Global Transformations: Politics, Economics and Culture*. Oxford: Polity.

Hellman, John. 1981. *Emmanuel Mounier and the New Catholic Left 1930–1959*. Toronto: University of Toronto Press.

Herrmann, Richard K., Thomas Risse, and Marilynn B. Brewer, eds. 2004. *Transnational Identities: Becoming European in the EU*. Lanham, MD: Rowman & Littlefield.

Herzfeld, Michael. 1987. *Anthropology through the Looking-Glass: Critical Ethnography in the Margins of Europe*. Cambridge: Cambridge University Press.

Hillmer, Norman. 2006. "Are Canadians Anti-American?" *Policy Options* 27(6): 63–5.

Hobsbawm, Eric. 1983. *The Invention of Tradition*. Cambridge: Cambridge University Press.

1987. *The Age of Empire*. New York: Pantheon Books.

Hoffman, Stanley. 1966. "Obstinate or Obsolete? The Fate of the Nation-State and the Case of Western Europe." *Dædalus*: 862–915.

Hollifield, James. 2004. "The Emerging Migration State." *International Migration Review* 38(3): 885–912.

Holmes, Douglas R. 1993. "Illicit Discourse," in George Marcus (ed.), *Perilous States: Conversations on Culture, Politics and Nation*. Late Editions 1. Chicago: University of Chicago Press.

2000. *Integral Europe: Fast-Capitalism, Multiculturalism, Neofascism*. Princeton, NJ: Princeton University Press.

2006. "Nationalism-Integralism-Supra-nationalism: A Schemata for the 21st Century," in Gerard Delanty and Krishan Kumar (eds.), *Handbook of Nations and Nationalism*. London: Sage Publications.

and George E. Marcus. 2006. "Fast Capitalism: Para-Ethnography and the Rise of the Symbolic Analyst," in Melissa S. Fisher and Greg Downey (eds.), *Frontiers of Capital*. Durham, NC: Duke University Press.

George E. Marcus, and David A. Westbrook. 2006. "Intellectual Vocations in the City of Gold." *Political and Legal Anthropology Review* 29(1): 154–79.

Hooghe, Liesbet. 2003. "Europe Divided?: Elites vs. Public Opinion on European Integration." *European Union Politics* 4: 281–304.

2005. "Several Roads Lead to International Norms, but Few via International Socialization: A Case Study of the European Commission." *International Organization* 59: 861–98.

and Gary Marks. Forthcoming. "A Postfunctional Theory of European Integration: From Permissive Consensus to Constraining Dissensus." *British Journal of Political Science*.

Hopf, Ted. 2002. *Social Construction of International Politics: Identities and Foreign Policies, Moscow, 1955 and 1999*. Ithaca, NY: Cornell University Press.

2006. "Ethnography and Rational Choice in David Laitin: From Equality to Subordination to Absence." *Qualitative Methods: Newsletter of the American Political Science Association Organized Section on Qualitative Methods* 4(1): 17–20.

"Hungary's Renewed Nation Policy" [last modified: 28 November 2005]. www.kulugyminiszterium.hu/kum/en/bal/Archivum/Archives/nation_policy_affairs.htm. Accessed September 14, 2007.

Huntington, Samuel. 1996. *The Clash of Civilizations and the Remaking of the New World Order*. Chicago: Chicago University Press.

2004. *Who Are We? The Challenges to American National Identity*. New York: Simon and Schuster.

Hyde-Price, Adrian. 2006. "'Normative' Power Europe: A Realist Critique." *Journal of European Public Policy* 13: 217–34.

International Commission to Inquire into the Causes and Conduct of the Balkan Wars. 1914. *Report of the International Commission to Inquire into the Causes and Conduct of the Balkan Wars*. Carnegie Endowment for International Peace. Divisions of Intercourse and Education. Publication. Vol. 4. Washington, DC: The Endowment.

International Commission to Inquire into the Causes and Conduct of the Balkan Wars, George F. Kennan, and International Commission to Inquire into the Causes and Conduct of the Balkan wars. 1993. *The Other Balkan Wars: A 1913 Carnegie Endowment Inquiry in Retrospect*. Washington, DC: Carnegie Endowment for International Peace: Brookings Institution Publications distributor.

Jachtenfuchs, Markus. 2002. *Die Konstruktion Europas: Verfassungsideen und institutionelle Entwicklung*. Baden-Baden: Nomos.

Joas, Hans and Klaus Wiegandt, eds. 2005. *Die kulturellen Werte Europas*. Frankfurt: Fischer.

Jochen, Peter and Claes H. de Vreese. 2003. "Agenda-Rich, Agenda-Poor: A Cross-National Comparative Investigation of Nominal and Thematic Public Agenda Diversity." *International Journal of Public Opinion Research* 15: 44–64.

Johnson, James. 2006. "Consequences of Positivism: A Pragmatist Assessment." *Comparative Political Studies* 39: 224–52.

Jones, Priska. 2007. "Shakespeare und zwölf Sterne. Europa-Karikaturen in Großbritannien während der Maastricht-Debatte 1991–1993," in Hartmut Kaelble and Martin Kirsch (eds.), *Selbstverständnis und Gesellschaft der Europäer. Soziale und kulturelle Europäisierung im 19. und 20. Jahrhundert*. Frankfurt: Lang.

Joppke, Christian and Ewa Morawska, eds. 2003. *Toward Assimilation and Citizenship: Immigrants in Liberal Nation States*. London: Palgrave Macmillan.

Judt, Tony. 2005. *Postwar: A History of Europe since 1945*. New York: Penguin.

Kaelble, Hartmut. 2001a. *Europäer über Europa. Die Entstehung des modernen europäischen Selbstverständisses im 19. und 20. Jahrhundert*. Frankfurt: Campus.

　　2001b. "European identity and national identities in Europe," in M. G. Melchionni (ed.), "Identità europea alla fine del XX secolo," *La Rivista di studi politici internazionali*. Florence: Biblioteca degli studi politici internazionali, pp. 423–39.

　　2002a. "European Self-Understanding in the 20th Century," in Dominic Sachsenmaier and Jens Riedel with Shmuel N. Eisenstadt (eds.), *Reflections on Multiple Modernities*. Leiden: Brill (different version in: Eder and Spohn 2005).

　　2002b. "The Historical Rise of a European Public Sphere?" *Journal of European Integration History* 8: 9–22.

　　2003. "European Symbols, 1945–2000: Concept, Meaning and Historical Change," in Luisa Passerini (ed.), *Figures d'Europe – Images and Myths of Europe*. Brussels: Peter Lang, pp. 47–61.

2004. "Social Peculiarities of Nineteenth- and Twentieth-Century Europe," in Hartmut Kaelble (ed.), *The European Way: European Societies in the 19th and 20th Centuries.* New York: Berghahn Books, pp. 276–317.

2007a. *The European Public Sphere.* Max Weber lectures, European University Institute, Florence.

2007b. *Sozialgeschichte Europas 1945 bis zur Gegenwart.* Munich: Beck.

2008. "L'Union européenne, une espace de démocratie?" in M.-T. Bitsch (ed.), *50 années de l'intégration européenne.* Luxembourg: Office for Official Publication of the European Communities.

Martin Kirsch, and Alexander Schmidt-Gernig, eds. 2002. *Transnationale Öffentlichkeit und Identitäten im 20. Jahrhundert.* Frankfurt: Campus.

Kantner, Cathleen. 2002. "Transnationale Öffentlichkeit und die Demokratiefähigkeit der Europäischen Union." Ph.D. Dissertation, Humboldt-Universität, Berlin.

2006. "What is a European Identity? The Emergence of a Shared Ethical Self-Understanding in the European Union." EUI Working Paper RSCAS, 2006/28.

Kastoryano, Riva. 1993. *Être turque en France.* Paris: L'Harmattan.

2002. *Negotiating Identities: States and Immigrants in France and Germany.* Trans. Barbara Harshav. Princeton, NJ: Princeton University Press.

Katzenstein, Peter. 1997a. "United Germany in an Integrated Europe." Working Paper Series. Center for German and European Studies, University of California, Berkeley.

ed. 1997b. *Tamed Power: Germany in Europe.* Ithaca, NY: Cornell University Press.

2005. *A World of Regions: Asia and Europe in the American Imperium.* Ithaca, NY: Cornell University Press.

2006. "Multiple Modernities as Limits to Secular Europeanization," in Byrnes and Katzenstein (eds.), *Religion in an Expanding Europe,* pp. 1–33.

2007. "Civilizational States, Secularisms and Religions." Paper prepared for the meeting of the Working Group on Religion, Secularism and International Affairs, Social Science Research Council, New York (May 11–12).

2008. *Rethinking Japanese Security: Internal and External Dimensions.* London and New York: Routledge.

and Timothy A. Byrnes. 2006. "Transnational Religion in an Expanding Europe." *Perspectives on Politics* 4: 679–94.

and Robert O. Keohane, eds. 2007. *Anti-Americanisms in World Politics.* Ithaca, NY: Cornell University Press.

and Takashi Shiraishi, eds. 2006. *Beyond Japan. The Dynamics of East Asian Regionalism.* Ithaca, NY: Cornell University Press.

and Rudra Sil. 2005. "What Is Analytic Eclecticism and Why Do We Need It? A Pragmatist Perspective on Problems and Mechanisms in the Study of World Politics." Paper presented at the Annual Convention of the American Political Science Association, Washington, DC (September).

Kenney, Padraic. 2002. *A Carnival of Revolution: Central Europe 1989.* Princeton, NJ: Princeton University Press.

Kielmansegg, Peter Graf. 1996. "Integration und Demokratie," in Markus Jachtenfuchs and Beate Kohler-Koch (eds.), *Europäische Integration.* Opladen: Leske & Budrich, pp. 47–71.

King, Russell. 2002. "Towards a New Map of European Migration." *International Journal of Population Geography* 8(2): 89–106.

and Enric Ruiz Gelices. 2003. "International Student Migration and the European 'Year Abroad': Effects on European Identity and Subsequent Migration Behaviour." *International Journal of Population Geography* 9: 229–52.

Tony Warnes, and Allan Williams. 2000. *Sunset Lives: British Retirement Migration to the Mediterranean.* Oxford: Berg.

Kletzin, Birgit. 2000. *Europa aus Rasse und Raum. Die nationalsozalistische Idee der Neuen Ordnung.* Münster: Litt.

Knill, Christoph. 2001. *The Europeanisation of National Administrations: Patterns of Institutional Change and Persistence.* Cambridge: Cambridge University Press.

Kohler-Koch, Beate, ed. 2003. *Linking EU and National Governance.* Oxford: Oxford University Press.

Kohli, Martin. 2000. "The Battle-grounds of European Identity." *European Societies* 2(2): 113–37.

Koopmans, Ruud. 2002. "Codebook for the Analysis of Political Mobilization and Communication in European Public Spheres." http://europub.wz-berlin.de.

2004a. "Integrated Report: Cross-National, Cross-Issue, Cross-Actor," http://europub.wz-berlin.de.

2004b. "Movements and Media: Selection Processes and Evolutionary Dynamics in the Public Sphere." *Theory and Society* 33: 367–91.

and Paul Statham. 1999. "Challenging the Liberal Nation-State? Postnationalism, Multiculturalism, and the Collective Claims-Making of Migrants and Ethnic Minorities in Britain and Germany." *American Journal of Sociology*: 105(3): 652–96.

Paul Statham, Marco Giugni, and Florence Passy. 2005. *Contested Citizenship: Immigration and Cultural Diversity in Europe.* Minneapolis: University of Minnesota Press.

Kornhauser, William. 1960. *The Politics of Mass Society*. London: Routledge.

Kosáry, Domokos. 2003. *Magyarország Európában*. Budapest: Nemzeti Tankönyvkiadó.

Koser, Khalid and Helma Lutz, eds. 1998. *The New Migration in Europe*. London: Macmillan.

Kundera, Milan. 1984. "The Tragedy of Central Europe." *New York Review of Books* (26 April): 33–8.

Laborde, Cecile. 2002. "From Constitutional to Civic Patriotism." *British Journal of Political Science* 32: 591–612.

Laffan, Brigid. 2004. "The European Union and its Institutions as 'Identity Builders,'" in Herrmann, Risse, and Brewer (eds.), *Transnational Identities*, pp. 75–96.

Rory O'Donnell, and Michael Smith. 2000. *Europe's Experimental Union*. London: Routledge.

Laitin, David. 1997. "The Cultural Identities of a European State." *Politics & Society* 25: 277–302.

1998. *Identity in Formation: The Russian-Speaking Populations in the Near Abroad*. Ithaca, NY: Cornell University Press.

Landfried, Christine. 2005. *Das politische Europa. Differenz als Potential der Europäischen Union*. 2nd ed. Baden-Baden: Nomos.

Laughland, John. 1997. *The Tainted Source: The Undemocratic Origins of the European Idea*. London: Little, Brown.

Le Goff, Jacques. 2003. *L'Europe est-elle née au Moyen Age?* Paris: Seuil.

Le Pen, Jean-Marie. 1984. *Les Français d'abord*. Paris: Carrere/Lafon.

1989. *Europe: Discours et interventions 1984–1989*. Paris: Groupes Droites européennes.

Le Torrec, Virginie, Philippe Blanchard, Guillaume Garcia, and Charles Patou. 2001. "Framing Europe: News Coverage and Legitimacy of the European Union in Five Countries." Seventh Biennial International Conference, European Community Studies Association, Madison, Wisconsin.

Lebow, Richard Ned and Mark Lichbach, eds. 2007. *Theory and Evidence in Comparative Politics and International Relations*. New York: Palgrave Macmillan.

Leibfried, S. and Paul Pierson, eds. 1995. *European Social Policy: Between Fragmentation and Integration*. Washington, DC: The Brookings Institution.

Lerner, Daniel and Morton Gordon. 1969. *Euratlantica: Changing Perspectives of the European Elites*. Cambridge, MA: MIT Press.

Lesthaege, Ron, ed. 2000. *Communities and Generations: Turkish and Moroccan Populations in Belgium*. Brussels: VUB Press.

Levine, Louis. 1914. "Pan-Slavism and European Politics." *Political Science Quarterly* 29(4): 664–86.

Li, Wei. 2007. *Deutsche Pläne zur europäischen wirtschaftlichen Neuordnung. Weltwirtschaft, kontinentaleuropäische Autarkie und mitteleuropäische Wirtschaftsintegration.* Hamburg: Verlag Kovac.

Lindberg, Leon N. and Stuart A. Scheingold. 1970a. *Europe's Would-Be Polity: Patterns of Change in the European Community.* Englewood Cliffs, NJ: Prentice-Hall.

   1970b. "Regional Integration: Theory and Research." *International Organization* 24 (Autumn).

Lipgens, Walter. 1984. *Documents on the History of European Integration,* vol. 1 *Continental Plans for European Union 1939–1945.* Berlin: Walter de Gruyter.

Loth, Wilfried. 1995. "Rettungsanker Europa? Deutsche Europa-Konzeptionen vom Dritten Reich bis zur Bundesrepublik," in H.-E. Volkmann (ed.), *Ende des Dritten Reiches – Ende des Zweiten Weltkriegs.* Munich: Piper.

Loth, Wilfried *et al.*, eds. In press. *Experiencing Europe. 50 years of European Construction.*

MacDonald, Maryann. 1996. "'Unity in Diversity:' Some Tensions in the Construction of Europe." *Social Anthropology* 4: 47–60.

   2006. "New Nationalism in the EU: Occupying the Available Space," in André Gingrich and Marcus Banks (eds.), *Neo-nationalism in Europe and Beyond: Perspectives from Social Anthropology.* Oxford: Berghahn Books, pp. 218–33.

Macdonald, Sharon, ed. 2000. *Approaches to European Historical Consciousness.* Hamburg: Körber.

Machill, Marcel, Markus Beiler, and Corinna Fischer. 2006. "Europe-topics in Europe's Media. The Debate about the European Public Sphere: A Meta-Analysis of Media Content Analyses." *European Journal of Communication* 21(1): 57–88.

Magyar Nemzet. 1990. (Oct. 15): 6.

Maier, Charles S. 1988. *The Unmasterable Past: History, Holocaust, and German National Identity.* Cambridge, MA: Harvard University Press.

Malmborg, Mikael af and Bo Stråth, eds. 2002. *The Meaning of Europe. Variety and Contention with and among Nations.* Oxford: Berg.

Mancini, G.F. 2000. *Democracy and Constitutionalism in the European Union.* Oxford: Hart.

Mann, Michael. 1993. *The Sources of Social Power,* vol. 2 *The Rise of Classes and Nation-States 1760–1914.* Cambridge: Cambridge University Press.

   2005. *The Dark Side of Democracy.* Cambridge: Cambridge University Press.

Manners, Ian. 2002. "Normative Power Europe: A Contradiction in Terms?" *Journal of Common Market Studies* 40: 235–58.

Maritain, Jacques. 1950. *Man and the State*. Chicago: University of Chicago Press.

Markovits, Andrei S. 2007. *Uncouth Nation: Why Europe Dislikes America*. Princeton, NJ: Princeton University Press.

Marks, Gary. 1999. "Territorial Identities in the European Union," in Jeffrey J. Anderson (ed.), *Regional Integration and Democracy: Expanding on the European Experience*. Lanham, MD: Rowman & Littlefield, pp. 69–91.

Liesbet Hooghe, and K. Blank. 1996. "European Integration from the 1980s: State-Centric vs. Multi-Level Governance." *Journal of Common Market Studies* 34: 341–78.

Martin, Benjamin George. 2006. *A New Order for European Culture: The German–Italian Axis and the Reordering of International Cultural Exchange, 1936–1943*. Dissertation, Columbia University.

Marx, Karl and Daniel De Leon. 1907. *The Eighteenth Brumaire of Louis Bonaparte*. Chicago: Charles H. Kerr & Co.

Marx Ferree, Myra, William Gamson, Jürgen Gerhards, and Dieter Rucht. 2002. "Four Models of the Public Sphere in Modern Democracies." *Theory and Society* 31: 289–324.

Masaryk, Tomas. 1943 [1915]. *Independent Bohemia*, in R.W. Seton-Watson, *Masaryk in England*. Cambridge and New York: Cambridge University Press/Macmillan. www.h-net.org/~habsweb/sourcetexts/masaryk1.htm. Accessed March 14, 2007.

Massey, Douglass, Jorge Durand, and Nolan Malone. 2002. *Beyond Smoke and Mirrors: Mexican Migration in an Era of Economic Integration*. New York: Sage.

Mazower, Mark. 1998. *Dark Continent: Europe's Twentieth Century*. London: Penguin.

Mazzini, Giuseppe. 1872. "Young Europe," in *Joseph Mazzini: His Life, Writings, and Political Principles*. New York: Hurd and Houghton, pp. 151–91.

McCormick, John. 2002. *Understanding the European Union*. London: Palgrave Macmillan.

McNamara, Kathleen. 1998. *The Currency of Ideas: Monetary Politics in the European Union*. Ithaca, NY: Cornell University Press.

Mead, Walter Russell. 2002. *Special Providence: American Foreign Policy and How It Changed the World*. New York: Knopf.

Meinhof, Ulrike. 2004. "Europe Viewed from Below: Agents, Victims and the Threat of the Other," in Herrmann, Risse, and Brewer (eds.), *Transnational Identities*, pp. 214–46.

Melchionni, Maria G., ed. 2001. "Identità europea alla fine del XX secolo," *La Rivista di studi politici internazionali*. Florence: Biblioteca degli studi politici internazionali.

Menand, Louis. 2005. "From the Ashes." *The New Yorker* (Nov. 28).

Mendras, Henri. 1997. *L'Europe des européens. Sociologie de l'Europe occidentale*. Paris: Gallimard.

Meyer, Jan-Henrik, 2007. "Was There a European Public Sphere at the Summit of The Hague 1969? An Analysis of Discourses on the Legitimacy of the EC," in M.-T. Bitsch, W. Loth, and C. Barthel (eds.), *Cultures politiques, opinion publique et ntégration européenne*. Brussels: Bruylant, pp. 227–45.

Meyer, John W. 2000. "The European Union and the Globalization of Culture." Paper presented at the Workshop on Institutional Approaches to the Study of the European Union, Oslo: Arena Centre for European Studies, University of Oslo (March).

Meyer, Thomas. 2004. *Die Identität Europas: Der EU eine Seele?* Frankfurt: Suhrkamp.

Mill, John S. 1991 [1861]. *Considerations on Representative Government*. New York: Prometheus Books.

Millar, David. 1995. *On Nationality*. Oxford: Oxford University Press.

2000. *Citizenship and National Identity*. Cambridge: Polity Press.

Millon-Delsol, Chantal. 1992. *L'État subsidiaire: Ingérence et non-ingérence de l'État: le principe de subsidiarité aux fondements de l'histoire européenne*. Paris: Presses Universitaires de France.

Miłosz, Czesław. 1990. *The Captive Mind* [Zniewolony umysł]. Vintage International ed. New York: Vintage International.

Milward, Alan. 1992. *The European Rescue of the Nation-state*. Berkeley: University of California Press.

2005. *The European Rescue of the Nation State*. 2nd ed. London: Routledge.

Moch, Leslie Page. 2003. *Moving Europeans: Migration in Western Europe Since 1650*. 2nd ed. Bloomington, IN: Indiana University Press.

Modood, Tariq and Pnina Werbner. 1997. *The Politics of Multiculturalism: Racism, Identity and Community in the New Europe*. London: Zed Books.

Monnet, Jean. 1978. *Jean Monnet: Memoir*. London: Collins.

Moravcsik, Andrew. 1998. *The Choices for Europe: Social Purpose and State Power from Messina to Maastricht*. Ithaca, NY: Cornell University Press.

2006. "What Can We Learn from the Collapse of the European Constitutional Project?" *Politische Vierteljahreschrift* 47: 219–41.

2007. "The European Constitutional Settlement," in Sophie Meunier and Kathleen R. McNamara (eds.), *Making History: European Integration and Institutional Change at Fifty*. Oxford: Oxford University Press.

Morawska, Ewa. 2002. "Transnational Migration in the Enlarged European Union: A Perspective from East and Central Europe," in Jan Zielonka (ed.), *Europe Unbound*. Oxford: Oxford University Press, pp. 161–90.

Morgan, Glyn. 2005. *The Idea of a European Superstate: Public Justification and European Integration*. Princeton and Oxford: Princeton University Press.

Morin, Edgar. 1987. *Penser l'Europe*. Paris: Gallimard.

Morozov, Viatcheslav. 2007. "Russia and the West: Dividing Europe, Constructing Each Other." Paper presented at the Annual Convention of the International Studies Association, Chicago (February 28–March 3).

"Muddled Amity: Improving the Moldovan-Romanian Relationship." Romanian Digest (2006) (9) www.hr.ro/digest/200609/digest.htm. Accessed March 3, 2007.

Muehlebach, Andrea Karin. 2007. "The Moral Neoliberal: Welfare State and Ethical Citizenship In Contemporary Italy." Ph.D. Thesis, University of Chicago, Dept. of Anthropology, June.

Müller, Hans-Peter. 2007. "Auf dem Weg in eine europäische Gesellschaft? Begriffsproblematik und theoretische Perspektiven." *Berliner Journal für Soziologie* 1: 7–31

Müller, Jan-Werner. 2007. *Constitutional Patriotism*. Princeton and Oxford: Princeton University Press.

Münch, Richard. 2001. *Offene Räume. Soziale Räume diesseits und jenseits des Natonalstaats*. Frankfurt: Suhrkamp.

Mussolini, Benito and Italy. 1935. *Fascism: Doctrine and Institutions*. Rome: "Ardita."

"Németh rendet teremtene Romániában." 2004. *Népszabadság* (July 20).

Neumann, Iver B. 1996. "Self and Other in International Relations." *European Journal of International Relations* 2: 139–74.

1999. *Uses of the Other: The East in European Identity Formation*. Minneapolis: University of Minnesota Press.

and Jennifer M. Welsh. 1991. "The Other in European Self-Definition: An Addendum to the Literature on International Society." *Review of International Studies* 17: 327–48.

Nexon, Daniel. 2006. "Religion, European Identity and Political Contention in Historical Perspective," in Byrnes and Katzenstein (eds.), *Religion in an Expanding Europe*, pp. 256–82.

Neidhardt, Friedhelm, Ruud Koopmans, and Barbara Pfetsch. 2000. "Konstitutionsbedingungen politischer Öffentlichkeit. Der Fall Europa," in Hans-Dieter Klingemann and Friedhelm Neidhardt (eds.), *Die Zukunft der Demokratie. Herausforderungen im Zeitalter der Globalisierung*. Berlin: WZB-Jahrbuch, pp. 263–94.

Nye, Joseph S., Jr. 1987 [1971]. *Peace in Parts: Integration and Conflict in Regional Integration*. Lanham, MD: University Press of America; repr. Boston: Little, Brown.

Offe, Claus. 2001. "Gibt es eine europäische Gesellschaft. Kann es sie geben?" *Blätter für deutsche und internationale Politik* 46: 423–35.

Olsen, Johan P. 2002. "The Many Faces of Europeanization." *Journal of Common Market Studies* 40(5): 921–52.

 2007. *Europe in Search of Political Order: An Institutional Perspective on Unity/Diversity, Citizens/Their Helpers, Democratic Design/ Historical Drift and the Co-existence of Orders*. Oxford: Oxford University Press.

Orbán, Viktor, 1989. "Viktor Orbán's Speech at the Reburial of Imre Nagy." *Uncaptive Minds*, vol. II, 4(8): 26.

Osterhammel, Jürgen. 1998. *Die Entzauberung Asiens. Europa und die asiatischen Reiche im 18. Jahrhundert*. Munich.

"Outrage at 'old Europe' Remarks," BBC News World Edition, January 23, 2003, http://news.bbc.co.uk/2/hi/europe/2687403.stm. Accessed March 10, 2007.

Pagden, Anthony, ed. 2002. *The Idea of Europe: From Antiquity to the EU*. Cambridge: Cambridge University Press.

Palmer, Alan Warwick. 1970. *The Lands between; a History of East-Central Europe since the Congress of Vienna*. 1st American ed. New York: Macmillan.

Parsons, Craig. 2003. *A Certain Idea of Europe*. Ithaca, NY: Cornell University Press.

Passerini, Luisa, ed. 1998. *Identità culturale europea. Idee, sentimenti, relazione*. Scandicci: La Nuova Italia.

 1999. *Europe in Love, Love in Europe. Imagination and Politics in Britain between the Wars*. London: I. B. Tauris.

 ed. 2003. *Figures d'Europe – Images and Myths of Europe*. Brussels: Peter Lang.

Pastor, Robert A. 2001. *Toward a North American Community: Lessons from the Old World for the New*. Washington, DC: Peterson Institute.

Patel, Kiran. 2004. "Integrationsgeschichte und Identitätssuche." *Internationale Politik* 52: 11–18.

Paxton, Robert O. 2005. *Europe in the Twentieth Century*. 2005 update, 4th ed. Belmont, CA: Thomson Wadsworth.

Pensky, Max. 2008. *The Ends of Solidarity: Discourse Theory in Ethics and Politics*. Albany, NY: State University of New York Press.

Pérez-Díaz, Victor. 1998. "The Public Sphere and a European Civil Society," in J.C. Alexander (ed.), *Real Civil Societies. Dilemmas of Institutionalization*. London: Sage, pp. 211–39.

Peri, Giovanni. 2005. "Skills and Talent of Immigrants: A Comparison between the European Union and the United States." Institute of European Studies Working Paper 050304. University of California, Berkeley.

Petőfi, Sándor. 1974. *Rebel or Revolutionary?: Sándor Petőfi as Revealed by his Diary, Letters, Notes, Pamphlets, and Poems: Selection, Foreword, and Notes* [Selections.]. Budapest: Corvina Press.

Phalet, Karen, Claudia van Lotringen, and Hans Entzinger. 2000. *Islam in de multiculturele samenleving*. Utrecht: ERCOMER.

Pierson, Paul. 1994. *Dismantling the Welfare State? Reagan, Thatcher and the Politics of Retrenchment*. New York: Cambridge University Press.

   1996. "The Path to European Integration: A Historical Institutionalist Analysis." *Comparative Political Studies* 29 (April).

Piore, Michael. 1979. *Birds of Passage: Migrant Labor in Industrial Societies*. Cambridge: Cambridge University Press.

Pocock, J.G.A. 1995. "Conclusion: Contingency, Identity, Sovereignty," in Alexander Grant and K.J. Stringer (eds.), *Uniting the Kingdom? The Making of British History*. London: Routledge, pp. 292–302.

Polcz, Alaine. 2002. *One Woman in the War: Hungary 1944–1945*. Budapest: Central European University Press.

Pomian, Krzysztof. 1990. *L'Europe et ses nations*. Paris: Gallimard.

Porunca Vremii, 20. June 1942; MOL [Magyar Országos Levéltár = Hungarian State Archives, Budapest], K63 [Külügyminisztérium, Politikai osztály], 257. csomó. 1940–27. tétel./7./E., Román-magyar viszony – Erdély, iktatlan, II. rész, p. 31.

"Présentation," *La Nouvelle Alternative*. www.nouvelle-alternative.org/revu/presentation.php. Accessed March 14, 2007.

Preuss, U.K. 2005. "Europa als politische Gemeinschaft," in G.F. Schuppert, I. Pernice, and U. Haltern (eds.), *Europawissenschaft*. Baden-Baden: Nomos, pp. 489–539.

Puchala, Donald J. 1972. "Of Blind Men, Elephants and International Integration." *Journal of Common Market Studies* 10: 267–84.

Rabinow, Paul. 1999. *French Modern: Norms and Forms of the Social Environment*. Chicago: University of Chicago Press.

Recchi, Ettore. 2006. "From Migrants to Movers: Citizenship and Mobility in the European Union," in Smith and Favell (eds.), *The Human Face of Global Mobility*, pp. 53–77.

   In press. "The Social Mobility of Mobile Europeans," in Recchi and Favell (eds.), *Pioneers of European Integration*.

   and Adrian Favell (eds.). In press. *Pioneers of European Integration*, Cheltenham: Elgar.

Rev, Istvan. 2005. *Retroactive Justice: Prehistory of Postcommunism*. Stanford, CA: Stanford University Press.

Riccio, Bruno. 2001. "From 'Ethnic Group' to 'Transnational Community': Senegalese Migrants' Ambivalent Experiences and Multiple Trajectories." *Journal of Ethnic and Migration Studies* 27(4): 583–99.

Risse, Thomas. 2002. "Zur Debatte über die (Nicht-)Existenz einer europäischen Öffentlichkeit." *Berliner Debatte* 13(5/6): 15–23.

2003. "An Emerging European Public Sphere: Theoretical Clarifications and Empirical Indicators." Paper presented to the Annual Meeting of the European Union Studies Association (EUSA), Nashville, Tennessee, March 27–30, 2003.

2004. "European Institutions and Identity Change: What Have We Learned?" in Herrmann, Brewer, and Risse (eds.), *Transnational Identities*, pp. 247–72.

and Matthias Maier, eds. 2003. *Europeanization, Collective Identities and Public Discourses – Draft Final Report submitted to the European Commission*. Florence: European University Institute and Robert Schuman Centre for Advanced Studies.

Daniel Engelmann-Martin, Hans Knopf, and Knut Rosher. 1999. "European Identity and National Politics." *European Journal of International Relations* 5: 147–88.

Rogers, Alisdair. 2000. "A European Space for Transnationalism?" Transnational Communities Programme Working Paper Series WPTC-2K-07. Oxford: COMPAS. www.transcomm.ox.ac.uk/working%20papers/rogers.pdf.

Rokkan, Stein. 1973. "Cities, States, Nations," in Samuel N. Eisenstadt and Stein Rokkan (eds.), *Building States and Nations*. London: Sage.

1983. *Economy, Territory, Identity: Politics of West European Peripheries*. London: Sage.

Ross, George. 1995. *Jacques Delors and European Integration*. New York: Oxford University Press.

Rößner, Susan. 2007. "Das verhinderte Europa: Historismus in der deutschen Europa- und Weltgeschichte," in Hartmut Kaelble and Martin Kirsch (eds.), *Selbstverständnis und Gesellschaft der Europäer. Soziale und kulturelle Europäisierung im 19. und 20. Jahrhundert*. Frankfurt: Lang.

Rother, Nina and Tina Nebe. In press. "More Mobile, More European? Free Movement and EU Identity," in Recchi and Favell (eds.), *Pioneers of European Integration*.

Sassen, Saskia. 2001. *The Global City*. 2nd ed. Princeton, NJ: Princeton University Press.

Scharpf, F.W. 1998. "Demokratie in der transnationalen Politik," in Ulrich Beck (ed.), *Politik der Globalisierung*. Frankfurt am Main: Suhrkamp, pp. 228–53.

Schimmelfennig, Frank and Ulrich Sedelmeier, eds. 2005. *The Europeanization of Central and Eastern Europe*. Ithaca, NY: Cornell University Press.

Schlesinger, Philip R. 1999. "Changing Spaces of Political Communication: The Case of the European Union." *Political Communication* 16: 263–79.

Schmale, Wolfgang. 2003. "Europa als Topos der Geschichtsschreibung," in Georg Michels (ed.), *Auf der Suche nach einem Phantom? Widerspiegelungen Europas in der Geschichtswissenschaft*. Baden-Baden: Nomos.

Schmidt-Gernig, Alexander. 1999. "Gibt es eine 'europäische Identität'? Konzeptionelle Überlegungen zum Zusammenhang transnationaler Erfahrungsräume, kollektiver Identitäten und öffentlicher Diskurse in Westeuropa seit dem Zweiten Weltkrieg," in Hartmut Kaelble and Jürgen Schriewer (eds.), *Diskurse und Entwicklungspfade. Gesellschaftsvergleiche in Geschichts- und Sozialwissenschaften*. Frankfurt: Campus.

Schumpeter, Joseph A. 1942. *Capitalism, Socialism, and Democracy*. London: George Allen and Unwin.

Shore, Cris. 2000. *Building Europe. The Cultural Politics of European Integration*. London: Routledge.

Sifft, Stephanie, Michael Brüggemann, Katharina Kleinen v. Königslöw, Bernhard Peters, and Andreas Wimmel. 2007. "Segmented Europeanization: Exploring the Legitimacy of the European Union from a Public Discourse Perspective." *Journal of Common Market Studies* 45(1): 127–55.

Skowronek, Stephen. 2006. "The Reassociation of Ideas and Purposes: Racism, Liberalism, and the American Political Tradition." *American Political Science Review* 100(3): 385–401.

Slack, Walter. 2006. *White Athena: The Afrocentrist Theft of Greek Civilization*. New York: iUniverse Inc.

Smith, Michael Peter and Adrian Favell, eds. 2006. *The Human Face of Global Mobility: International High Skilled Migrants in Europe, North America and the Asia Pacific*. New Brunswick, NJ: Transaction Press.

Smith, Rogers M. 1993. "Beyond Tocqueville, Myrdal, and Hartz: The Multiple Traditions in America." *American Political Science Review* 87(3): 549–65.

Soysal, Yasemin Nuhoglu. 2002. "Locating Europe." *European Societies* 4: 265–84.

Steeg, Marianne van de. 2004. "Does a Public Sphere exist in the EU? An Analysis of the Debate on the Haider Case," EUI Working Paper SPS 2004/5.

2006. "Does a Public Sphere Exist in the European Union? An Analysis of the Debate of the Haider Case." *European Journal of Political Research* 45(4): 609–34.

Sternhell, Zeëv. 1996. *Neither Right Nor Left: Fascist Ideology in France*, trans. David Maisel. Princeton, NJ: Princeton University Press.

Stolcke, Verena. 1995. "Talking Culture: New Boundaries, New Rhetorics of Exclusion in Europe." *Current Anthropology* 36: 1–24.

Stråth, Bo, ed. 2001. *Europe and the Other and Europe as the Other*. 2nd ed. Brussels: Lang.

2002. "A European Identity. To the Historical Limits of a Concept." *European Journal of Social Theory* 5: 387–401.

Swedberg, R. 1994. "The Idea of 'Europe' and the Origin of the EU – a Sociological Approach." *Zeitschrift für Soziologie* 23.

Sweig, Julia E. 2006. *Friendly Fire: Losing Friends and Making Enemies in the Anti-American Century*. New York: Public Affairs.

Symposium. 2006. "Ethnography Meets Rational Choice: David Laitin, for Example." *Qualitative Methods: Newsletter of the American Political Science Association Organized Section on Qualitative Methods* 4(1): 2–33.

Tajfel, Henri. 1981. *Human Groups and Social Categories*. Cambridge: Cambridge University Press.

Tamir, Yael. 1993. *Liberal Nationalism*. Princeton, NJ: Princeton University Press.

Taylor, Charles. 1998. "The Dynamics of Democratic Exclusion." *Journal of Democracy* 9(4): 143–56.

1989. "Cross-Purposes: The Liberal-Communitarian Debate," in Nancy L. Rosenblum (ed.), *Liberalism and the Moral Life*. Cambridge, MA: Harvard University Press, pp. 159–82.

Temkin, Gabriel. 1998. *My Just War: The Memoir of a Jewish Red Army Soldier in World War II*. Novato, CA: Presidio.

Therborn, Göran. 1995. *European Modernity and Beyond. The Trajectory of European Societies 1945–2000*. London.

Thibaud, Paul. 1992. "L'Europe par les nations (et réciproquement)," in Jean-Marc Ferry and Paul Thibaud, *Discussion sur l'Europe*. Paris: Calmann-Levy.

Thomas, Daniel C. Forthcoming. "Constitutionalization through Enlargement: The Contested Origins of the EU's Democratic Identity." *Journal of European Public Policy*.

Tilly, Charles. 1975. "Reflections on the History of European State Making," in Charles Tilly and Gabriel Ardant (eds.), *The Formation of National States in Western Europe*. Princeton, NJ: Princeton University Press.

Todorova, Maria Nikolaeva. 1997. *Imagining the Balkans*. New York: Oxford University Press.

"Togliatti on Nagy, 30 October 1956: Missing Cable Found." *Cold War International History Project Bulletin 8/9* (Winter 1996): 357.

Tönnies, Ferdinand. 2001. *Community and Civil Society*, ed. Jose Harris; trans. Jose Harris and Margaret Hollis. Cambridge: Cambridge University Press.

Torpey, John. 2000. *The Invention of the Passport*. Cambridge: Cambridge University Press.

Trenz, Hans-Jörg. 2002. *Zur Konstituiton politischer Öffentlichkeit in der Europäischen Union*. Baden-Baden: Nomos.

    2004. "Media Coverage on European Governance. Exploring the European Public Sphere in National Quality Newspapers." *European Journal of Communication* 19(3): 291–319.

    2006. "A Transnational Space of Contention? Patterns of Europeanisation of Civil Society in Germany," in Vincent della Sala and Carlo Ruzza (eds.), *Normative Basis of Governance and Civil Society in the EU*. Manchester: Manchester University Press.

Trichet, Jean-Claude. 2005. "Monetary Policy Strategies: A Central Bank Panel," A Symposium Sponsored by the Federal Reserve Bank of Kansas City. Jackson Hole, Wyoming, August 25–27, 2005.

Türk Ceza Kanunu, Kanun No. 5237, Kabul Tarihi: 26.9.2004, www.tbmm. gov.tr/kanunlar/k5237.html. Accessed March 14, 2007.

Turner, Jonathan. 1975. "Social Comparisons and Social Identity." *European Journal of Social Psychology* 5: 5–34.

Union of International Associations. 2000. *Yearbook of International Organizations*. Frankfurt, FRG: Sauer.

Ustawa z dnia 18 października 2006 r. o ujawnianiu informacji o dokumentach organów bezpieczeństwa państwa z lat 1944–1990 oraz treści tych dokumentów, http://orka.sejm.gov.pl/opinie5.nsf/nazwa/333_u/$file/ 333_u.pdf. Accessed March 14, 2007.

Vaculik, Ludvik. 1968. "Two Thousand Words," June 27, http://library. thinkquest.org/C001155/index1.htm. Accessed March 14, 2007.

Valéry, Paul. 1919. "What is to Become of the European Spirit?" Cited from The European Prospect, www.ellopos.net/politics/eu_valery.html. Accessed March 14, 2007.

Viehoff, Reinhold and Rien T. Segers. 1999. *Kultur, Identität, Europa*. Frankfurt am Main: Suhrkamp.

Viereck, Peter. 1941. *Metapolitics from the Romantics to Hitler*. New York: A.A. Knopf.

Walker, N. 2002. "The Idea of a European Constitution and the Finalité of Integration." Faculdade de Direito da Universidade Nova de Lisboa,

Francisco Lucas Pires Working Papers Series on European Constitutionalism, Working Paper 2002/01.

Wallace, Claire and Dariusz Stola, eds. 2001. *Patterns of Migration in Central Europe*. London: Palgrave.

Walters, E. Garrison. 1987. *The Other Europe: Eastern Europe to 1945*. 1st ed. Syracuse, NY: Syracuse University Press.

Weber, Max. 1968. *Economy and Society: An Outline of Interpretive Sociology*, ed. Guenther Roth and Claus Wittich. New York: Bedminster.

Weiler, J.H.H. 1999. *The Constitution of Europe – Do the New Clothes Have an Emperor? And Other Essays on European Integration*. Cambridge: Cambridge University Press.

Westbrook, David A. 2004. *City of Gold: An Apology for Global Capitalism in a Time of Discontent*. New York: Routledge.

Wheeler-Bennett, John. 1941. "Britain and the Future." *New Europe* (Oct.).

Wilson, Kevin, Jan van der Dussen and Pim den Boer. 1995. *The History of the Idea of Europe*. London: Routledge and The Open University.

Wilson, Thomas M. and M. Estellie Smith, eds. 1993. *Cultural Change and the New Europe: Perspectives on the European Community*. Boulder, CO: Westview.

"Winston Churchill on Europe." In David De Giustino, *A Reader in European Integration*. London; New York: Longman, 1996, pp. 44–6.

Winter, Jay. 2007. "Generations of Memory: War Narratives and Collective Remembrance." Unpublished paper, Yale University.

Wolf, Christa. 1996. *Medea: Stimmen*. Munich: Deutsche Taschenbuch Verlag GmbH & Co. KG.

Wolff, Larry. 1994. *Inventing Eastern Europe: The Map of Civilization on the Mind of the Enlightenment*. Stanford, CA: Stanford University Press.

2003. "The Rise and Fall of Morlacchismo: Identity in the Mountains of Dalmatia," in Norman M. Naimark and Holly Case (eds.), *Yugoslavia and its Historians: Understanding the Balkan Wars of the 1990s*. Stanford, CA: Stanford University Press.

Wood, Nicholas. 2007. "A Croatian Rock Star Flirts with Nazi Past." *International Herald Tribune*, www.iht.com/articles/2007/07/01/europe/croatia.php.

Young, Iris M. 1996. "Communication and the Other: Beyond Deliberative Democracy," in Seyla Benhabib (ed.), *Democracy and Difference: Contesting the Boundaries of the Political*. Princeton, NJ: Princeton University Press, pp. 120–36.

Zaller, John R. 1992. *The Nature and Origins of Mass Opinion*. Cambridge: Cambridge University Press.

Zathureczky, Gyula. 1943. "A magyarság helyzete Európában," in *Erdélyi kérdések – magyar kérdések*. Minerva: Kolozsvár.

Zorgbibe, Charles. 1993. *Histoire de la construction européenne*. Paris: Presses Universitaires de France.

Zürn, Michael and Jeffrey T. Checkel. 2005. "Getting Socialized to Build Bridges: Constructivism and Rationalism, Europe and the Nation State." *International Organization* 59(4): 1045–79.

Index